Reborn as a Vending Machine, I Now Wander the DUNGEON

2

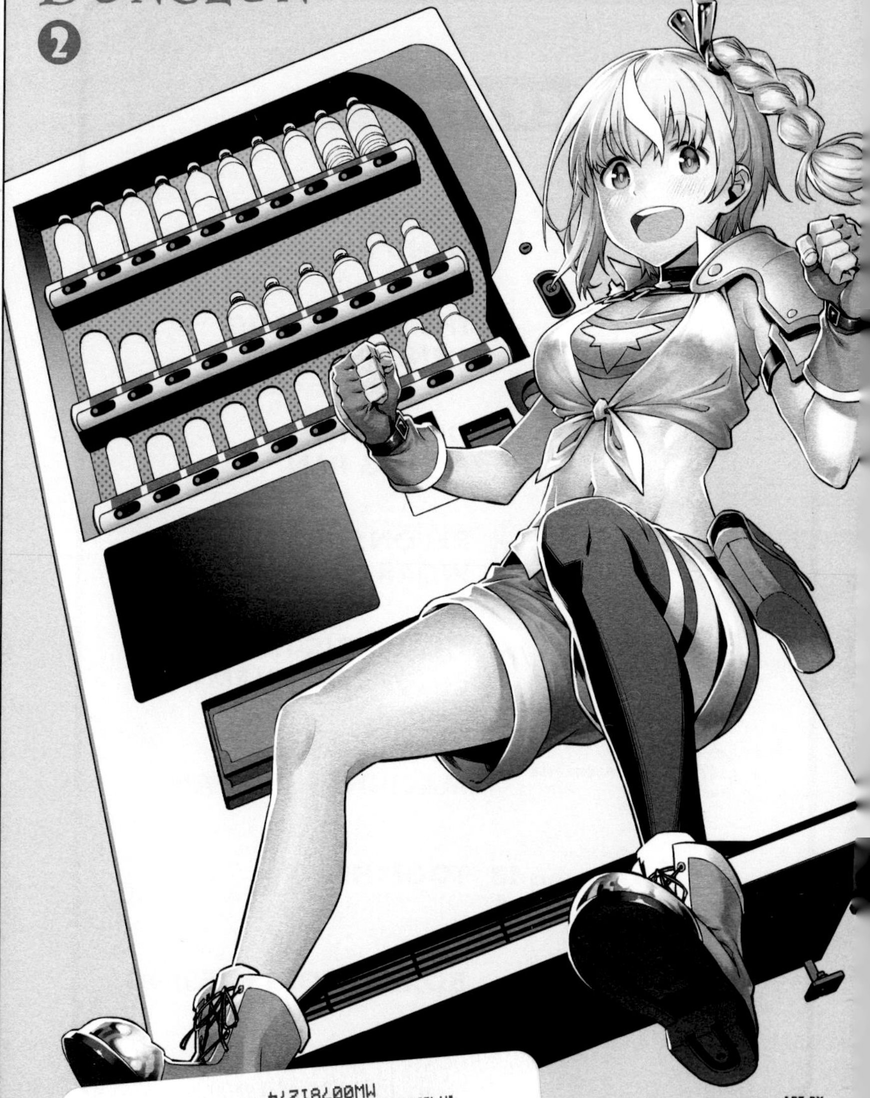

ART BY
Kunieda

ORIGINAL STORY BY
Hirukuma

CHARACTER DESIGN BY
Hagure Yuuki

CONTENTS

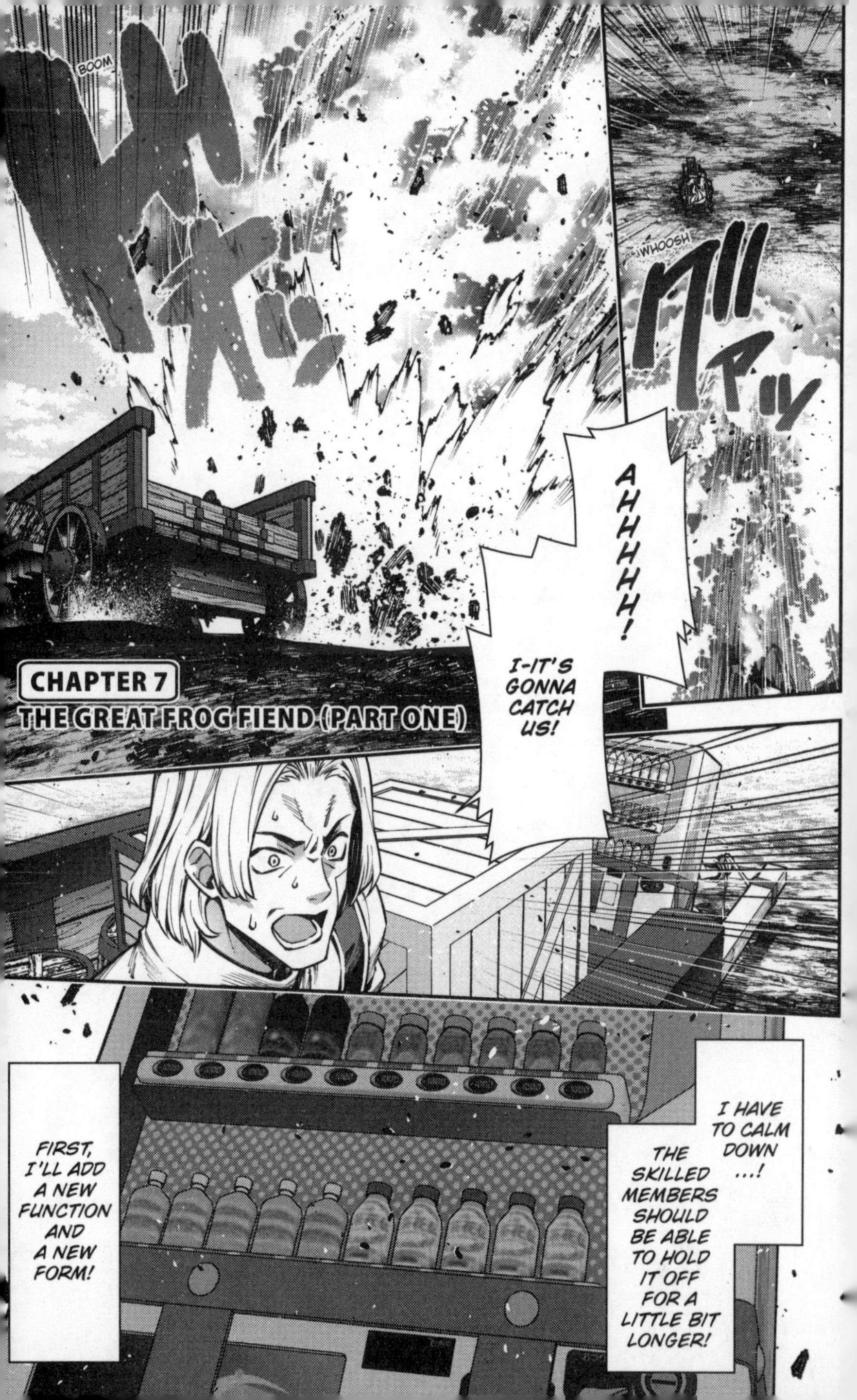
WHOOSH
BOOM
CHAPTER 7
THE GREAT FROG FIEND (PART ONE)
AHHHHHH!
I-IT'S GONNA CATCH US!
I HAVE TO CALM DOWN ...!
THE SKILLED MEMBERS SHOULD BE ABLE TO HOLD IT OFF FOR A LITTLE BIT LONGER!
FIRST, I'LL ADD A NEW FUNCTION AND A NEW FORM!

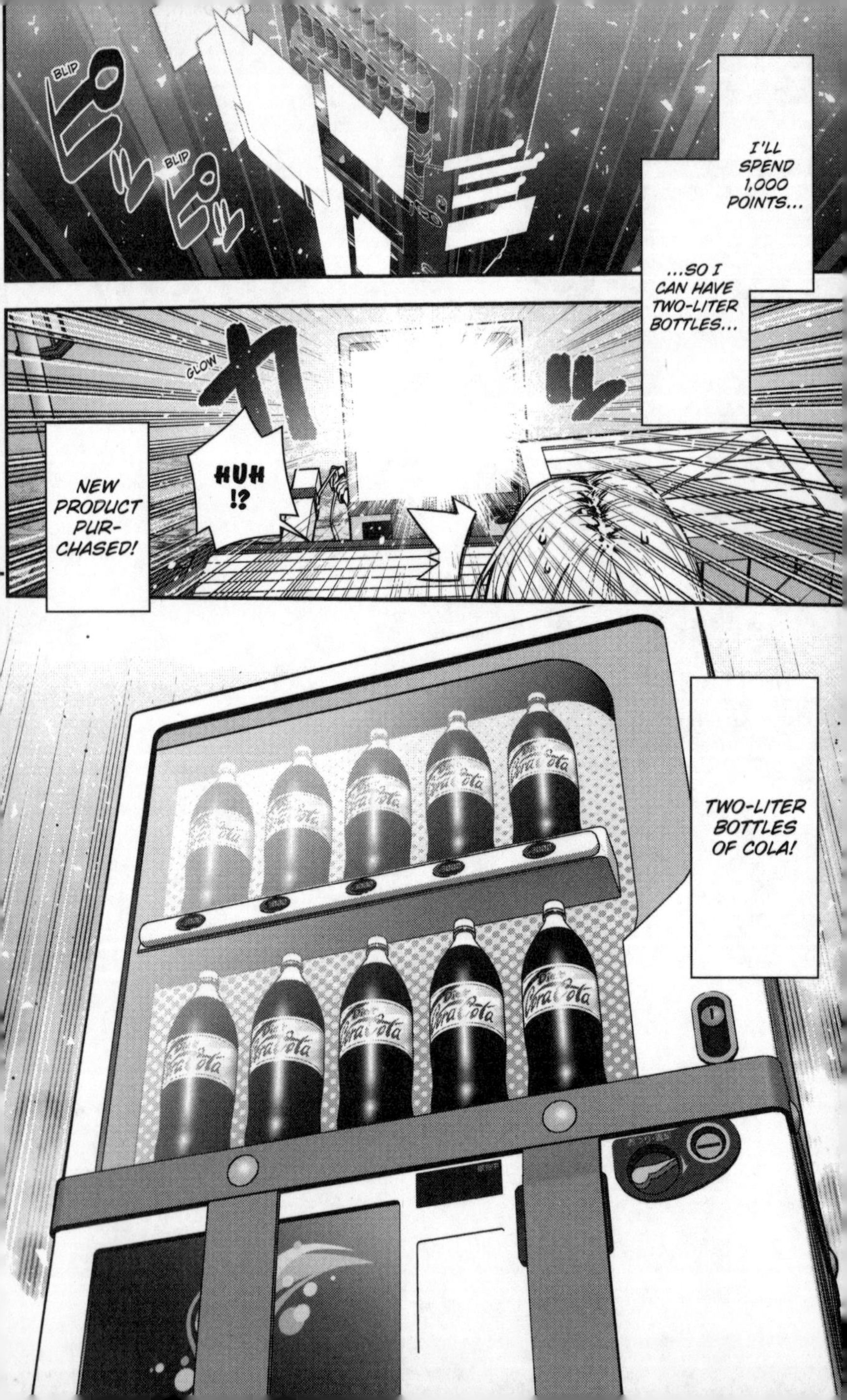
I'LL SPEND 1,000 POINTS...
...SO I CAN HAVE TWO-LITER BOTTLES...
BLIP
BLIP
GLOW
HUH !?
NEW PRODUCT PUR-CHASED!
TWO-LITER BOTTLES OF COLA!

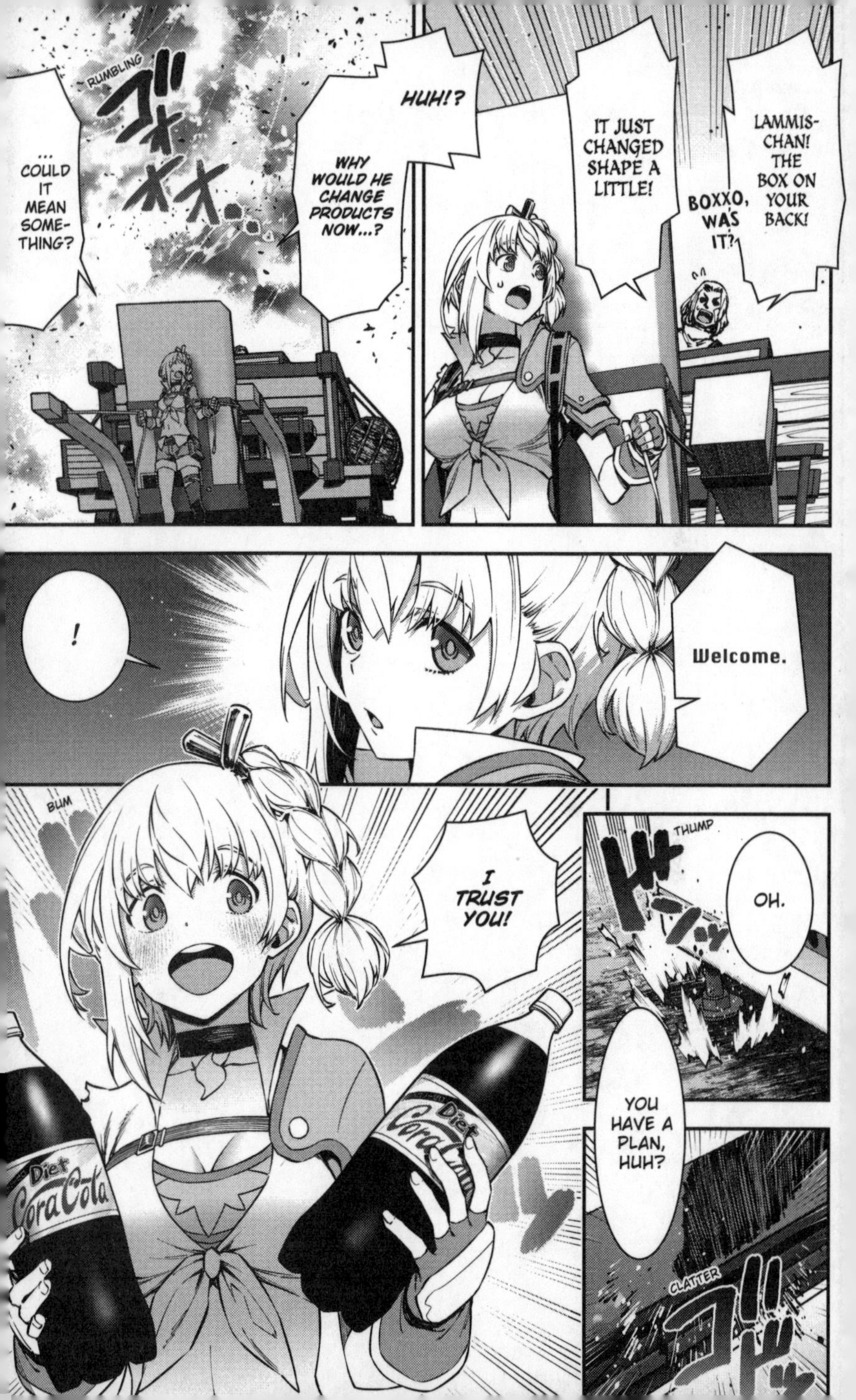
LAMMIS-CHAN! THE BOX ON YOUR BACK!
BOXXO, WAS IT?
IT JUST CHANGED SHAPE A LITTLE!
HUH!?
WHY WOULD HE CHANGE PRODUCTS NOW...?
RUMBLING
... COULD IT MEAN SOME-THING?
Welcome.
!
THUMP
OH.
YOU HAVE A PLAN, HUH?
CLATTER
BUM
I TRUST YOU!
Diet Cora Cola
Diet Cora Cola

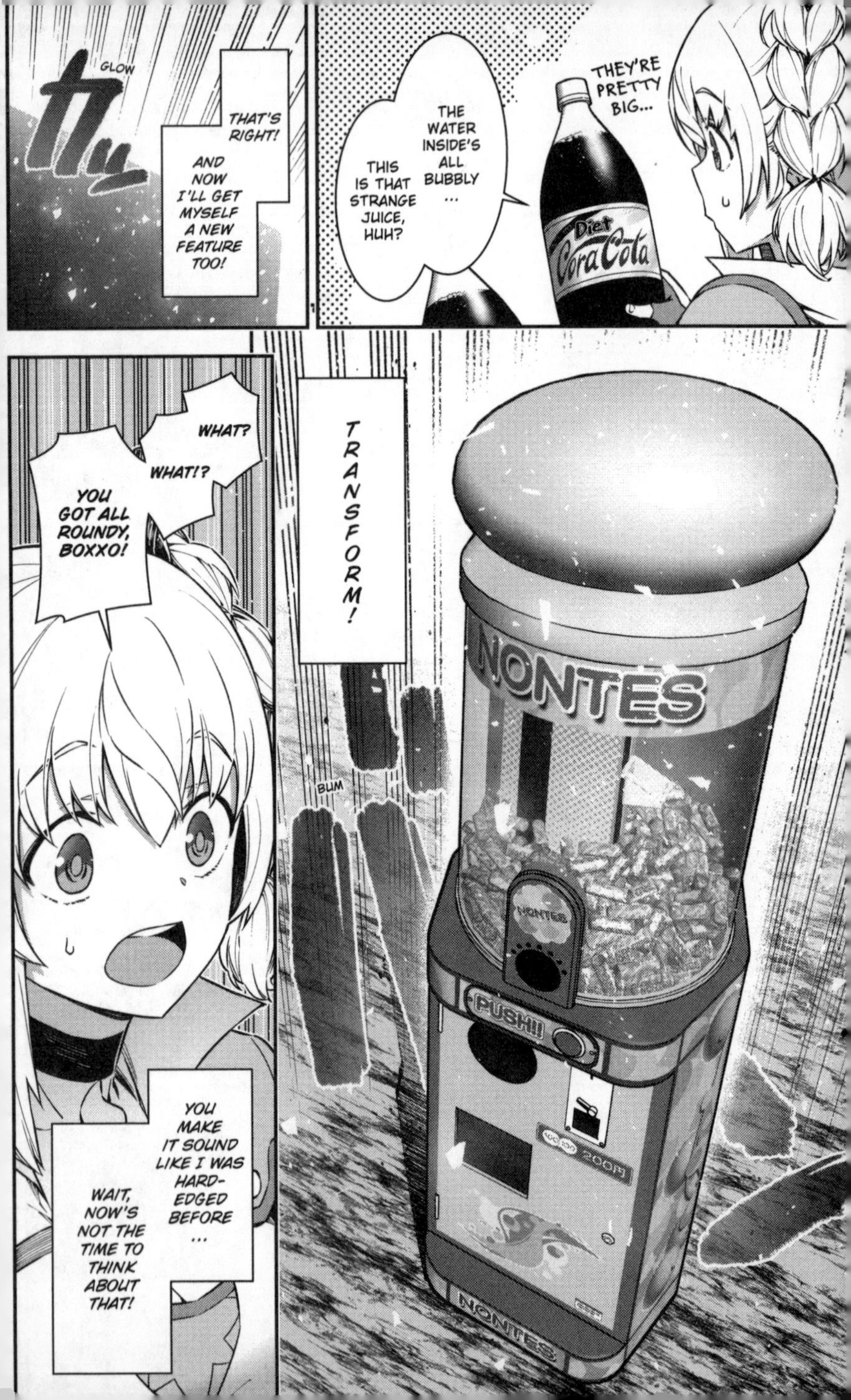
THEY'RE PRETTY BIG...
THE WATER INSIDE'S ALL BUBBLY ...
THIS IS THAT STRANGE JUICE, HUH?
Diet
CoraCola
GLOW
THAT'S RIGHT!
AND NOW I'LL GET MYSELF A NEW FEATURE TOO!
TRANSFORM!
NONTES
BUM
NONTES
PUSH!!
NONTES
WHAT?
WHAT!?
YOU GOT ALL ROUNDY, BOXXO!
YOU MAKE IT SOUND LIKE I WAS HARD-EDGED BEFORE ...
WAIT, NOW'S NOT THE TIME TO THINK ABOUT THAT!

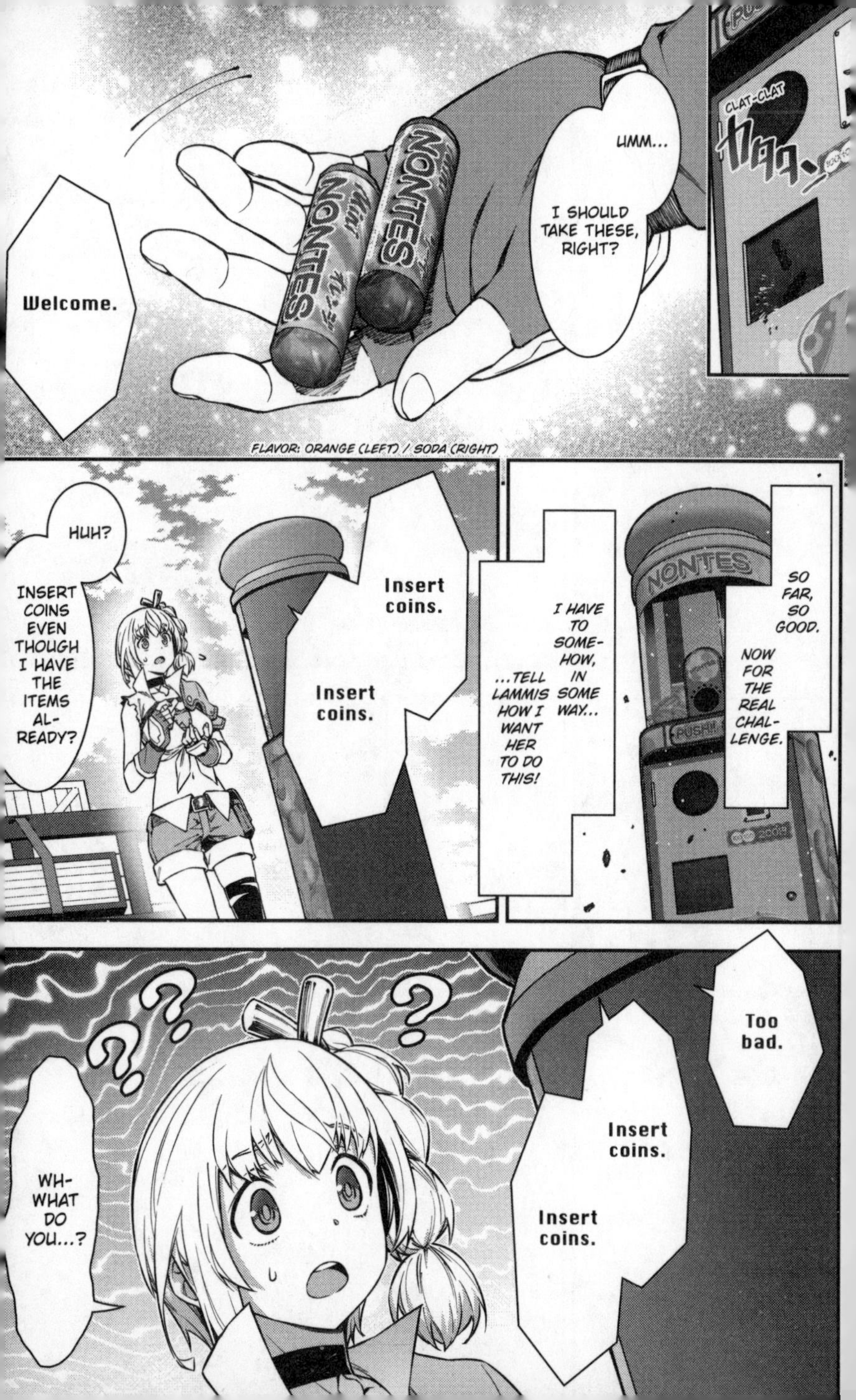
CLAT-CLAT
UMM...
I SHOULD TAKE THESE, RIGHT?
Welcome.
FLAVOR: ORANGE (LEFT) / SODA (RIGHT)
SO FAR, SO GOOD.
NOW FOR THE REAL CHALLENGE.
I HAVE TO SOMEHOW, IN SOME WAY...
...TELL LAMMIS HOW I WANT HER TO DO THIS!
Insert coins.
Insert coins.
HUH?
INSERT COINS EVEN THOUGH I HAVE THE ITEMS ALREADY?
Too bad.
Insert coins.
Insert coins.
WH-WHAT DO YOU...?

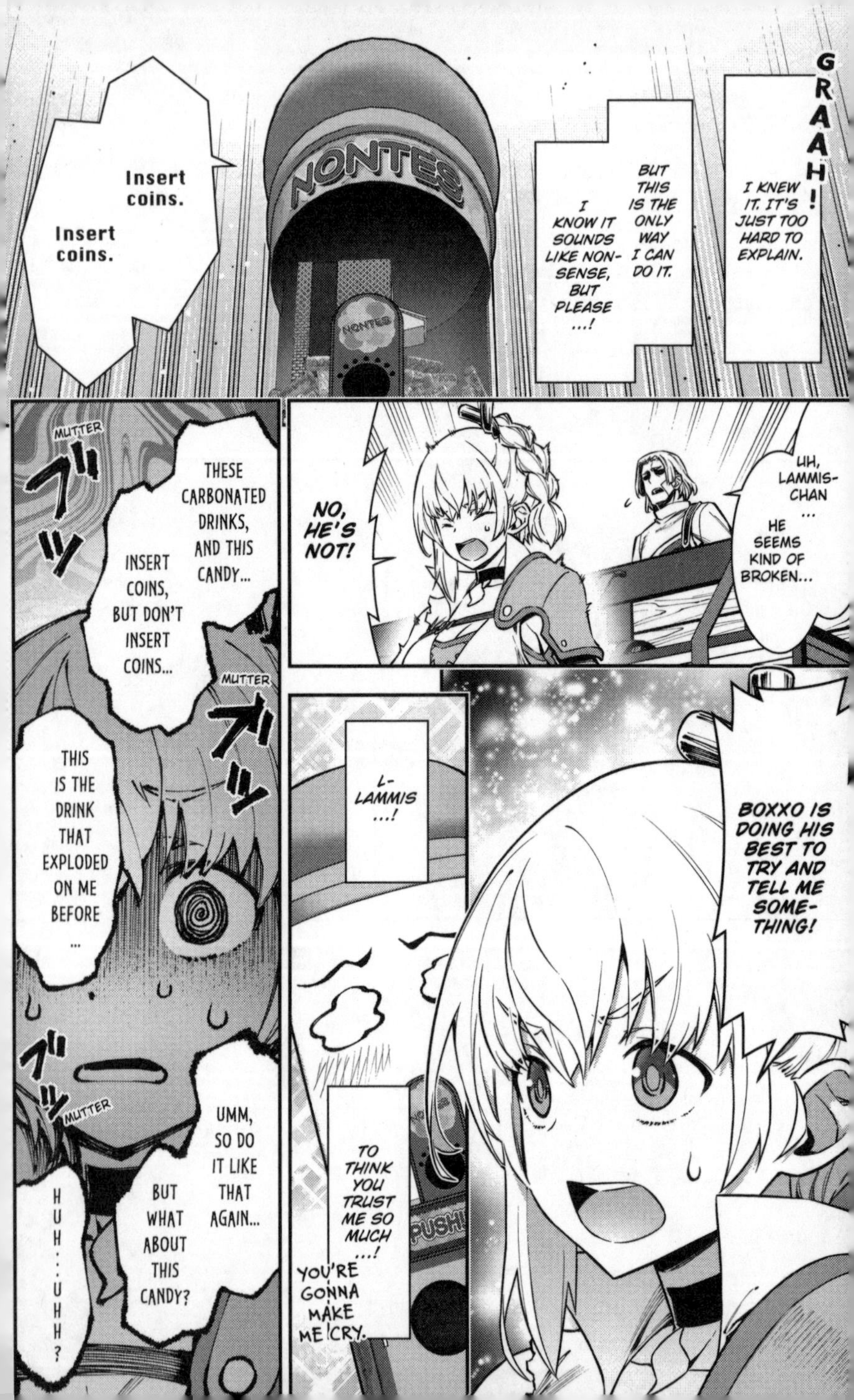
GRAAAH!
I KNEW IT. IT'S JUST TOO HARD TO EXPLAIN.
BUT THIS IS THE ONLY WAY I CAN DO IT.
I KNOW IT SOUNDS LIKE NON-SENSE, BUT PLEASE...!
Insert coins.
Insert coins.
UH, LAMMIS-CHAN... HE SEEMS KIND OF BROKEN...
NO, HE'S NOT!
BOXXO IS DOING HIS BEST TO TRY AND TELL ME SOME-THING!
L-LAMMIS...!
TO THINK YOU TRUST ME SO MUCH...!
YOU'RE GONNA MAKE ME CRY.
MUTTER
THESE CARBONATED DRINKS, AND THIS CANDY...
INSERT COINS, BUT DON'T INSERT COINS...
MUTTER
THIS IS THE DRINK THAT EXPLODED ON ME BEFORE...
UMM, SO DO IT LIKE THAT AGAIN...
BUT WHAT ABOUT THIS CANDY?
MUTTER
HUH...UHH?

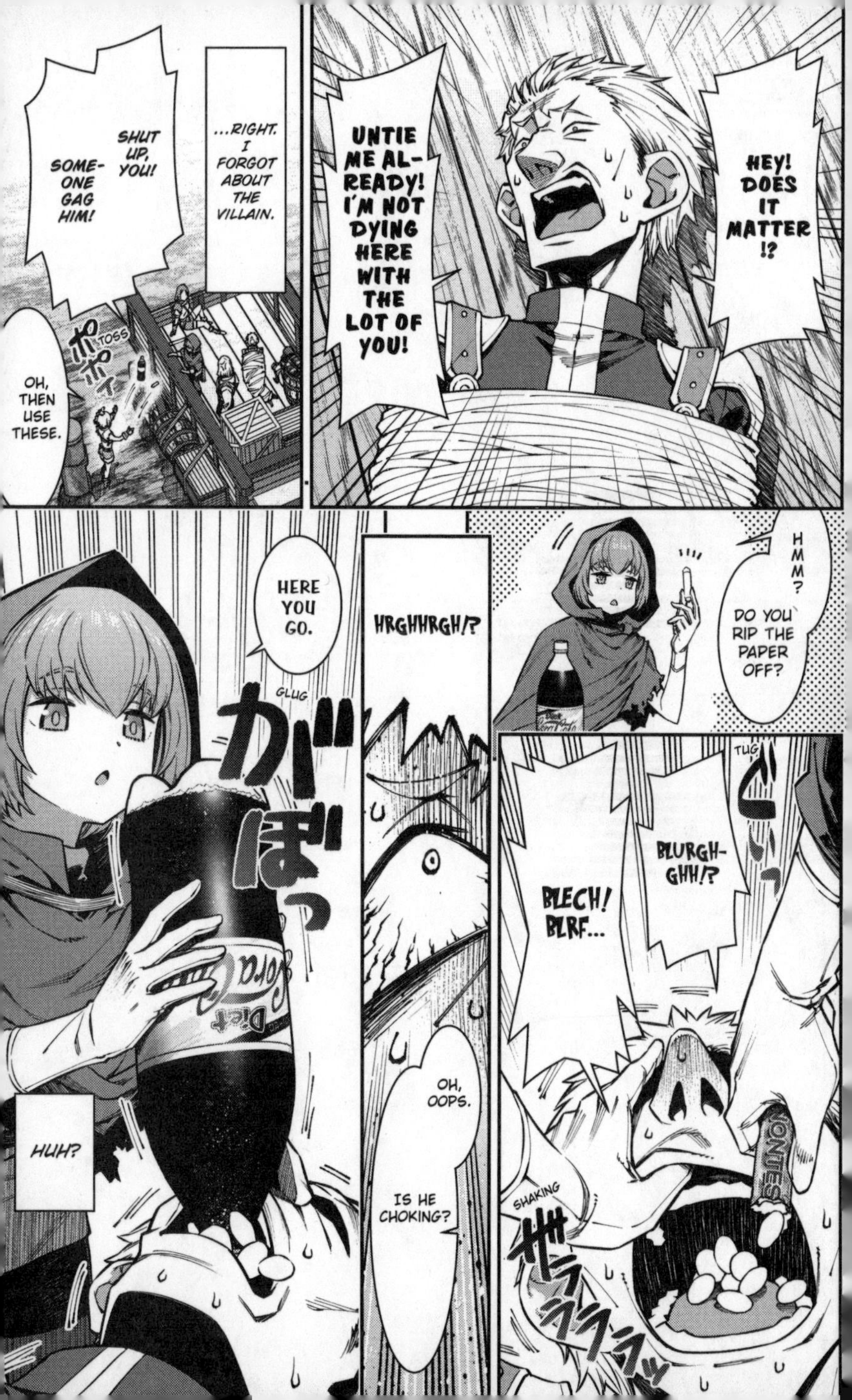
HEY! DOES IT MATTER!?
UNTIE ME AL-READY! I'M NOT DYING HERE WITH THE LOT OF YOU!
...RIGHT. I FORGOT ABOUT THE VILLAIN.
SHUT UP, YOU!
SOME-ONE GAG HIM!
TOSS
OH, THEN USE THESE.
HMM? DO YOU RIP THE PAPER OFF?
TUG
BLURGH-GHH!?
BLECH! BLRF...
SHAKING
HRGHHRGH!?
OH, OOPS.
IS HE CHOKING?
HERE YOU GO.
GLUG
HUH?

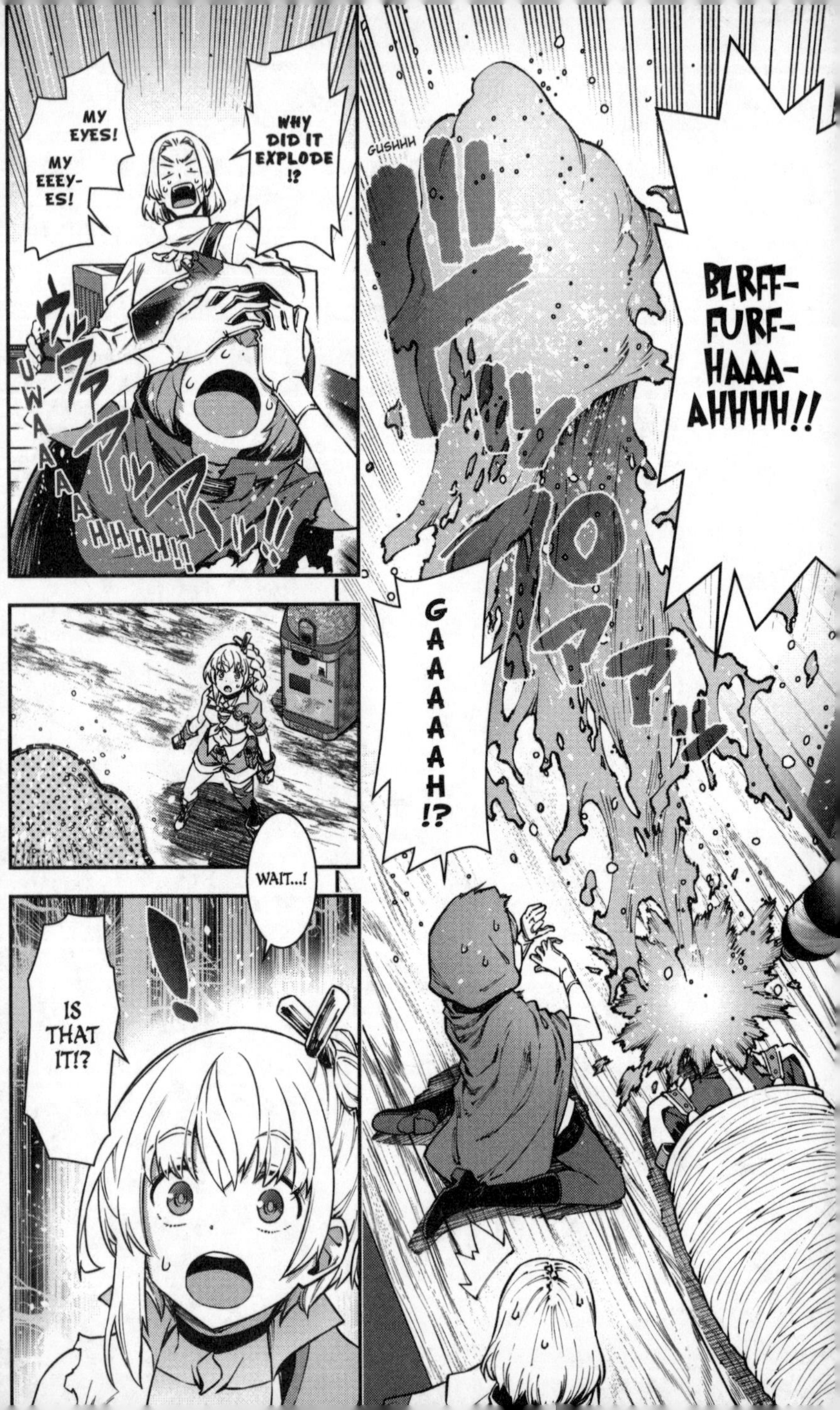
BLRFF-FURF-HAAA-AHHHH!!
GUSHHH
GAAAAAAAH!?
WHY DID IT EXPLODE!?
MY EYES!
MY EEEY-ES!
UWAAAAAAHHHHH!!
WAIT...!
IS THAT IT!?

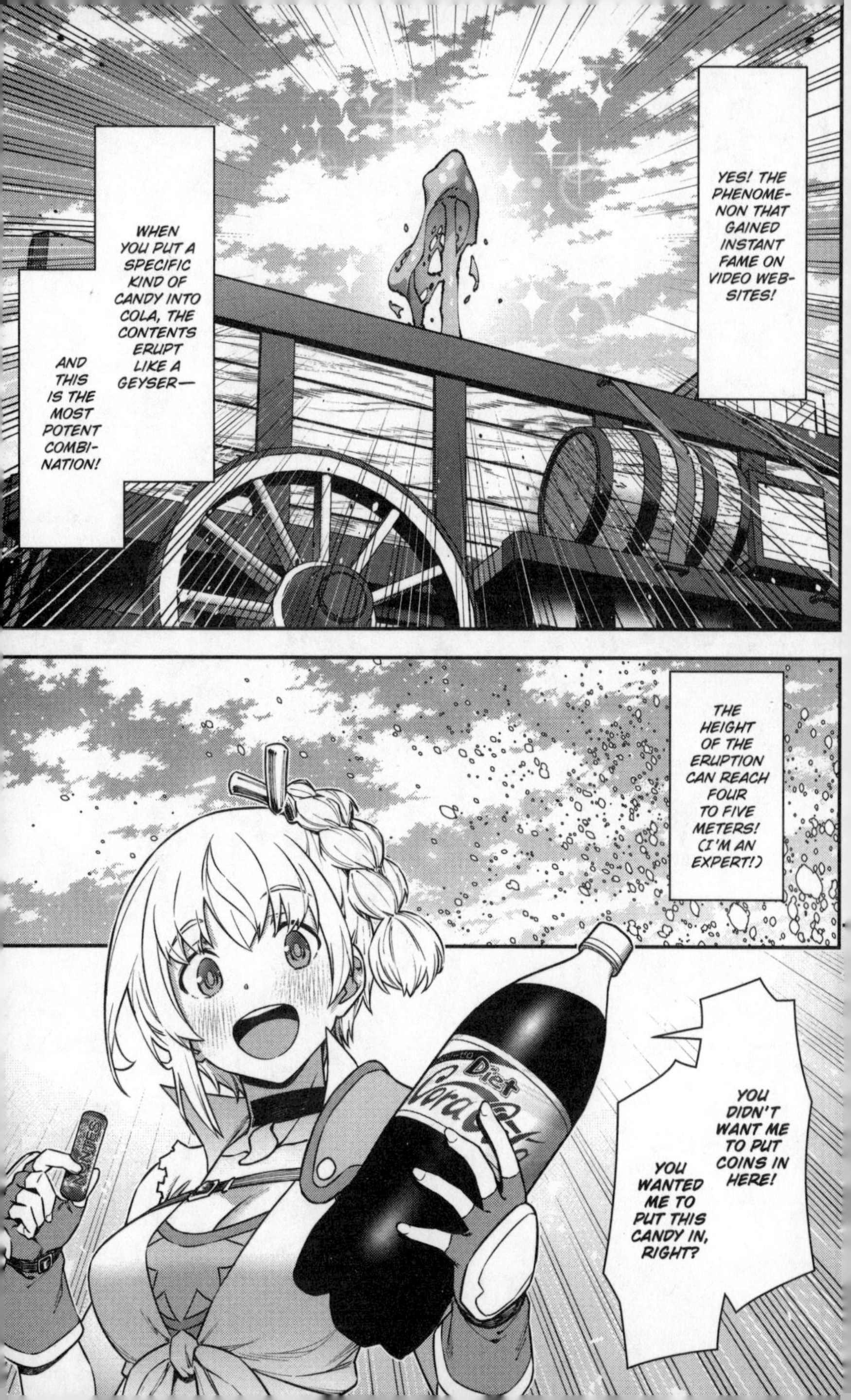
YES! THE PHENOME-NON THAT GAINED INSTANT FAME ON VIDEO WEB-SITES!
WHEN YOU PUT A SPECIFIC KIND OF CANDY INTO COLA, THE CONTENTS ERUPT LIKE A GEYSER—
AND THIS IS THE MOST POTENT COMBI-NATION!
THE HEIGHT OF THE ERUPTION CAN REACH FOUR TO FIVE METERS! (I'M AN EXPERT!)
YOU DIDN'T WANT ME TO PUT COINS IN HERE!
YOU WANTED ME TO PUT THIS CANDY IN, RIGHT?

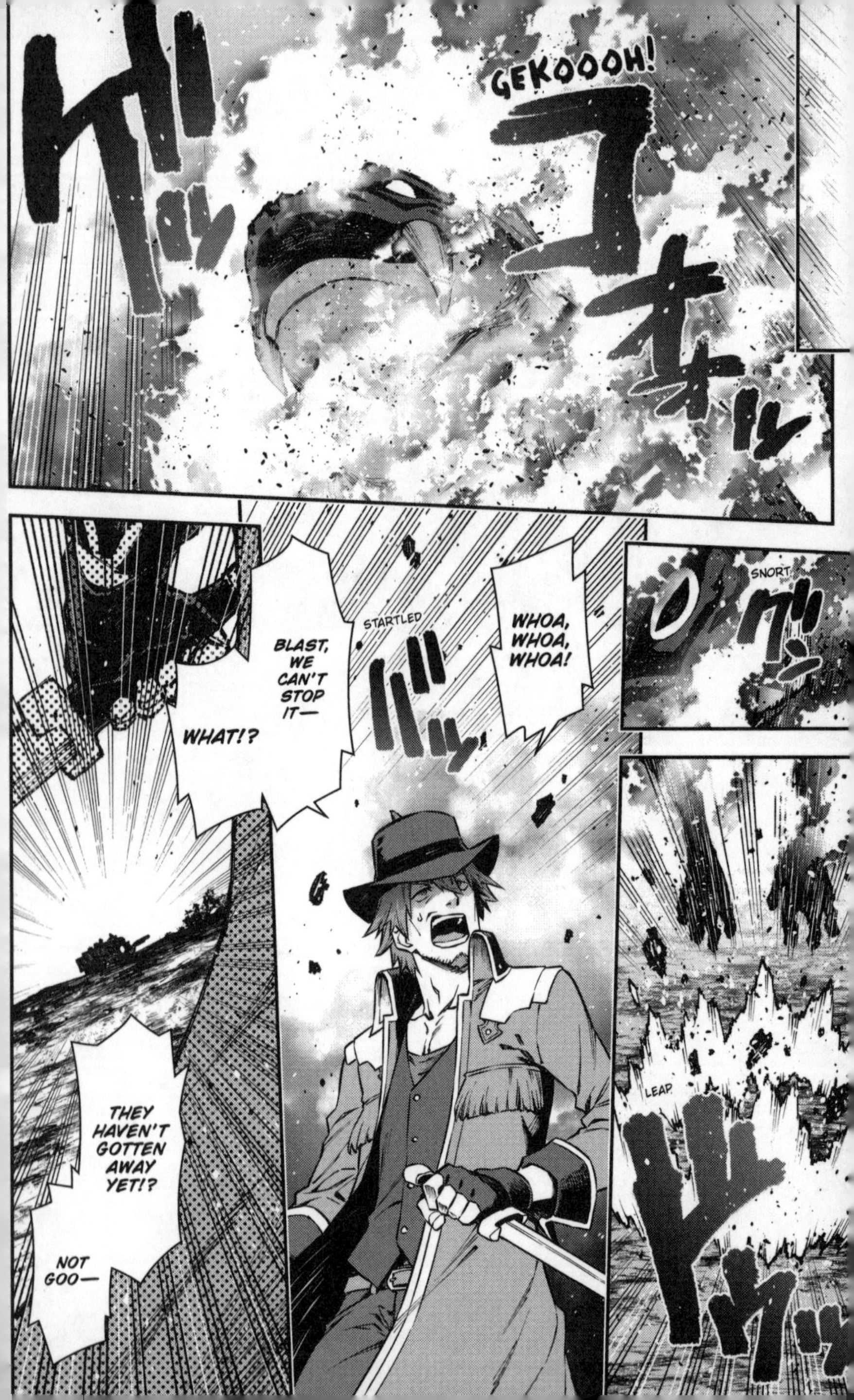
GEKOOOH!
SNORT
LEAP
WHOA, WHOA, WHOA!
STARTLED
BLAST, WE CAN'T STOP IT—
WHAT!?
THEY HAVEN'T GOTTEN AWAY YET!?
NOT GOO—

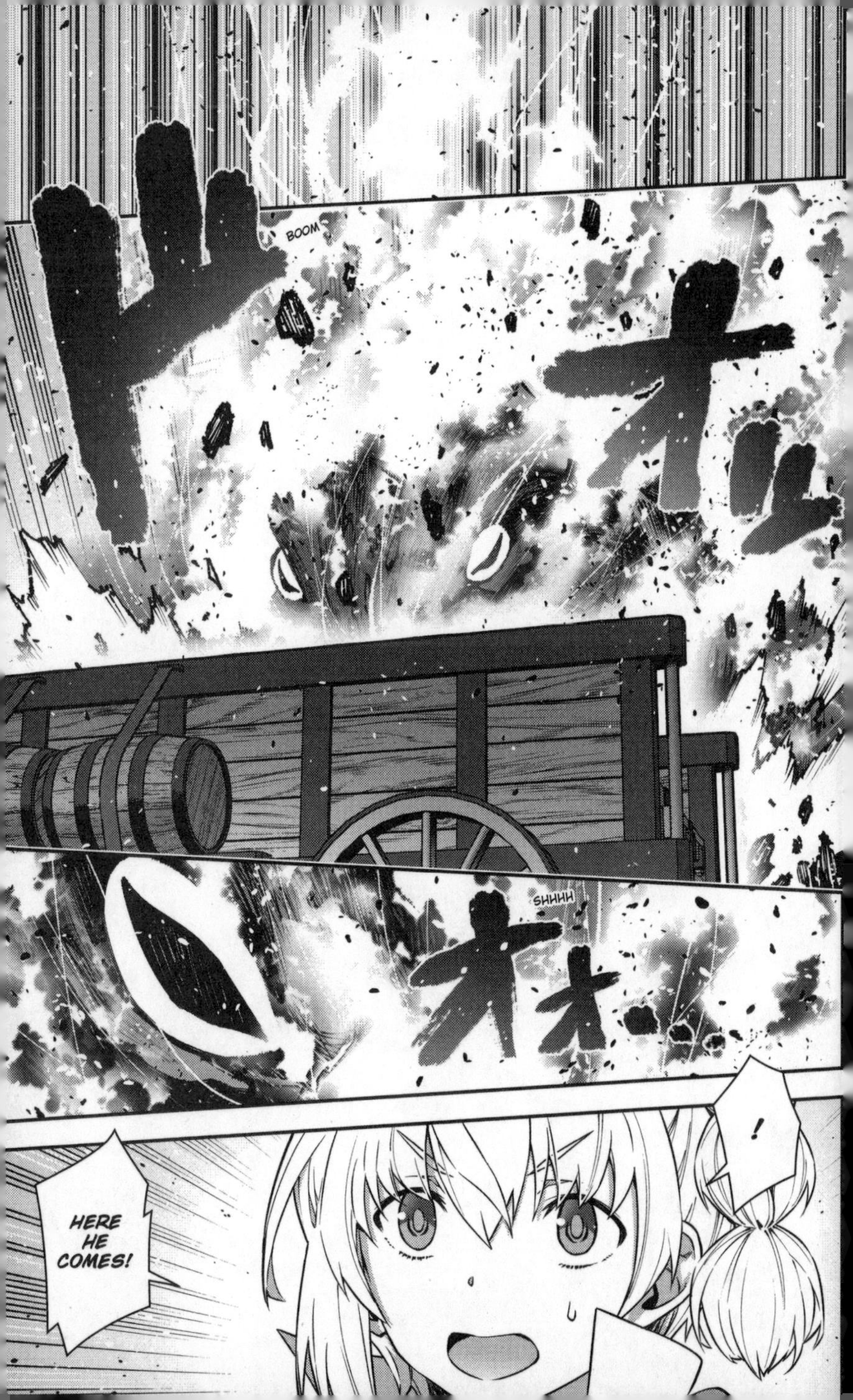
BOOM
SHHHH
!
HERE HE COMES!

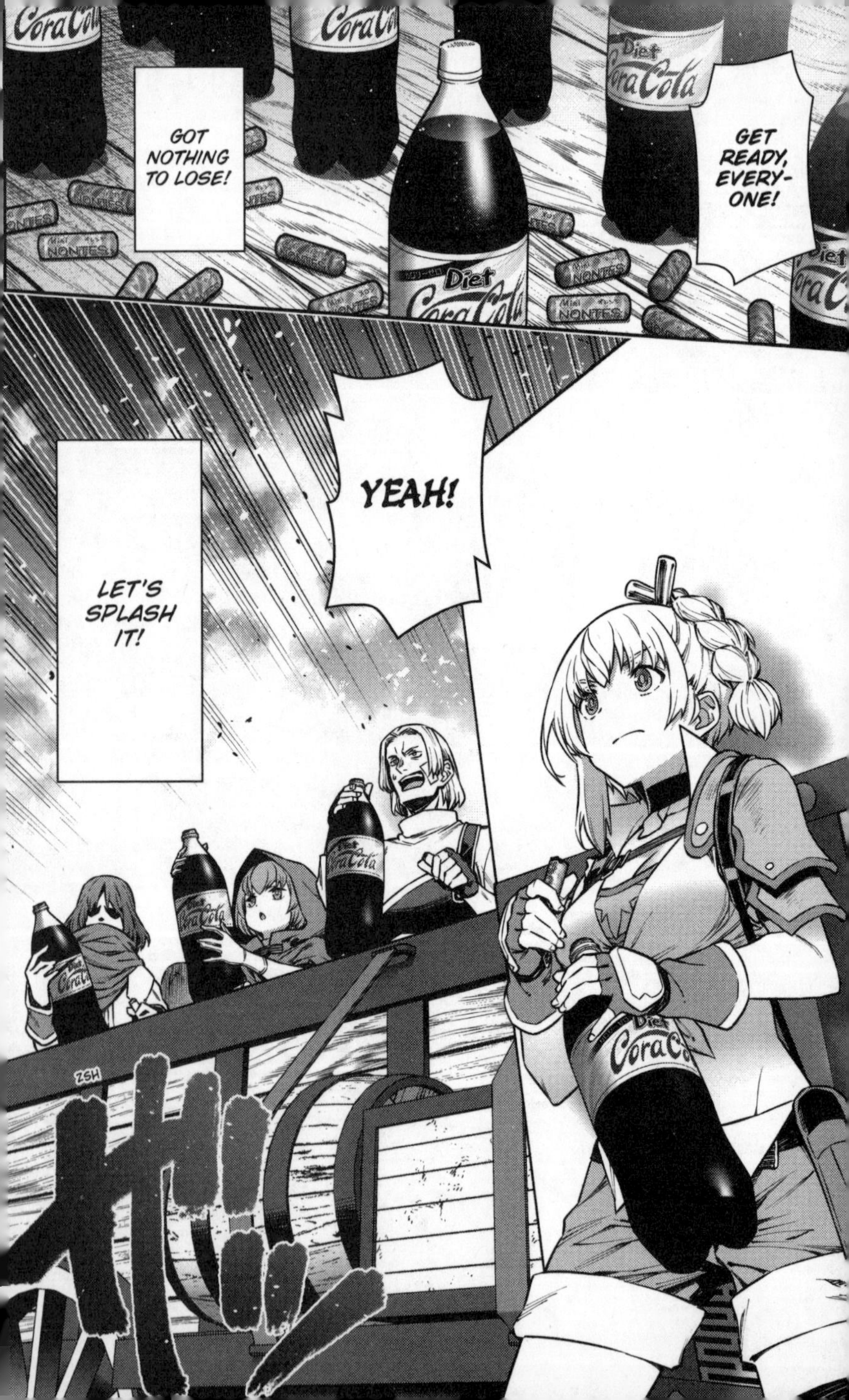
GET READY, EVERY-ONE!
GOT NOTHING TO LOSE!
YEAH!
LET'S SPLASH IT!
ZSH

CHAPTER 8 THE GREAT FROG FIEND (PART TWO)

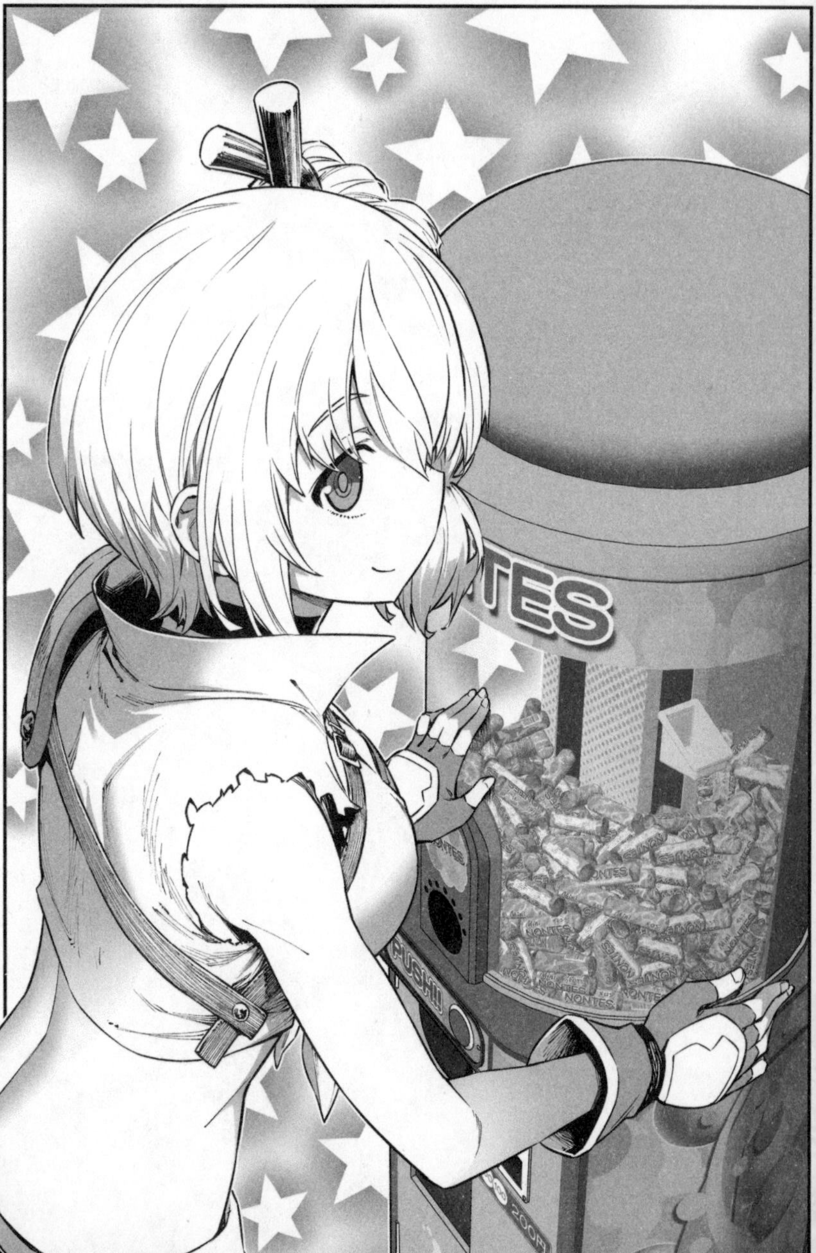
TES
NONTES
PUSH!

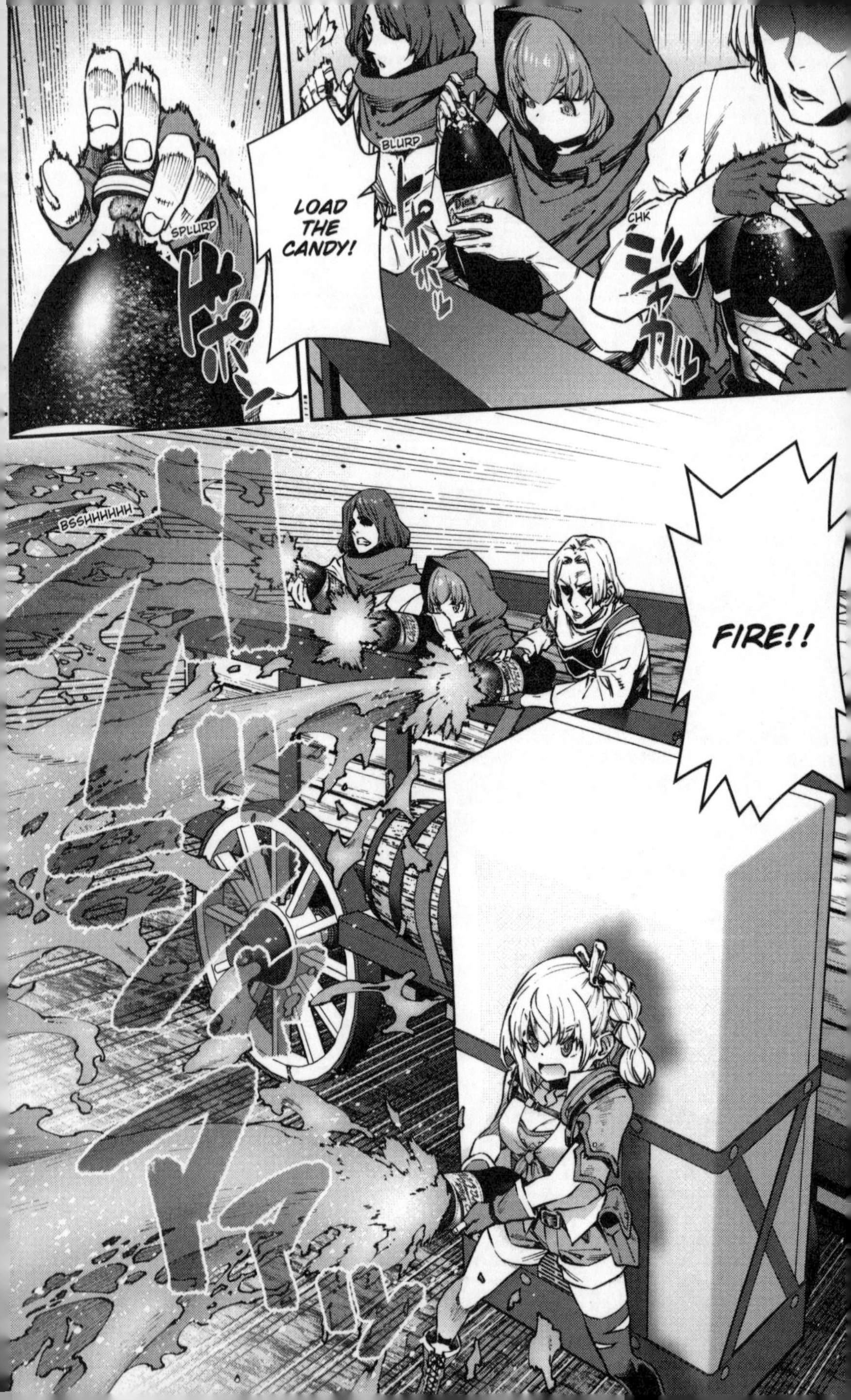
LOAD THE CANDY!
CHK
BLURP
SPLURP
FIRE!!
BSSHHHHHH

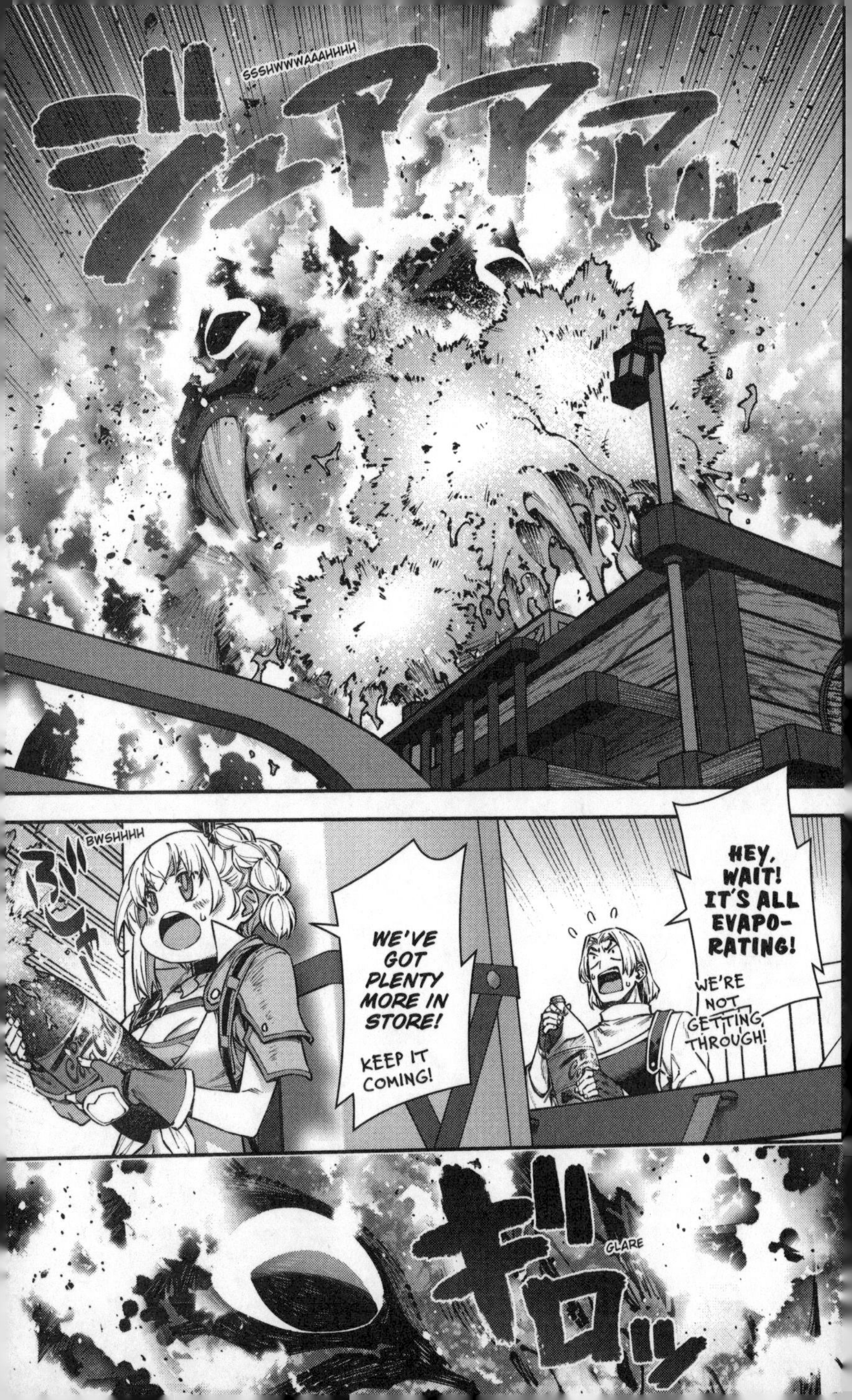
SSSHWWWAAAHHHH
HEY, WAIT! IT'S ALL EVAPO-RATING!
WE'RE NOT GETTING THROUGH!
WE'VE GOT PLENTY MORE IN STORE!
KEEP IT COMING!
BWSHHHH
GLARE

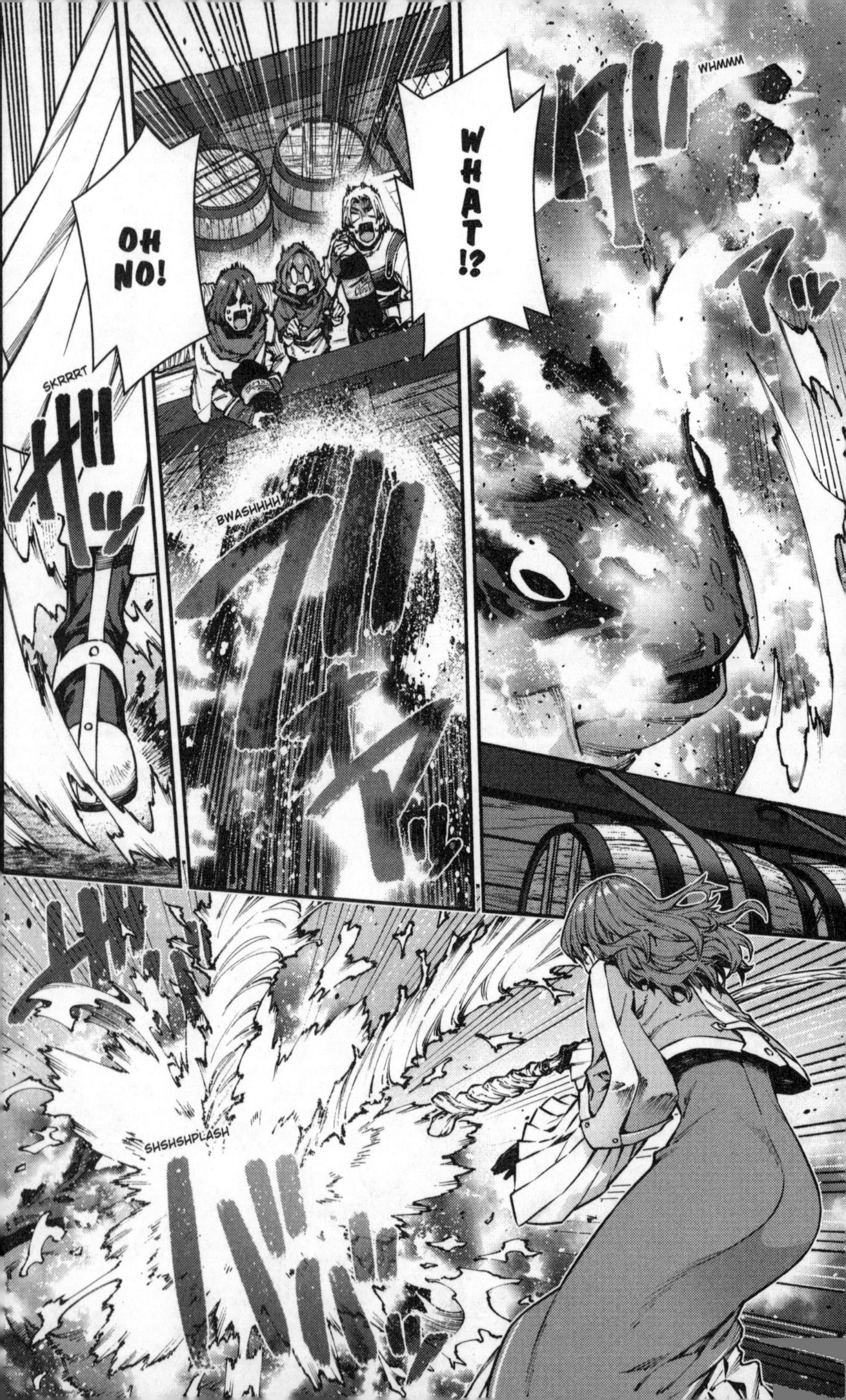
WHMMM
WHAT!?
OH NO!
BWASHHHH
SKRRRT
SHSHSHPLASH

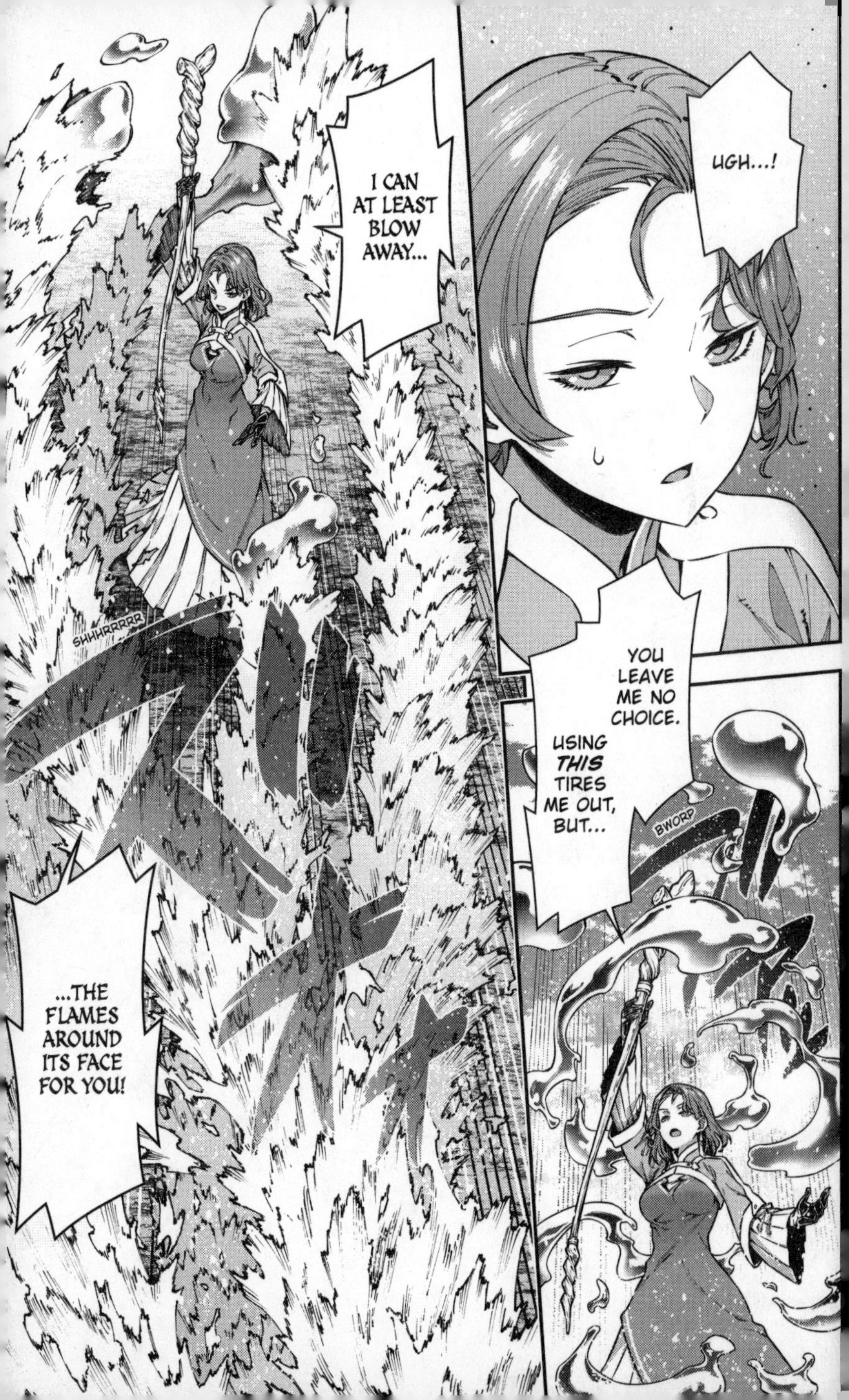
UGH...!
YOU LEAVE ME NO CHOICE.
USING *THIS* TIRES ME OUT, BUT...
BWORP
I CAN AT LEAST BLOW AWAY...
SHHHRRRRR
...THE FLAMES AROUND ITS FACE FOR YOU!

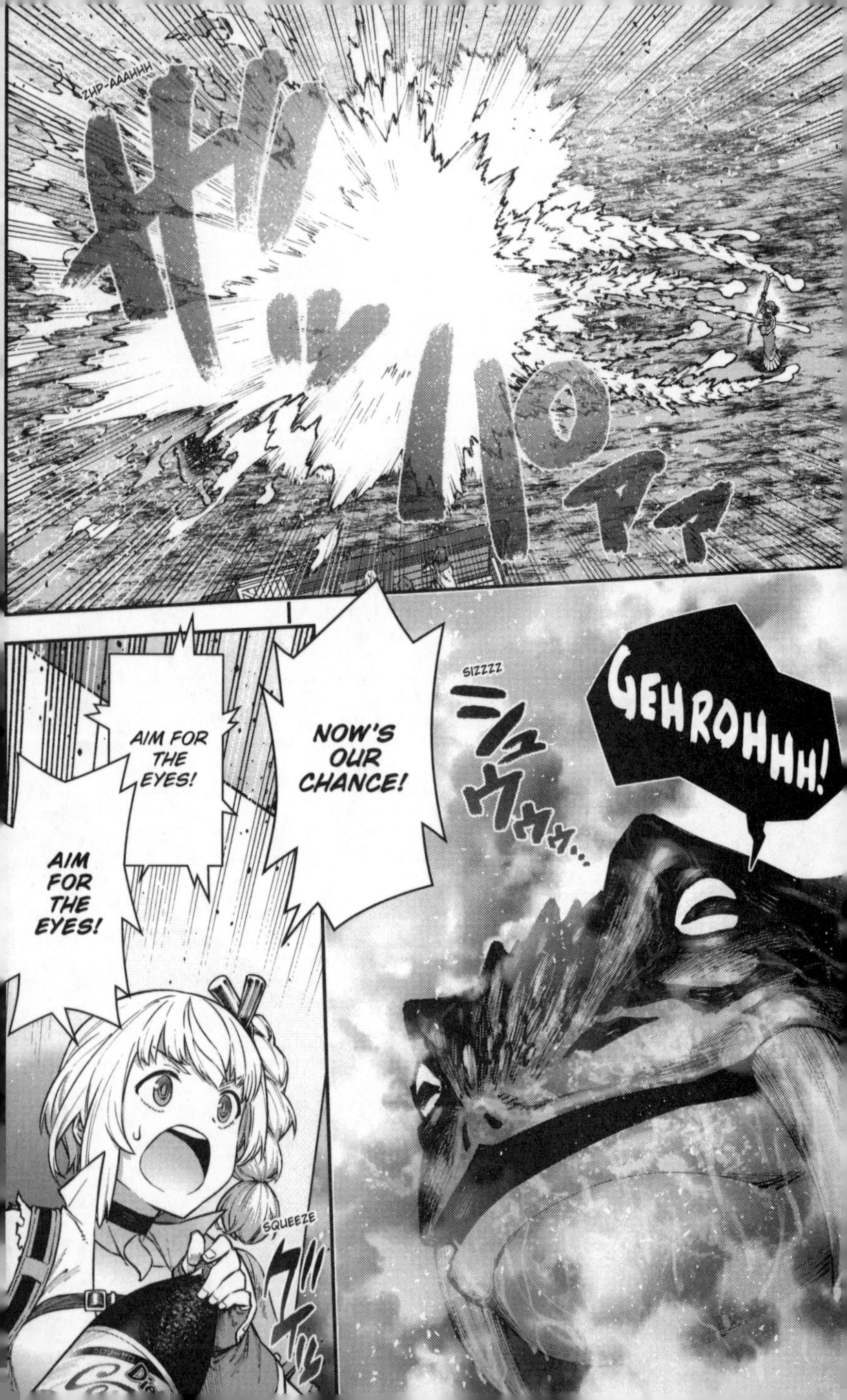
ZHP-AAAHHH
GEHROHHH!
SIZZZZ
NOW'S OUR CHANCE!
AIM FOR THE EYES!
AIM FOR THE EYES!
SQUEEZE

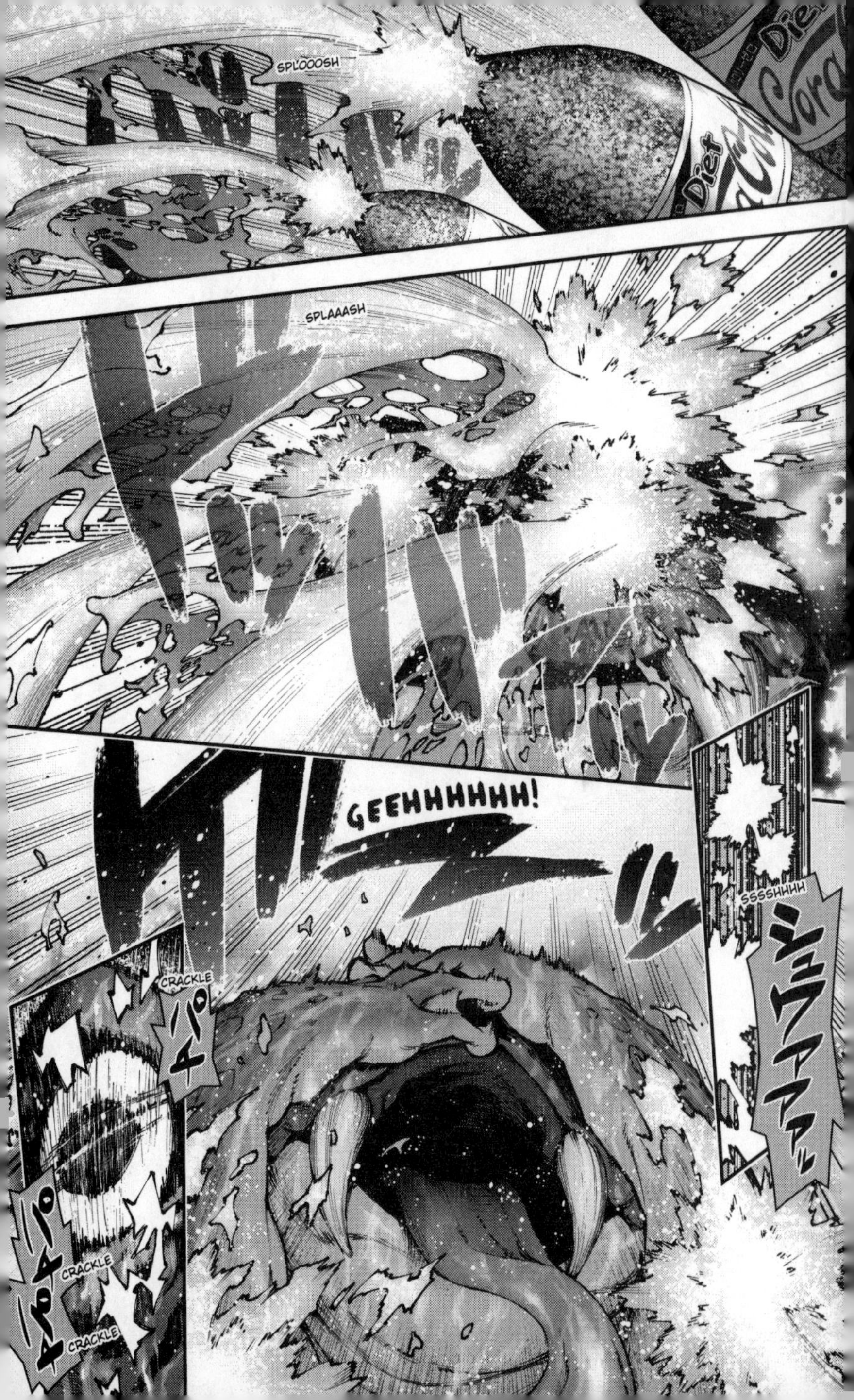

Diet
SPLOOOSH
Diet
SPLAAASH
SSSSHHHH
GEEHHHHHH!
CRACKLE
CRACKLE
CRACKLE

GEKOHH-HHH!
FSSSSHHHH
OOORH!
AHH!
GEKUHHH!
GEROGE-KOHH...!
THE FIRES...
THEY'RE WEAKER NOW!

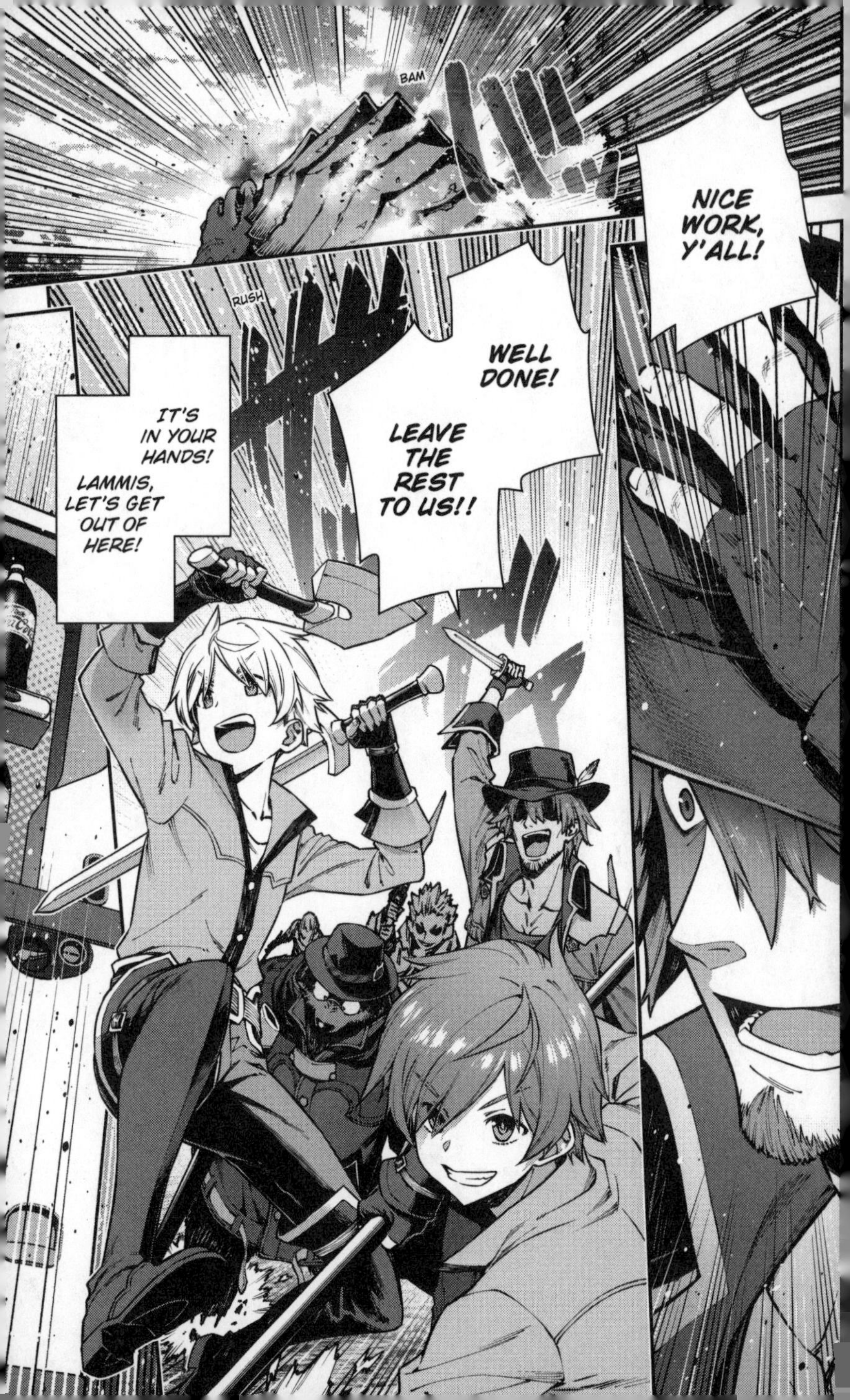
BAM
NICE WORK, Y'ALL!
RUSH
WELL DONE!
LEAVE THE REST TO US!!
IT'S IN YOUR HANDS!
LAMMIS, LET'S GET OUT OF HERE!

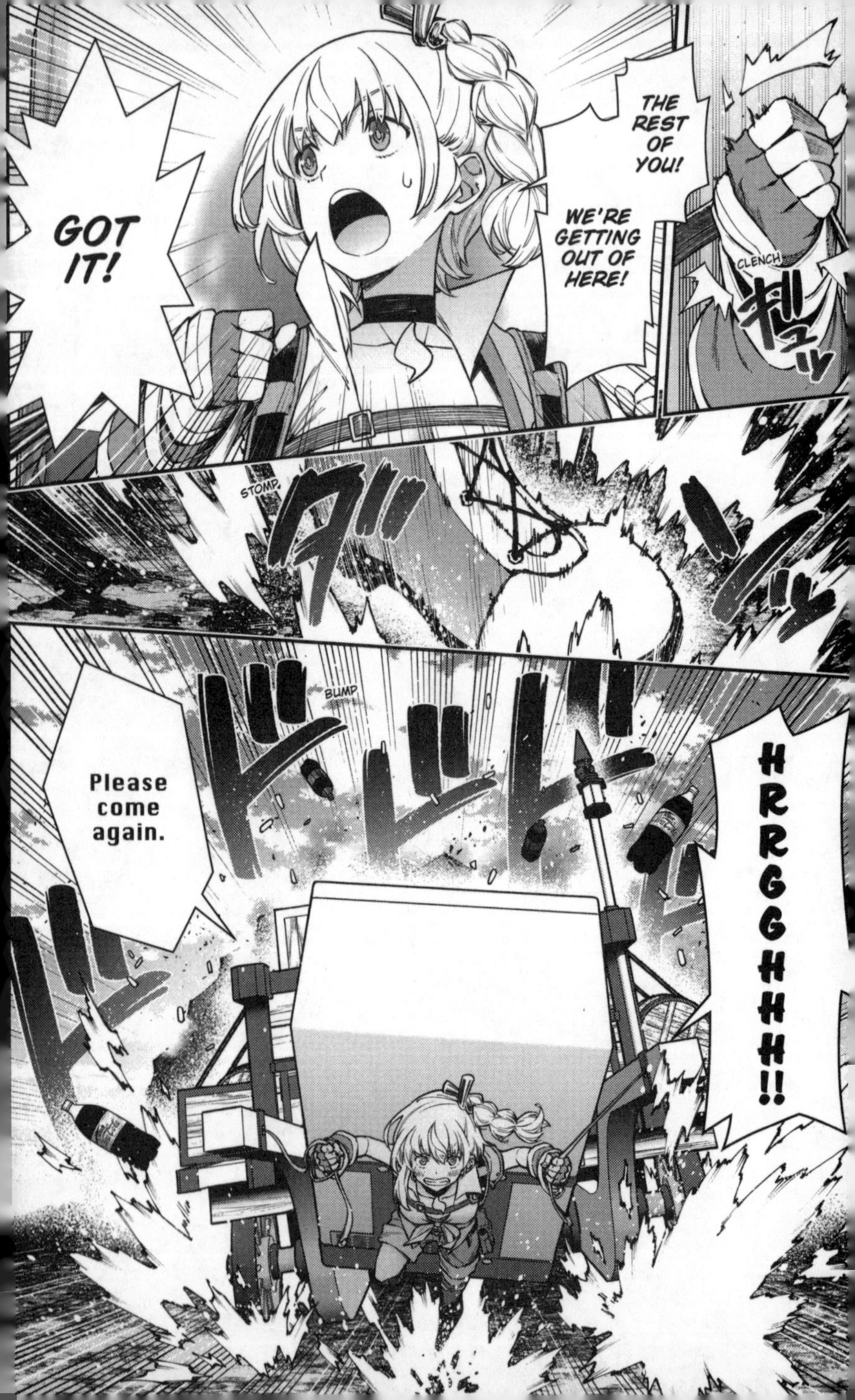
CLENCH
THE REST OF YOU!
WE'RE GETTING OUT OF HERE!
GOT IT!
STOMP
BUMP
HRRGGHHHH!!
Please come again.

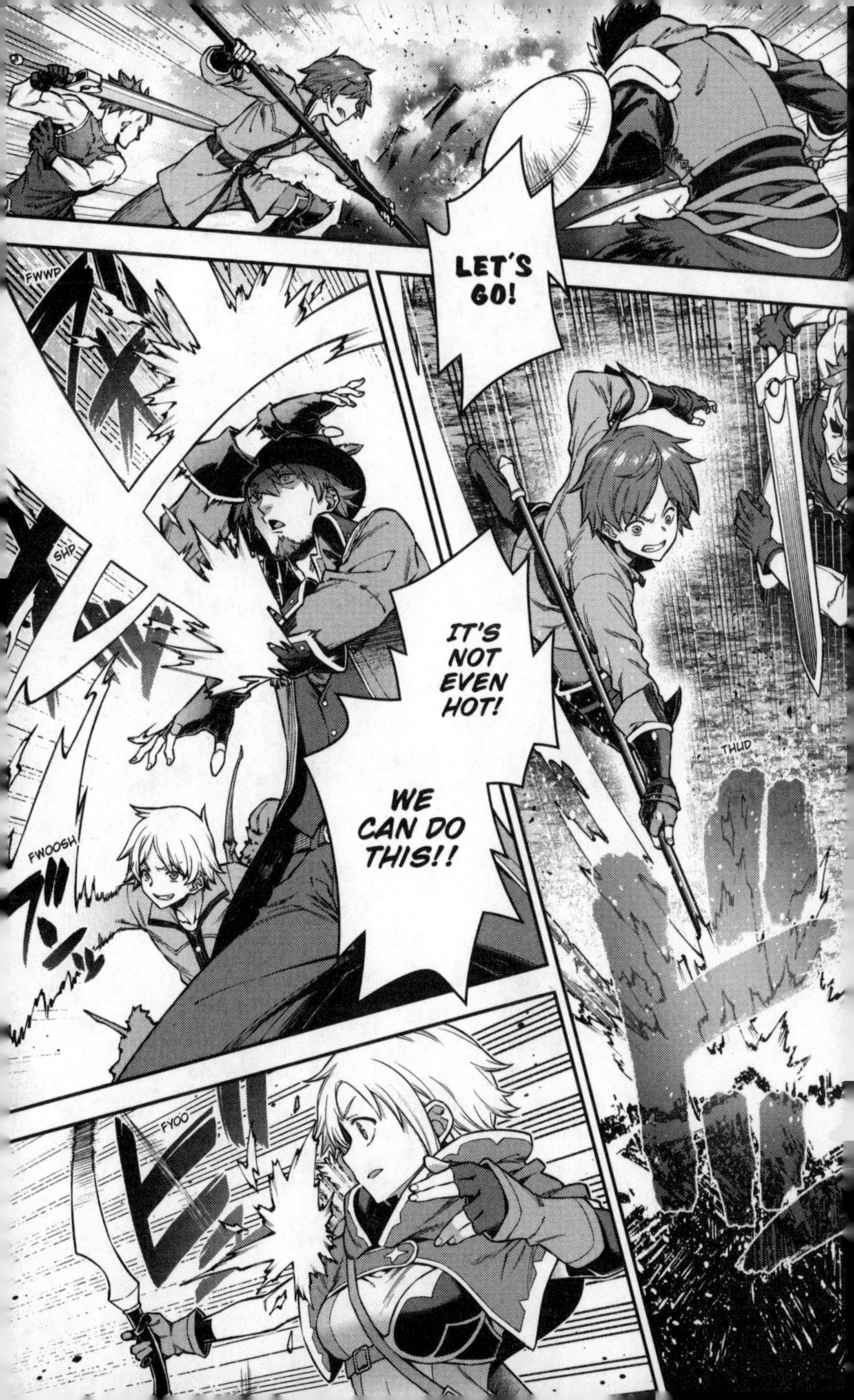
LET'S GO!
THUD
FWWP
SHP
IT'S NOT EVEN HOT!
WE CAN DO THIS!!
FWOOSH
FYOO

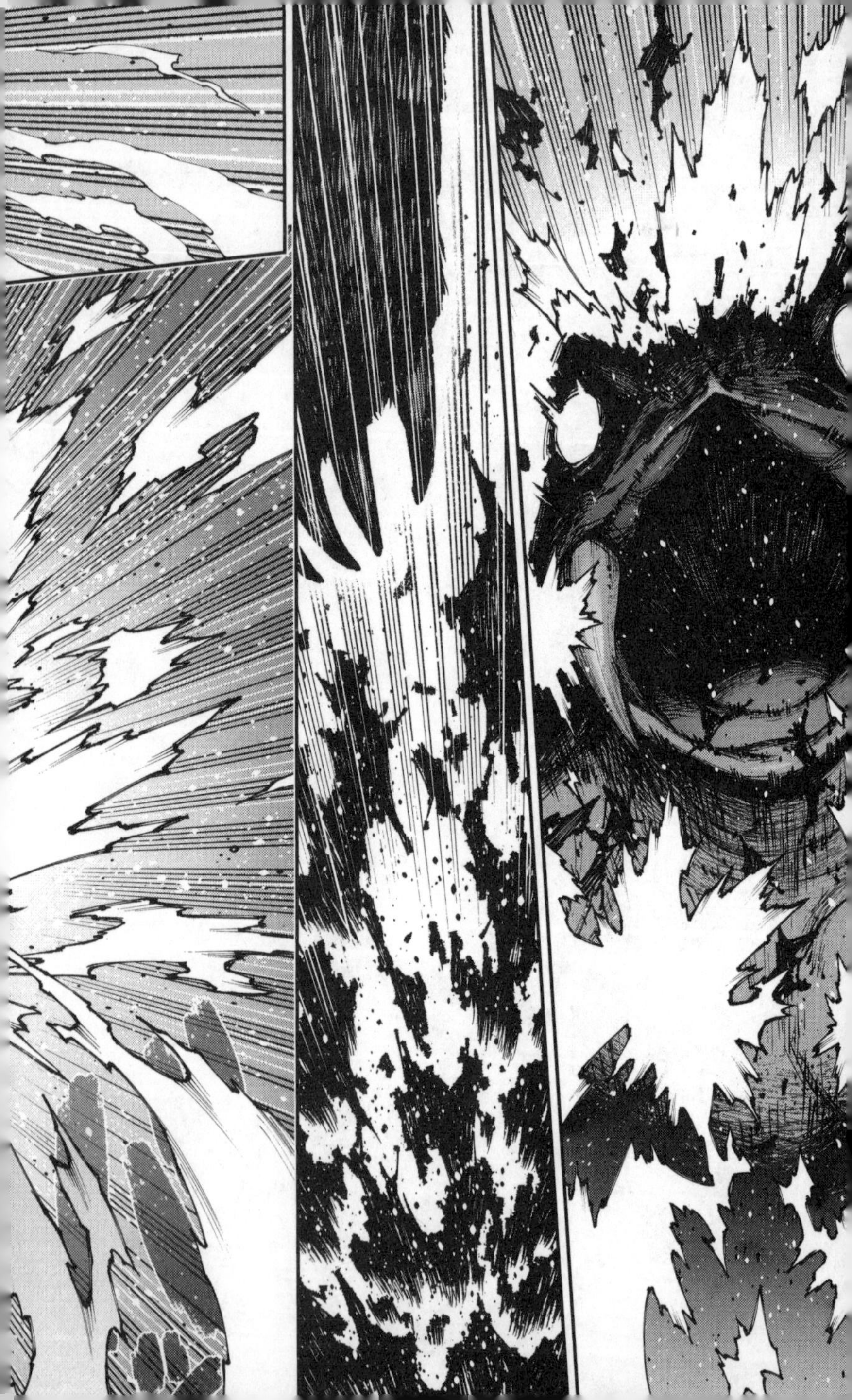

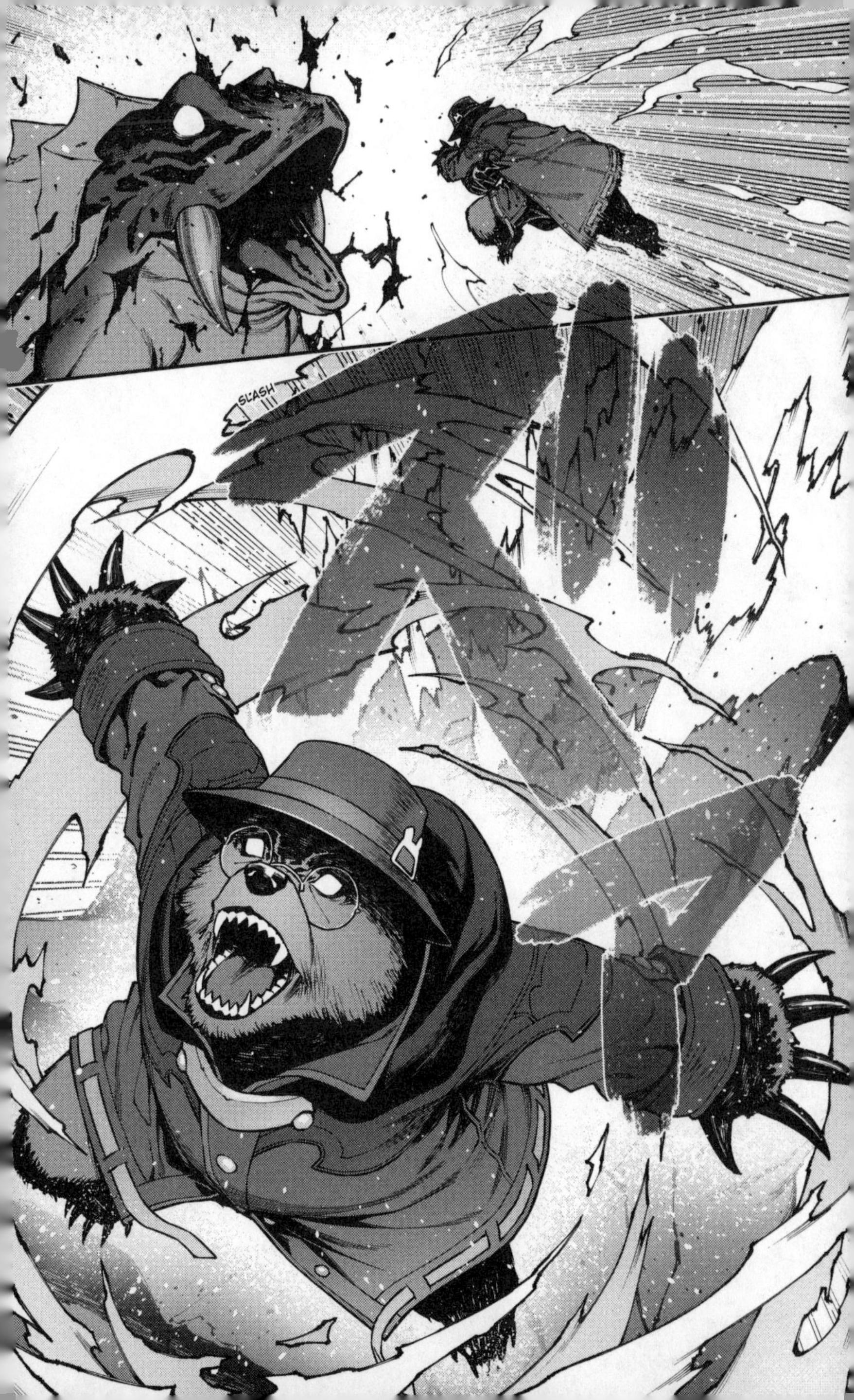
SLASH

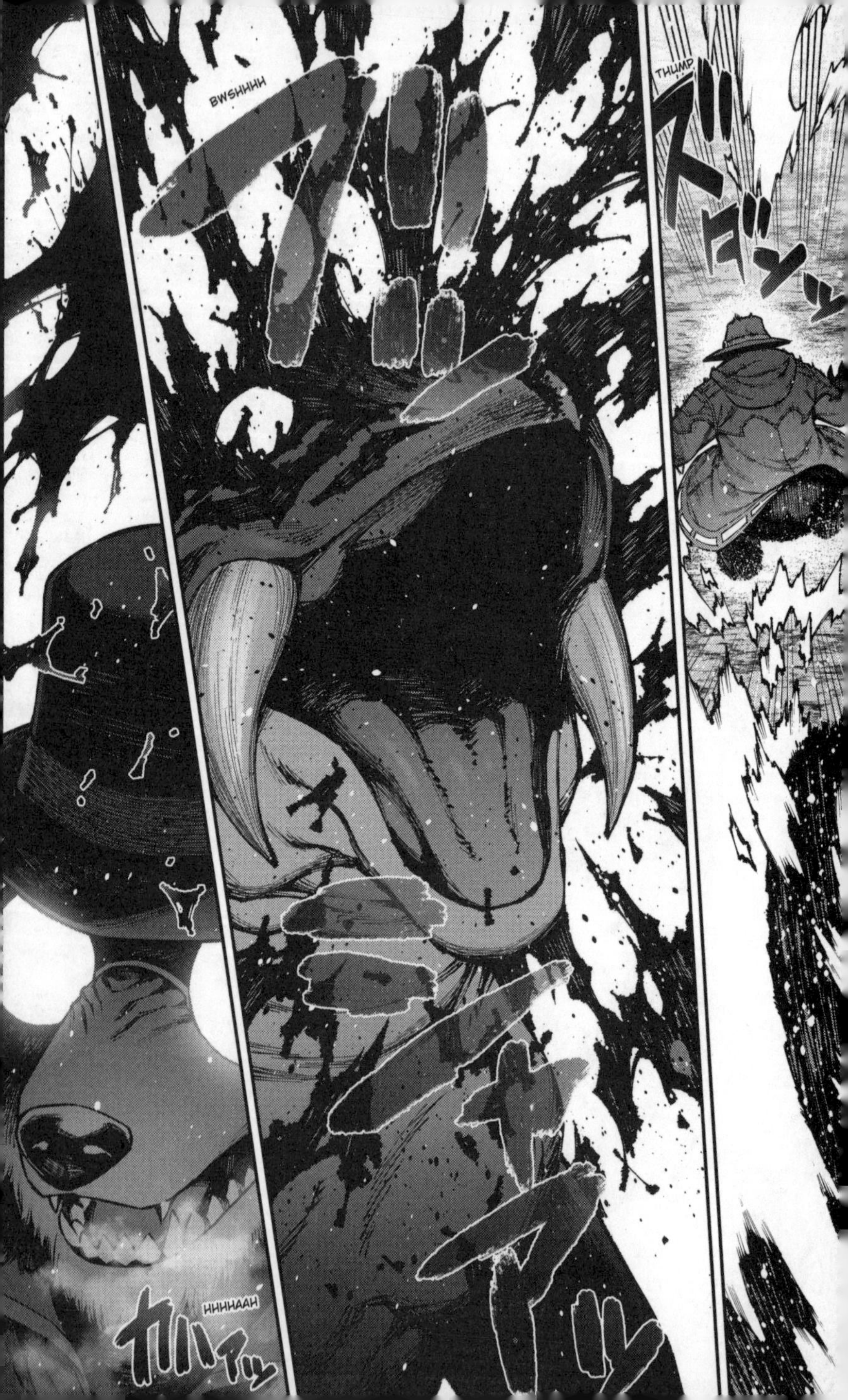
THUMP
BWSHHHH
HHHHAAH

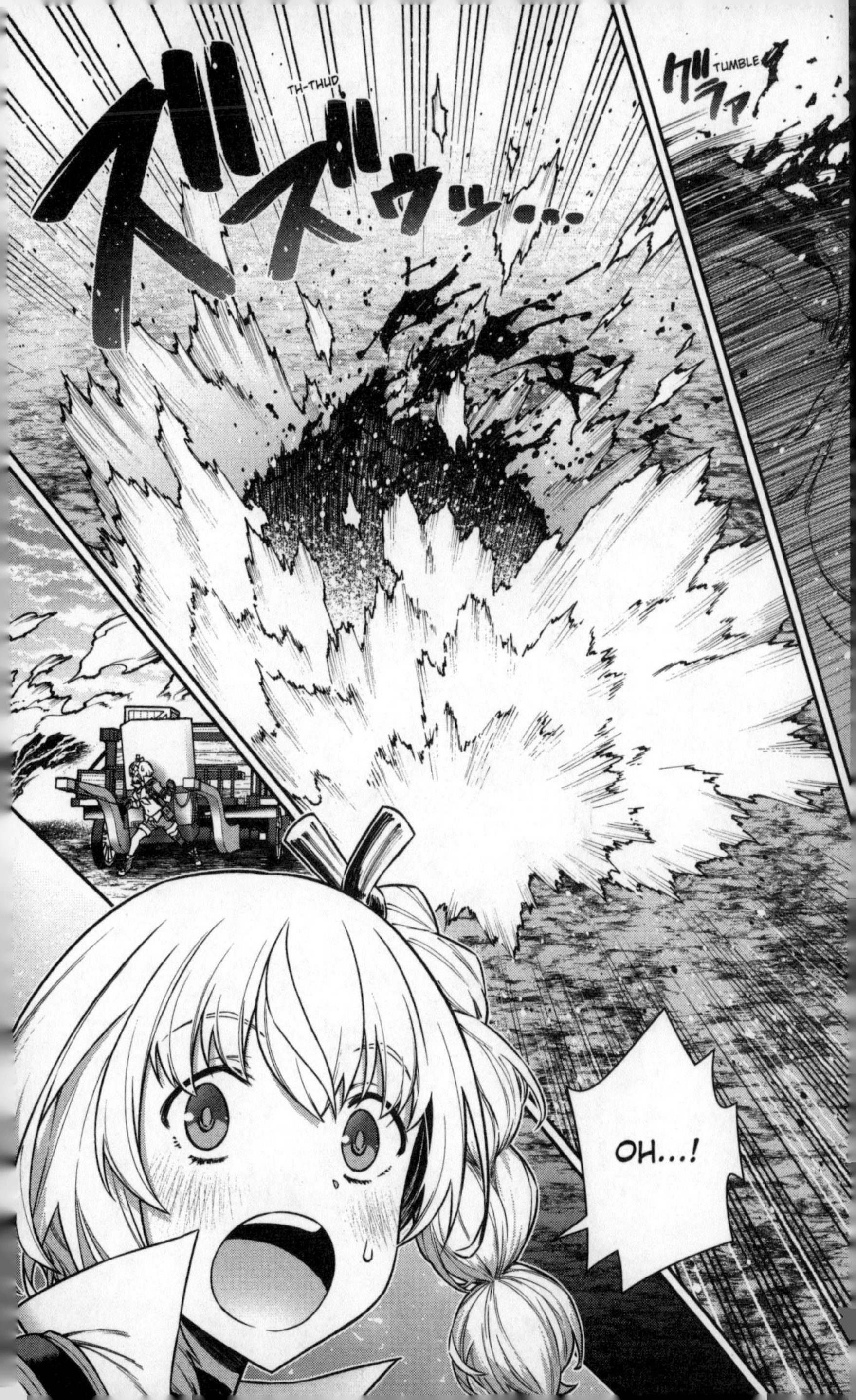
グラァ
TUMBLE
ズズゥッ…
TH-THUD
OH...!

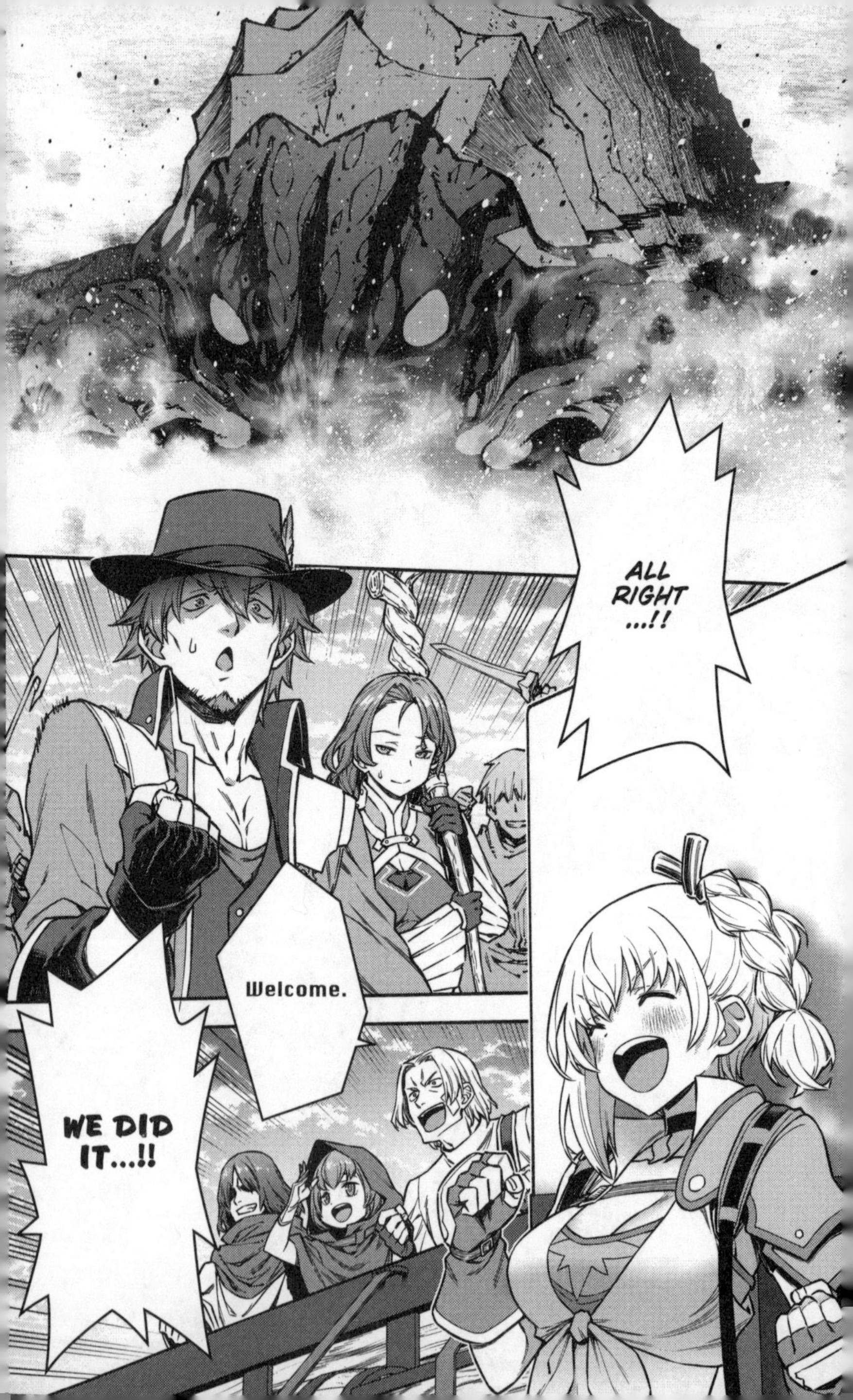
ALL RIGHT ...!!
Welcome.
WE DID IT...!!

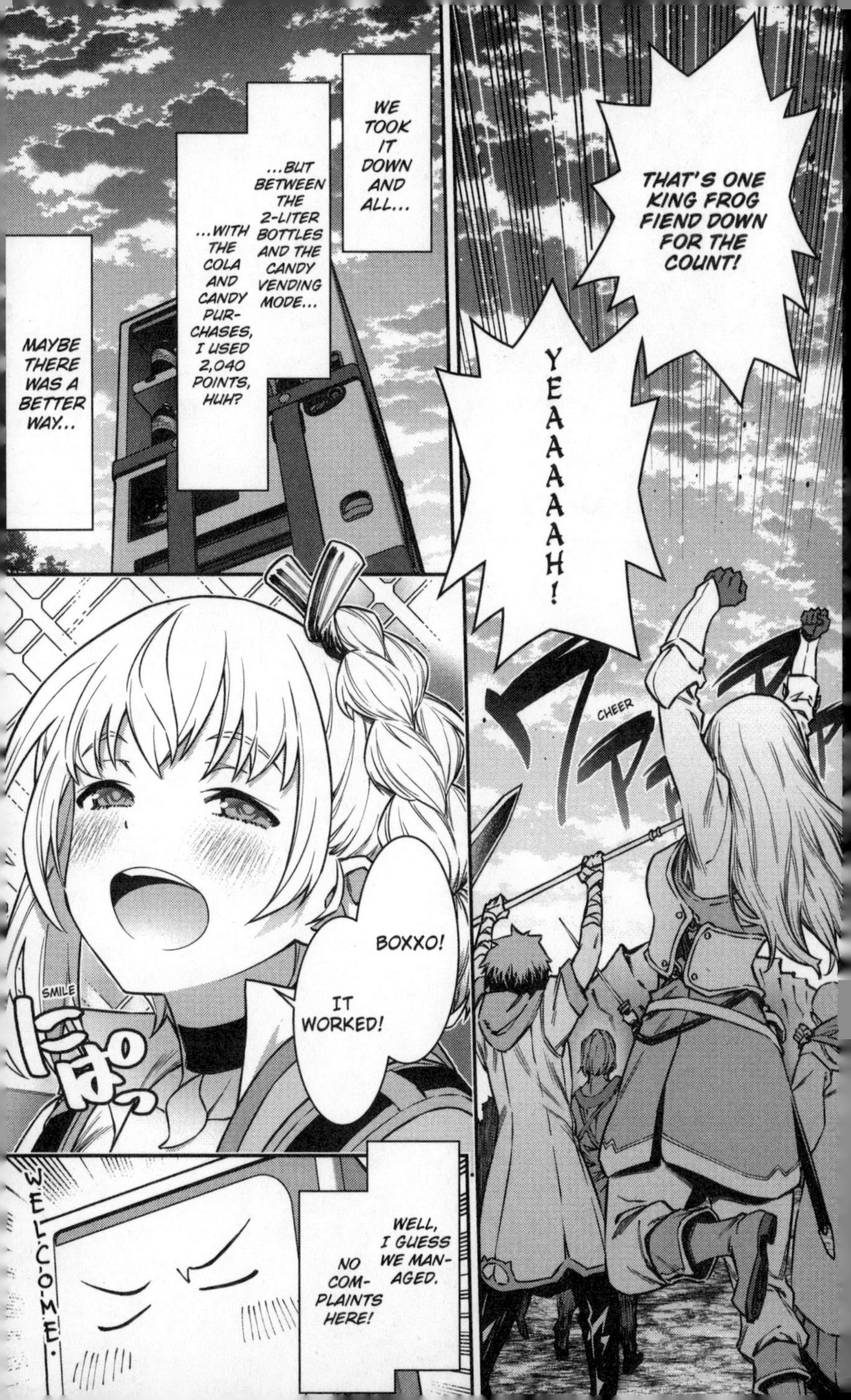
THAT'S ONE KING FROG FIEND DOWN FOR THE COUNT!
YEAAAAAAH!
CHEER
WE TOOK IT DOWN AND ALL...
...BUT BETWEEN THE 2-LITER BOTTLES AND THE CANDY VENDING MODE...
...WITH THE COLA AND CANDY PURCHASES, I USED 2,040 POINTS, HUH?
MAYBE THERE WAS A BETTER WAY...
BOXXO!
IT WORKED!
SMILE
WELCOME.
WELL, I GUESS WE MANAGED.
NO COMPLAINTS HERE!

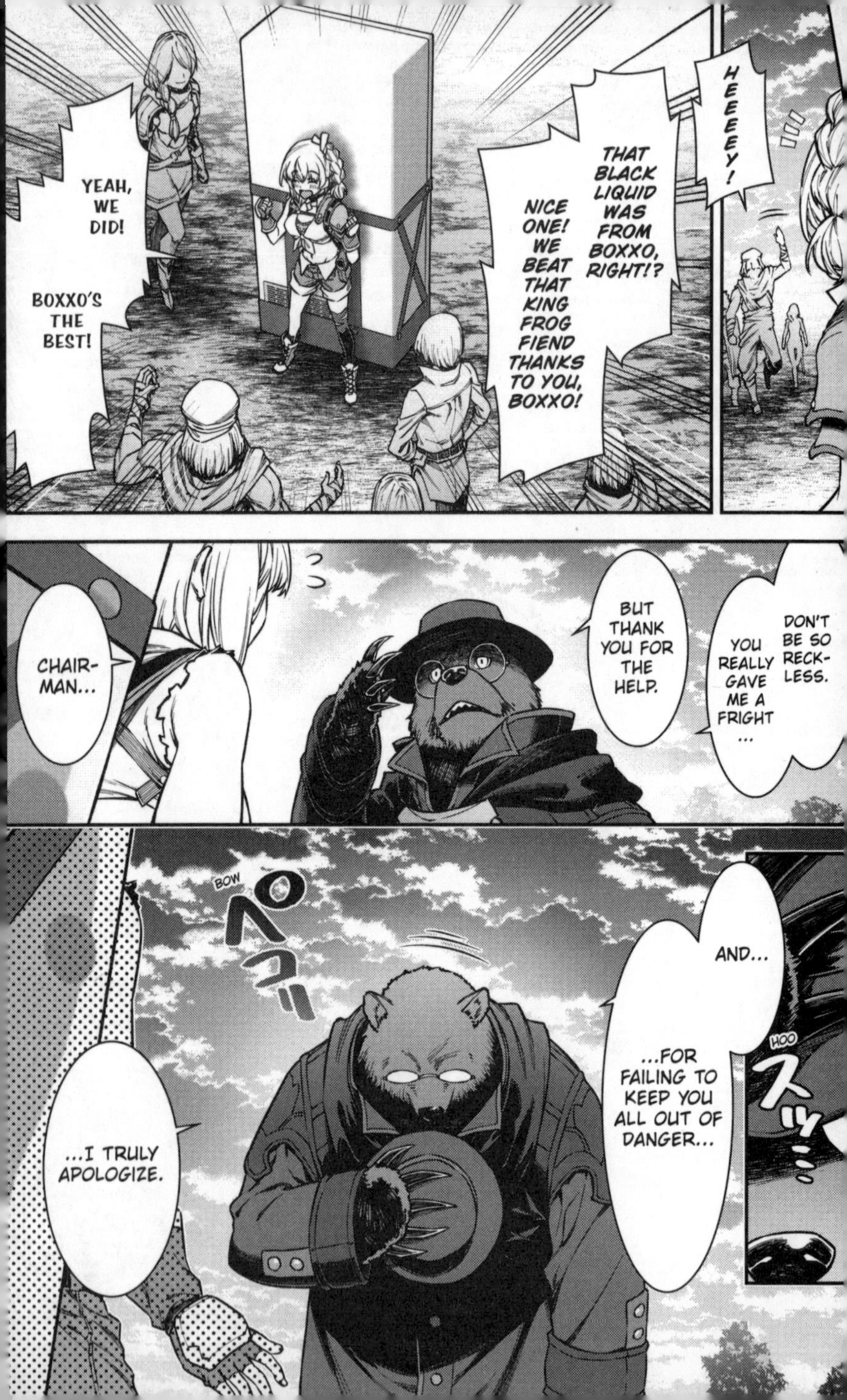
HEEEEEY!
THAT BLACK LIQUID WAS FROM BOXXO, RIGHT!?
NICE ONE! WE BEAT THAT KING FROG FIEND THANKS TO YOU, BOXXO!
YEAH, WE DID!
BOXXO'S THE BEST!
DON'T BE SO RECK-LESS.
YOU REALLY GAVE ME A FRIGHT...
BUT THANK YOU FOR THE HELP.
CHAIR-MAN...
HOO
AND...
BOW
...FOR FAILING TO KEEP YOU ALL OUT OF DANGER...
...I TRULY APOLOGIZE.

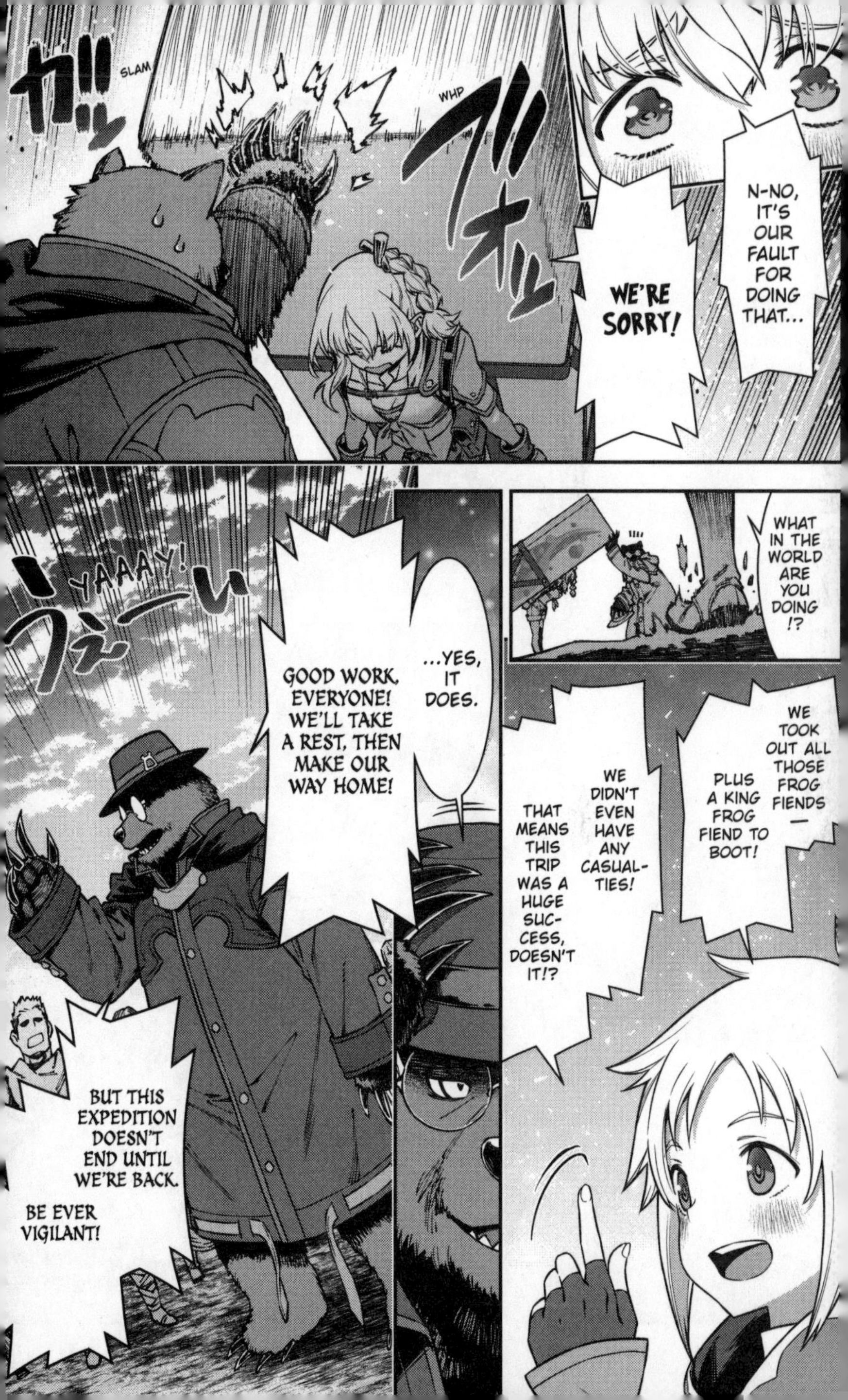
N-NO, IT'S OUR FAULT FOR DOING THAT...
WE'RE SORRY!
WHP
SLAM
WHAT IN THE WORLD ARE YOU DOING!?
WE TOOK OUT ALL THOSE FROG FIENDS—
PLUS A KING FROG FIEND TO BOOT!
WE DIDN'T EVEN HAVE ANY CASUAL-TIES!
THAT MEANS THIS TRIP WAS A HUGE SUC-CESS, DOESN'T IT!?
...YES, IT DOES.
GOOD WORK, EVERYONE! WE'LL TAKE A REST, THEN MAKE OUR WAY HOME!
YAAAY!
BUT THIS EXPEDITION DOESN'T END UNTIL WE'RE BACK.
BE EVER VIGILANT!

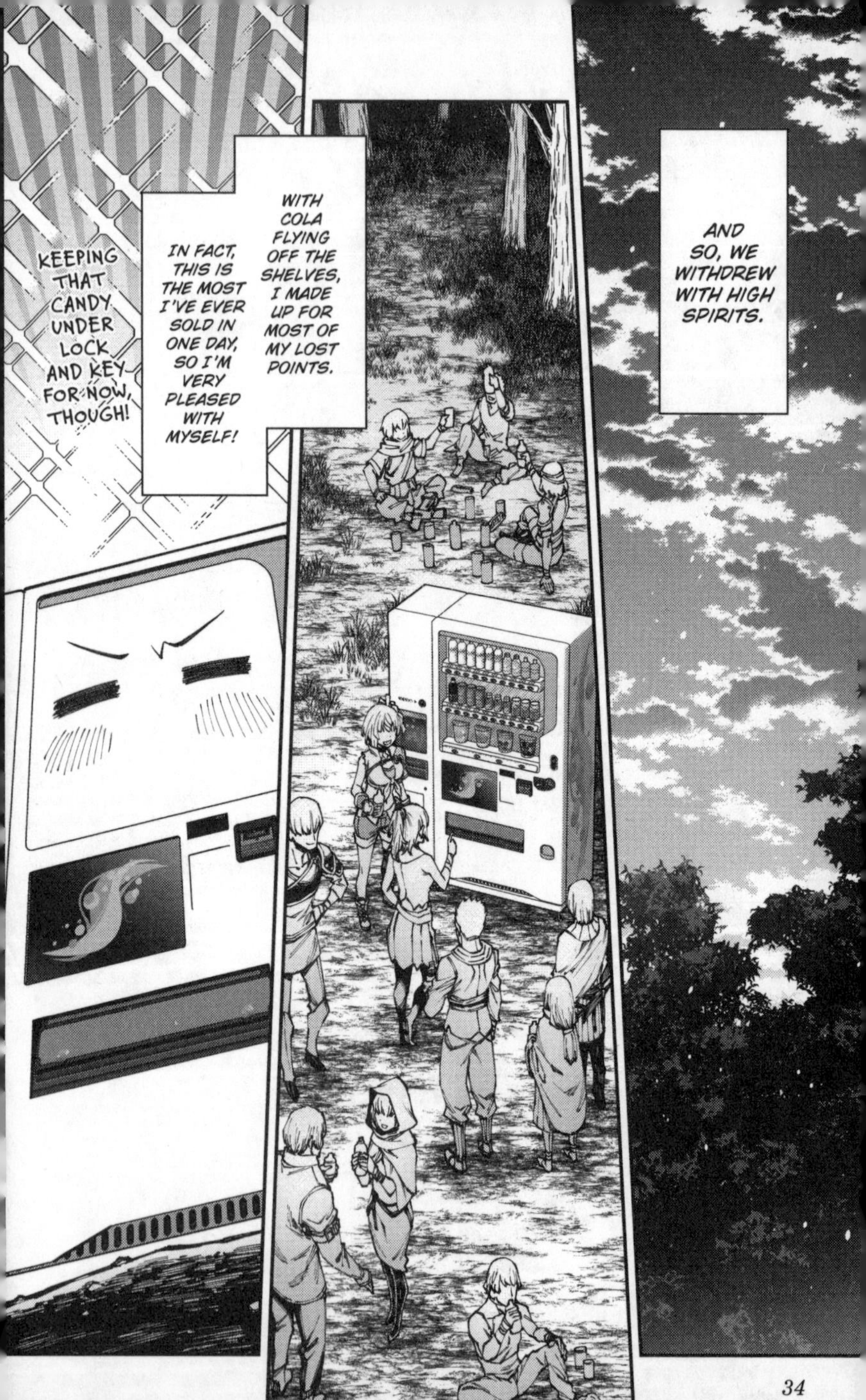
AND SO, WE WITHDREW WITH HIGH SPIRITS.
WITH COLA FLYING OFF THE SHELVES, I MADE UP FOR MOST OF MY LOST POINTS.
IN FACT, THIS IS THE MOST I'VE EVER SOLD IN ONE DAY, SO I'M VERY PLEASED WITH MYSELF!
KEEPING THAT CANDY UNDER LOCK AND KEY FOR NOW, THOUGH!

AFTER A NIGHT IN THE WOODS, WE GOT ON OUR WAY...

WE'RE ALMOST BACK TO THE SETTLEMENT.

SO MUCH HAPPENED ON THIS EXPEDITION THAT I'M EXHAUSTED......

MENTALLY.

WHEN WE GET BACK, I'M GONNA HAVE LAMMIS GIVE ME A REAL GOOD WIPING DOWN—

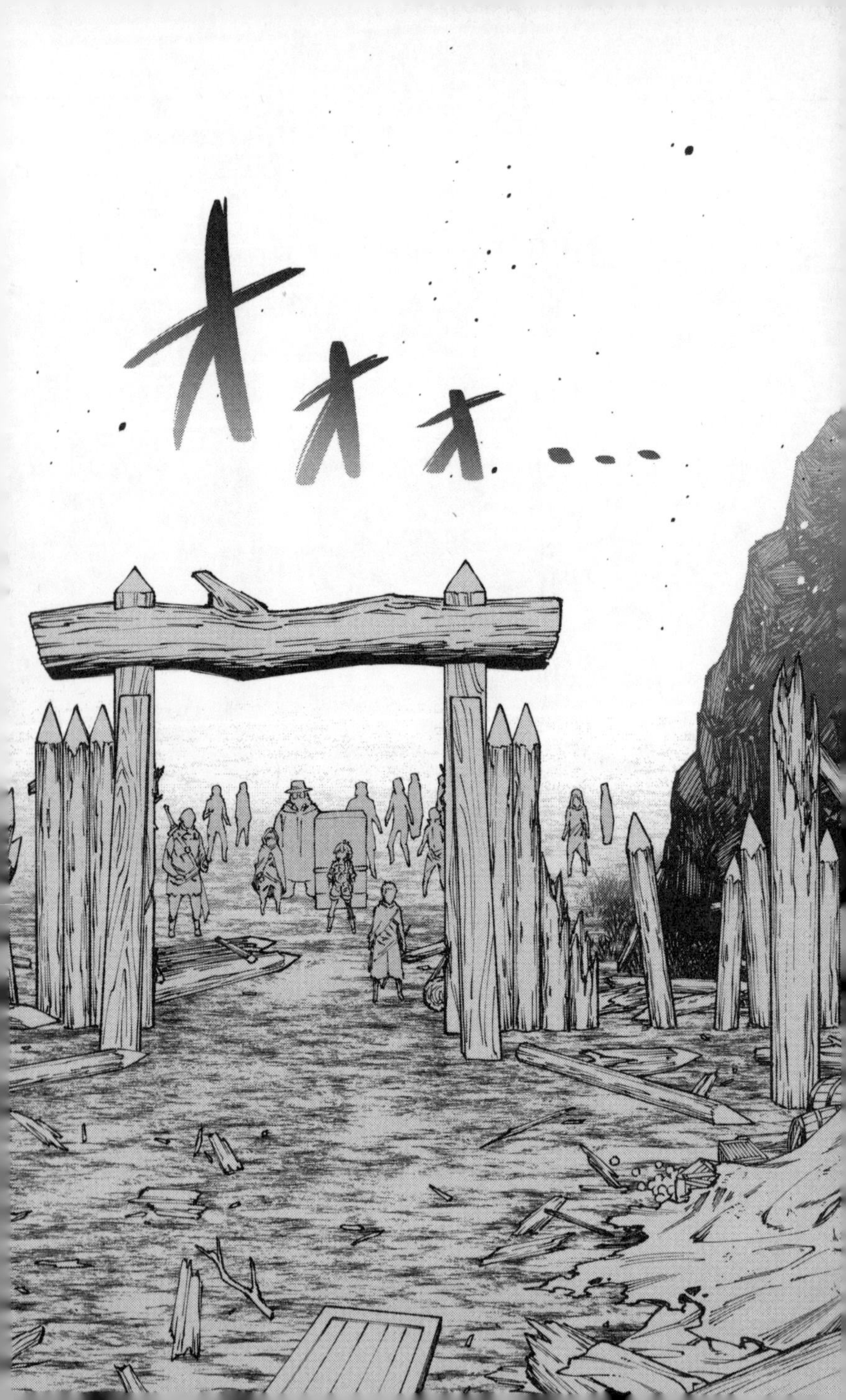
オォォ…

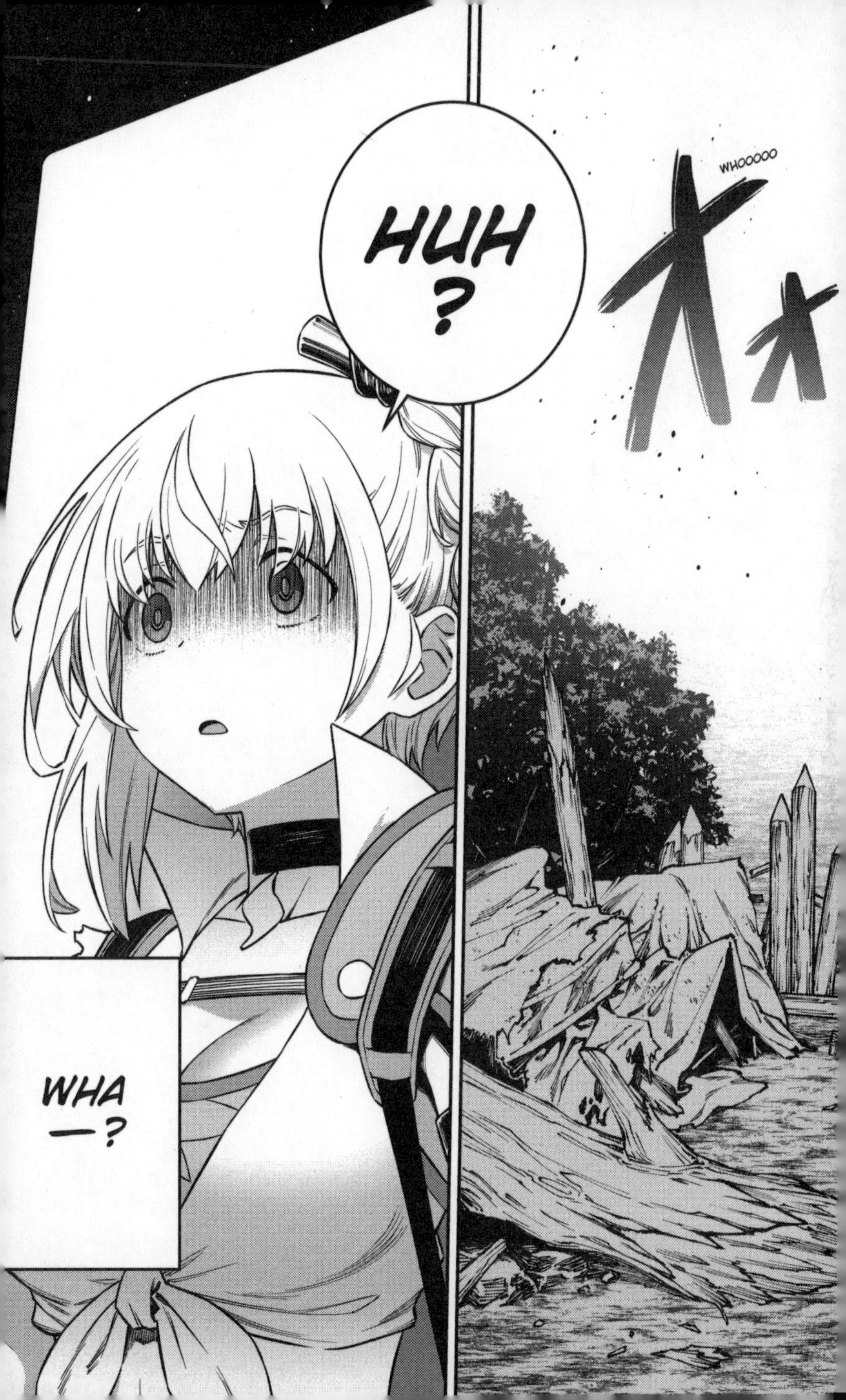
WHOOOOO
HUH ?
WHA —?

Reborn as a Vending Machine, I Now Wander the Dungeon

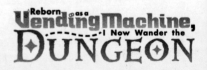

CHAPTER 9 OUT OF THE FRYING PAN

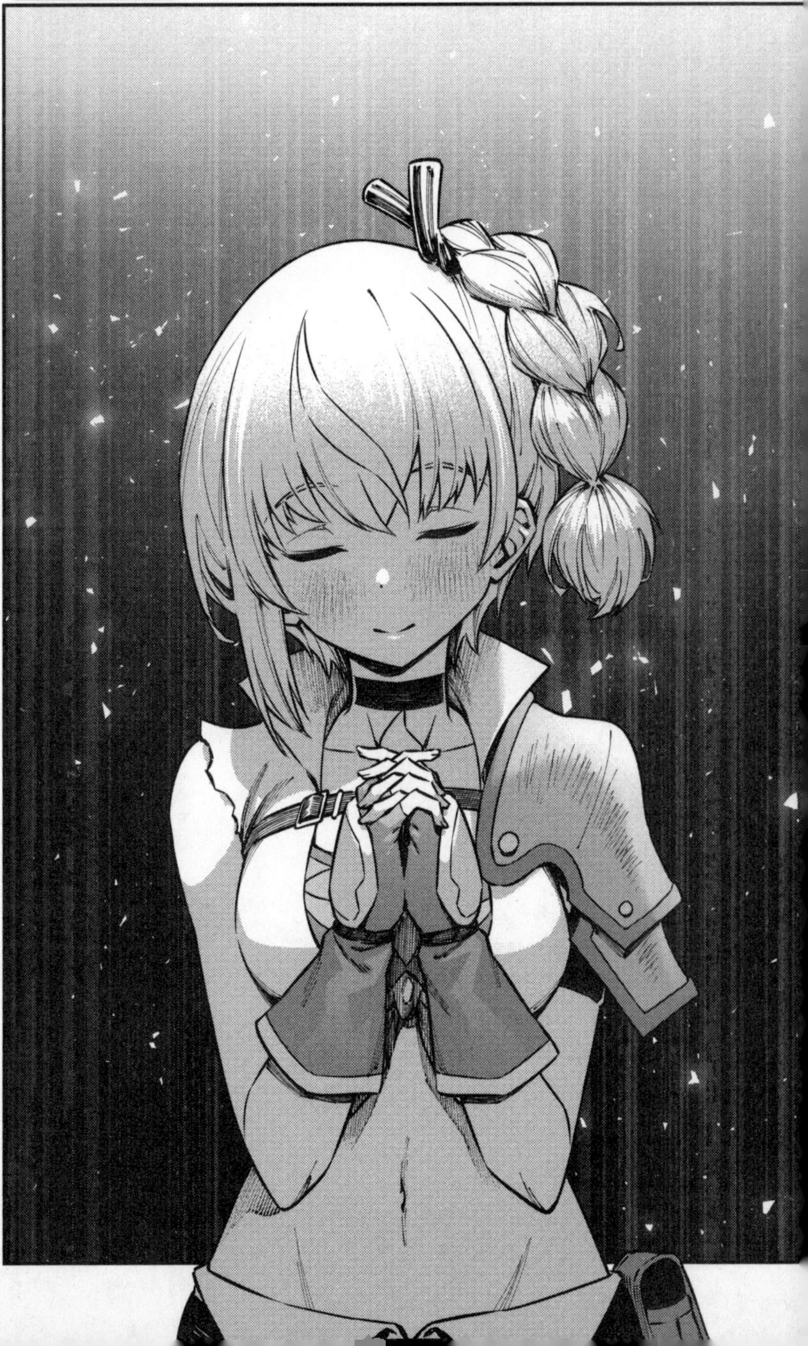

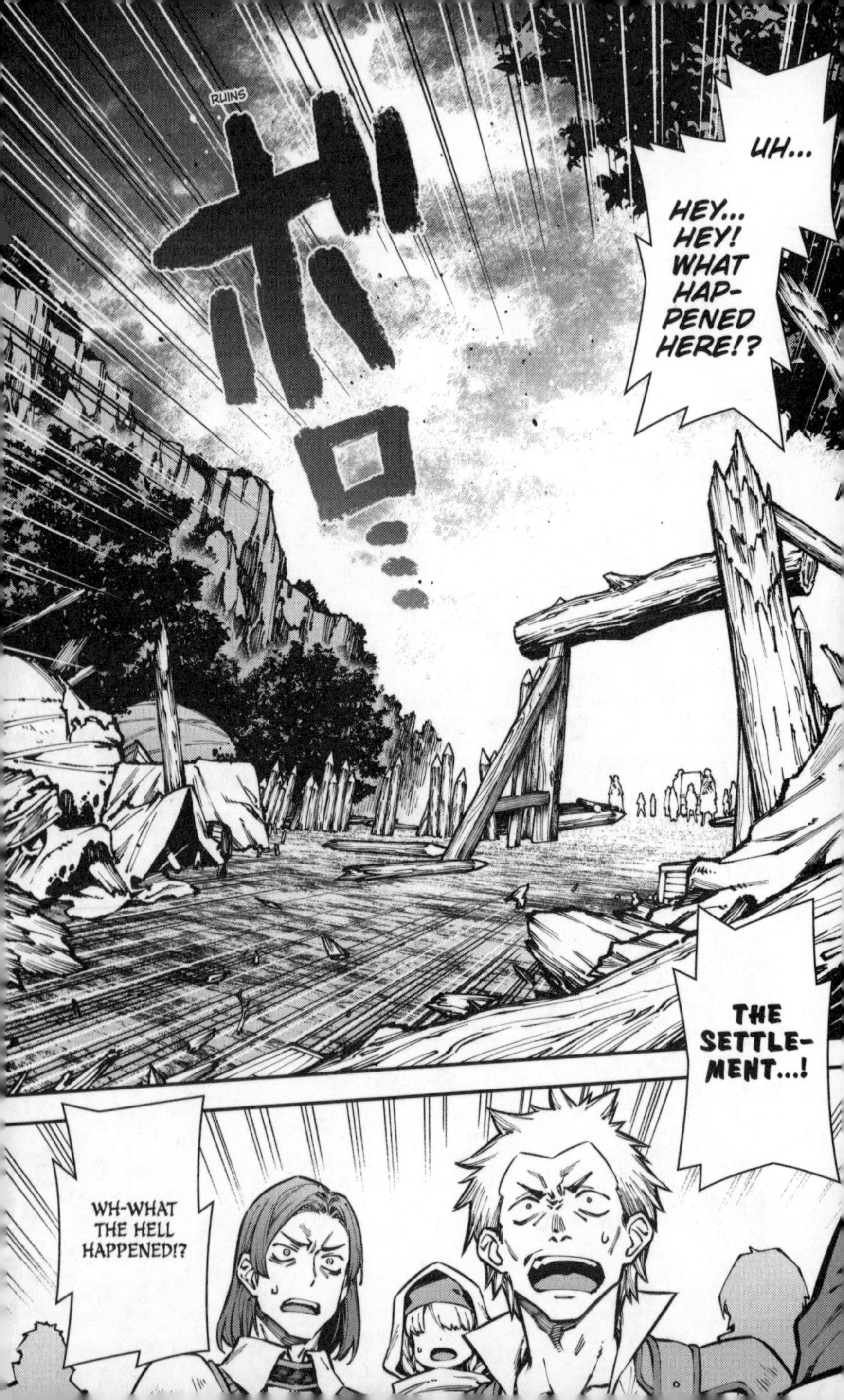
UH...
HEY... HEY! WHAT HAP-PENED HERE!?
RUINS
THE SETTLE-MENT...!
WH-WHAT THE HELL HAPPENED!?

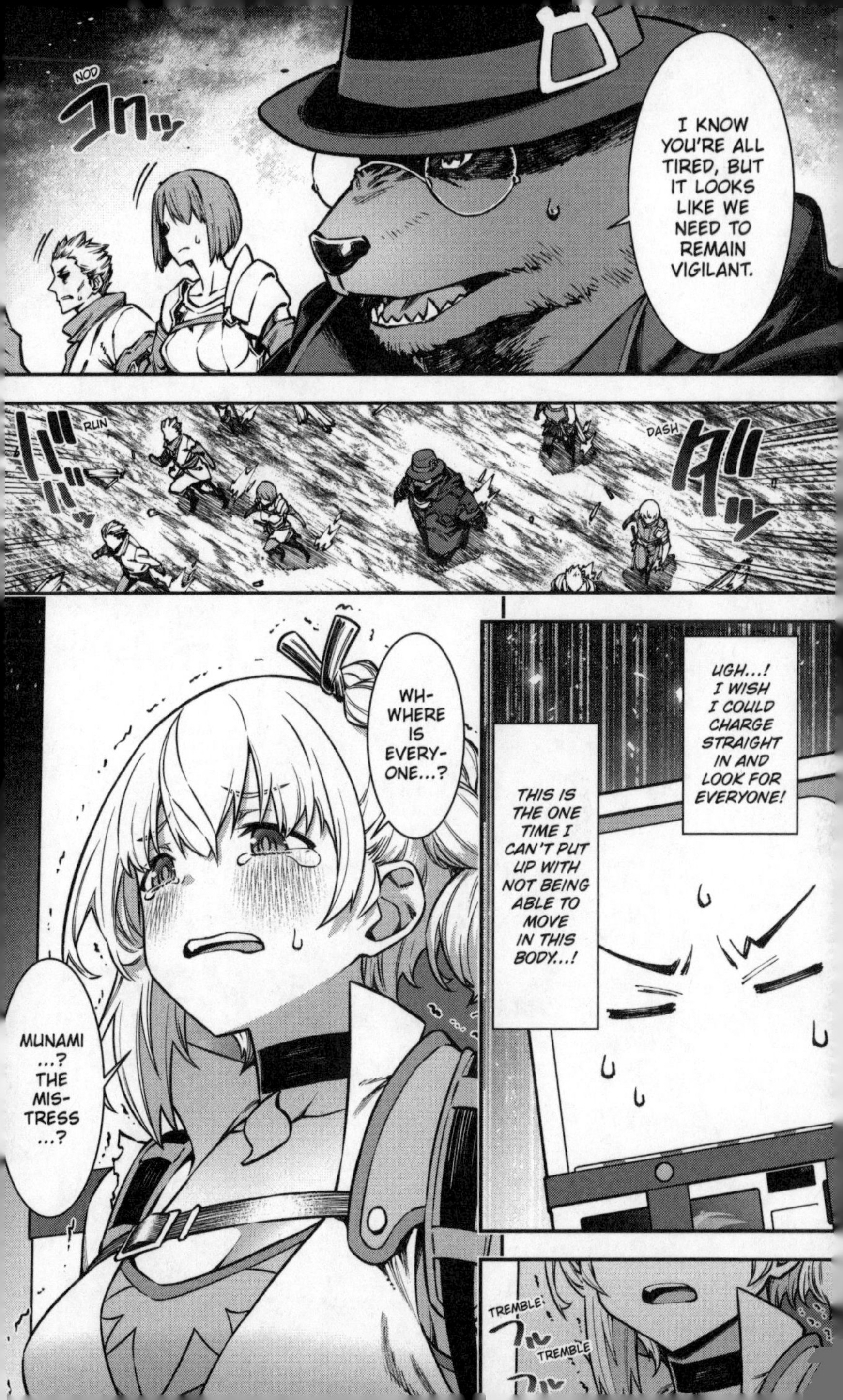
I KNOW YOU'RE ALL TIRED, BUT IT LOOKS LIKE WE NEED TO REMAIN VIGILANT.
NOD
DASH
RUN
UGH...! I WISH I COULD CHARGE STRAIGHT IN AND LOOK FOR EVERYONE!
THIS IS THE ONE TIME I CAN'T PUT UP WITH NOT BEING ABLE TO MOVE IN THIS BODY...!
TREMBLE
TREMBLE
WH-WHERE IS EVERY-ONE...?
MUNAMI ...? THE MIS-TRESS ...?

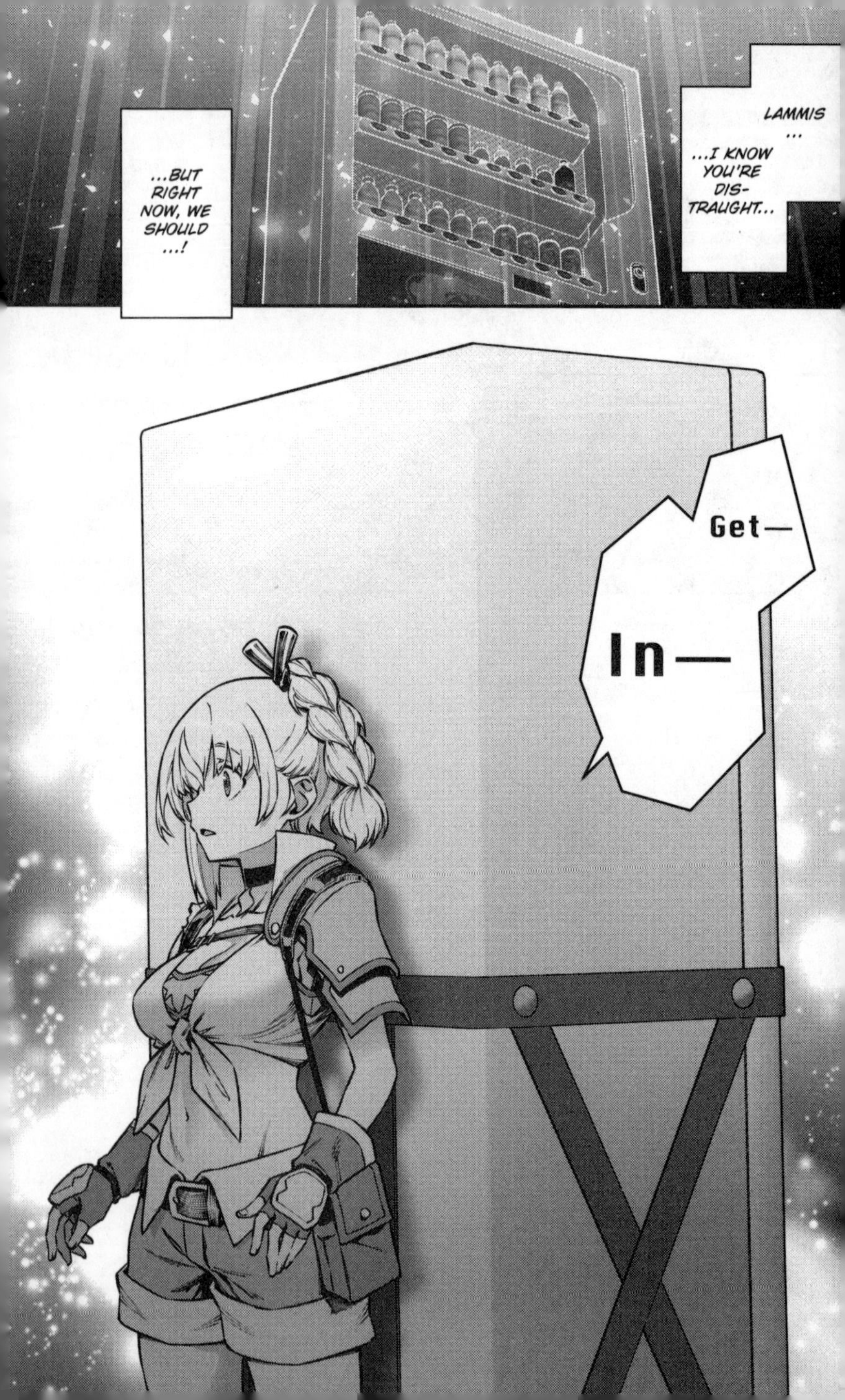
LAMMIS ...
...I KNOW YOU'RE DIS-TRAUGHT...
...BUT RIGHT NOW, WE SHOULD ...!
Get—
In—

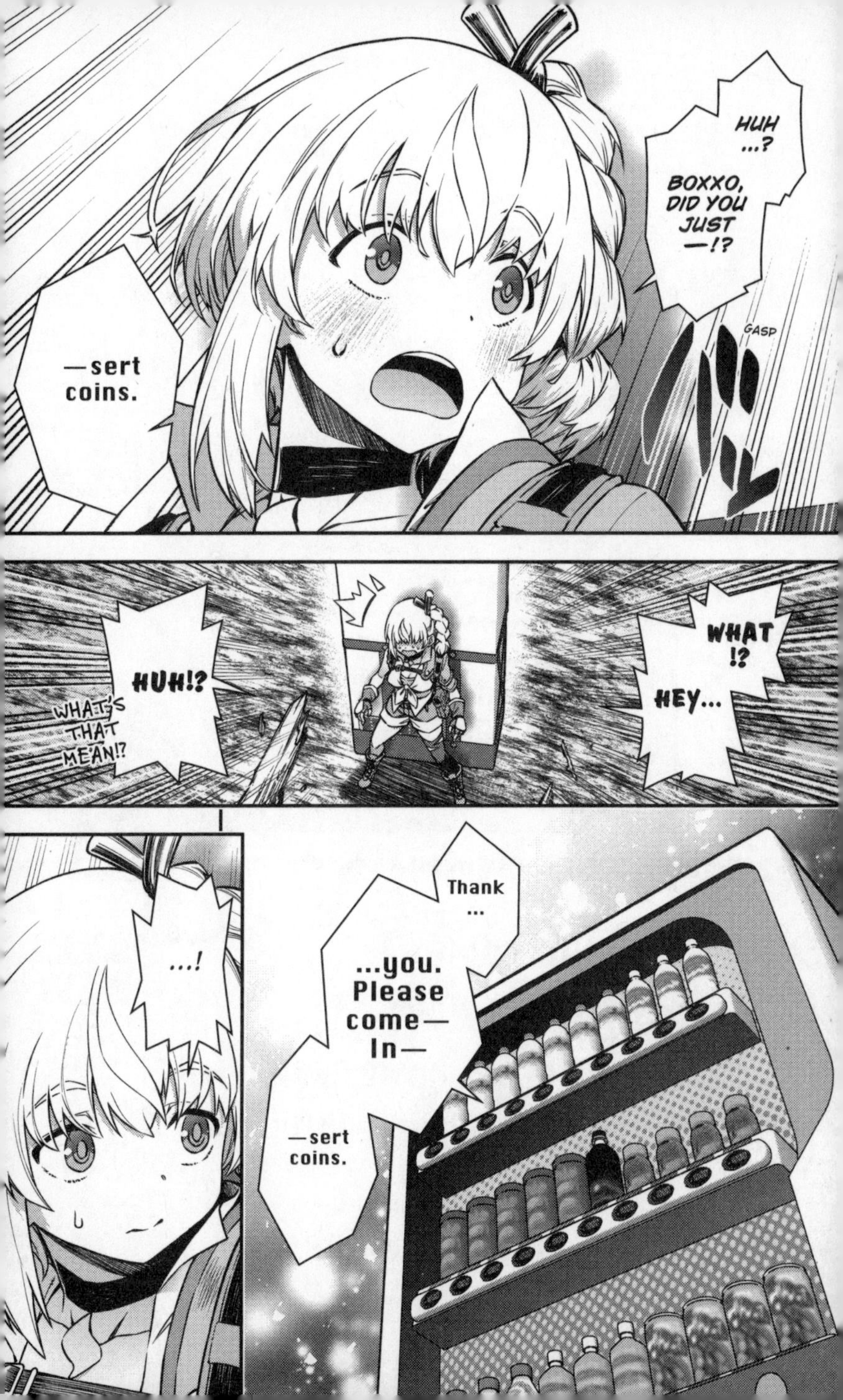
HUH ...? BOXXO, DID YOU JUST —!?
GASP
—sert coins.
WHAT !?
HEY...
HUH!?
WHAT'S THAT MEAN!?
Thank ...
...you. Please come— In—
—sert coins.
...!

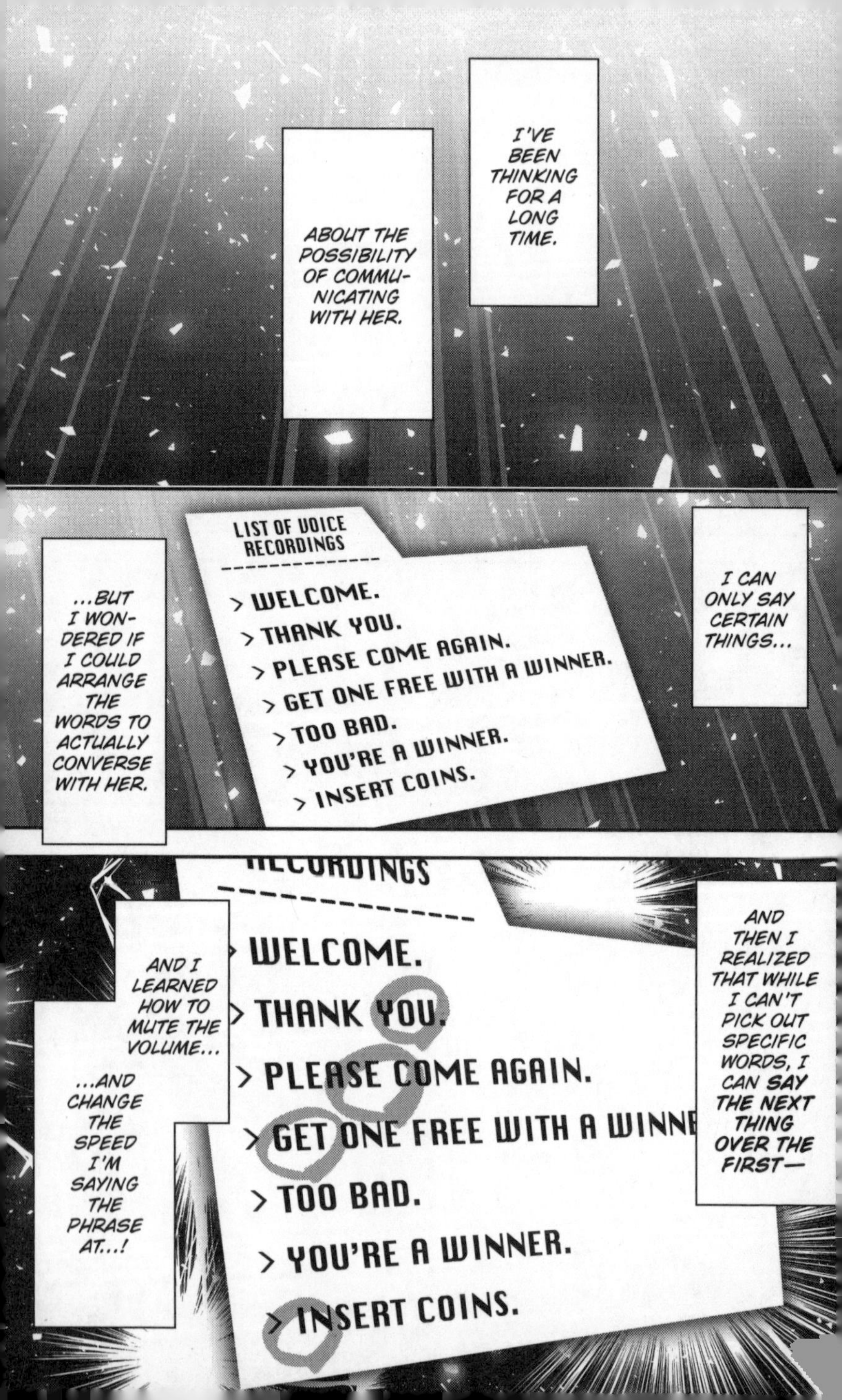
I'VE BEEN THINKING FOR A LONG TIME.
ABOUT THE POSSIBILITY OF COMMUNICATING WITH HER.
I CAN ONLY SAY CERTAIN THINGS...
LIST OF VOICE RECORDINGS
> WELCOME.
> THANK YOU.
> PLEASE COME AGAIN.
> GET ONE FREE WITH A WINNER.
> TOO BAD.
> YOU'RE A WINNER.
> INSERT COINS.
...BUT I WONDERED IF I COULD ARRANGE THE WORDS TO ACTUALLY CONVERSE WITH HER.
AND THEN I REALIZED THAT WHILE I CAN'T PICK OUT SPECIFIC WORDS, I CAN SAY THE NEXT THING OVER THE FIRST—
> WELCOME.
> THANK YOU.
> PLEASE COME AGAIN.
> GET ONE FREE WITH A WINNE
> TOO BAD.
> YOU'RE A WINNER.
> INSERT COINS.
AND I LEARNED HOW TO MUTE THE VOLUME...
...AND CHANGE THE SPEED I'M SAYING THE PHRASE AT...!

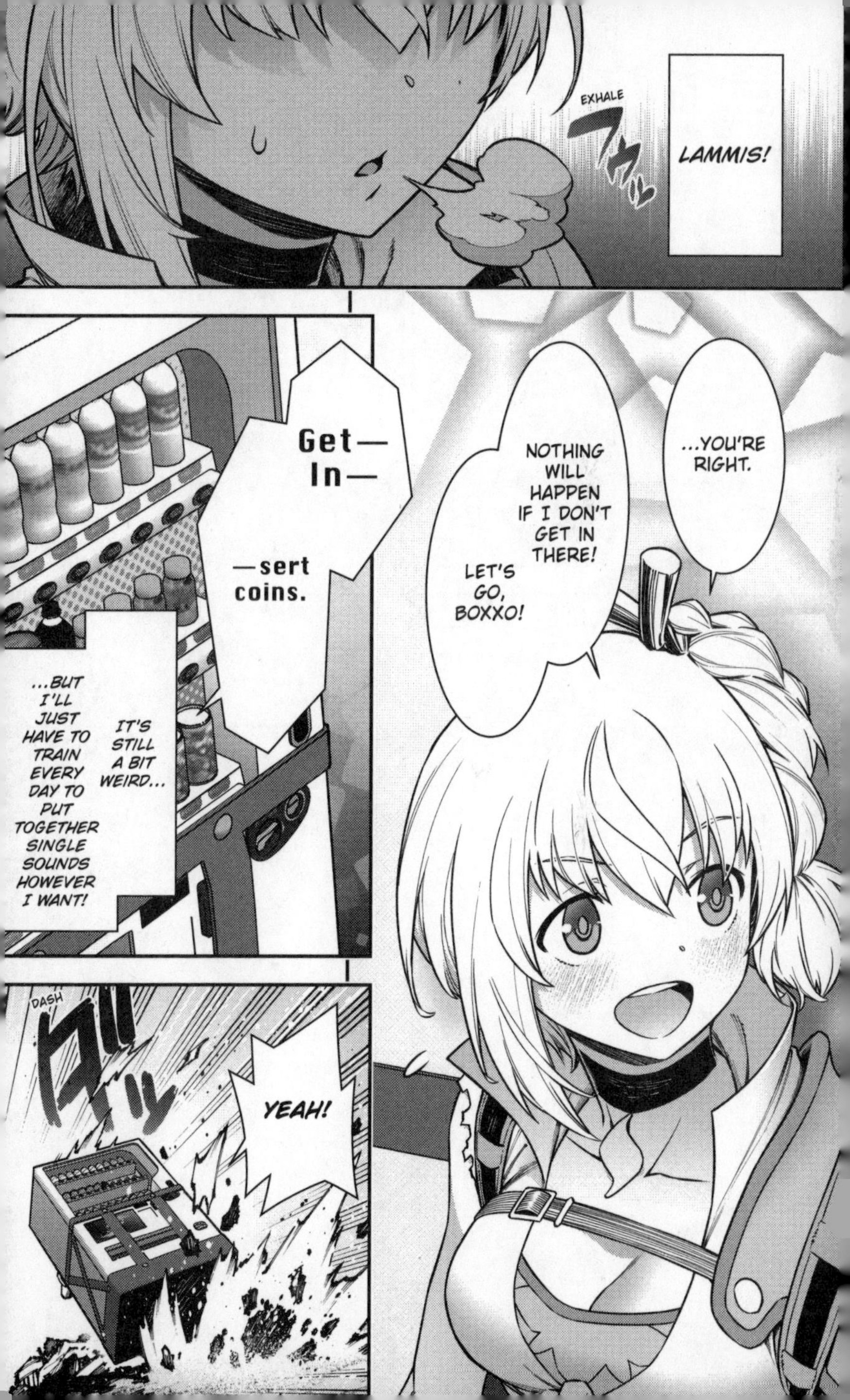
LAMMIS!
EXHALE
...YOU'RE RIGHT.
NOTHING WILL HAPPEN IF I DON'T GET IN THERE!
LET'S GO, BOXXO!
Get— In—
—sert coins.
IT'S STILL A BIT WEIRD...
...BUT I'LL JUST HAVE TO TRAIN EVERY DAY TO PUT TOGETHER SINGLE SOUNDS HOWEVER I WANT!
DASH
YEAH!

HOW ODD...

EVERYTHING IS A TOTAL WRECK, BUT I DON'T SEE ANYONE —

NO BLOOD OR CORPSES EITHER.

SSHK

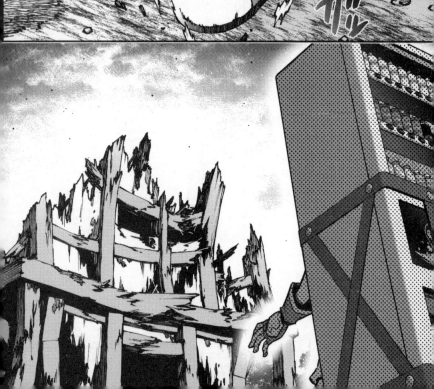

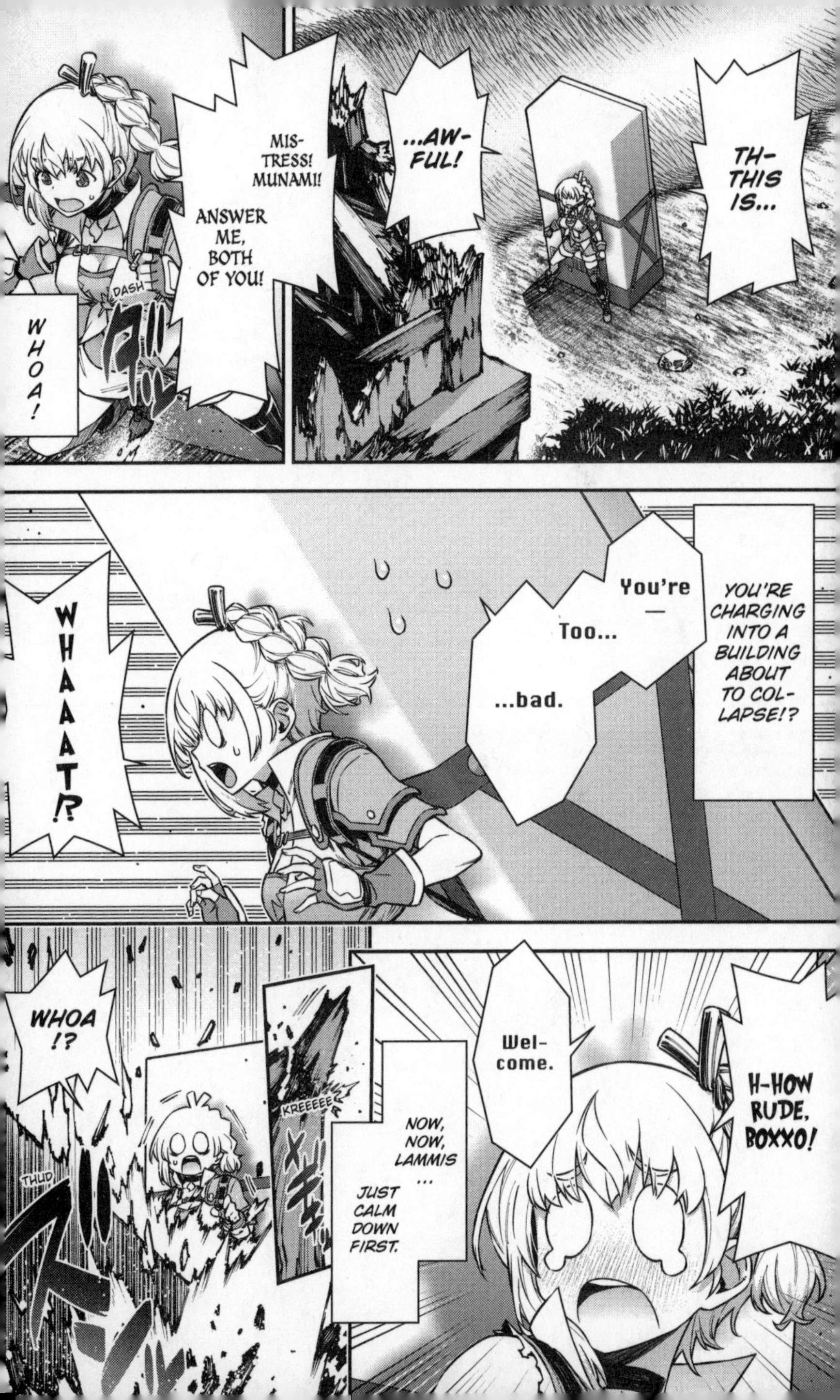
TH-THIS IS...
...AW-FUL!
MIS-TRESS! MUNAMI!
ANSWER ME, BOTH OF YOU!
DASH
WHOA!
YOU'RE CHARGING INTO A BUILDING ABOUT TO COL-LAPSE!?
You're —
Too...
...bad.
WHAAAAT!?
H-HOW RUDE, BOXXO!
Wel-come.
NOW, NOW, LAMMIS...
JUST CALM DOWN FIRST.
KREEEEE
WHOA!?
THUD

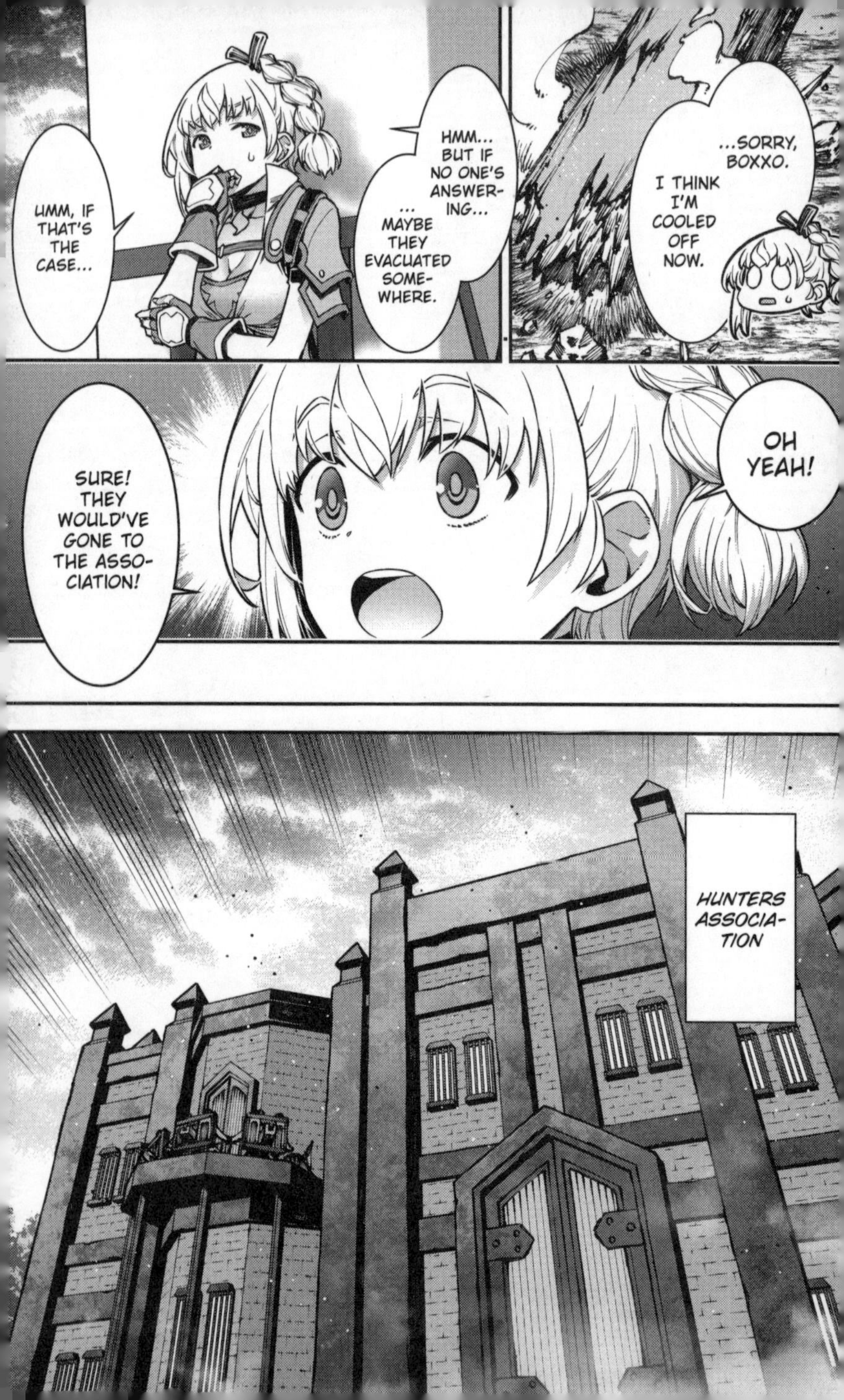

...SORRY, BOXXO. I THINK I'M COOLED OFF NOW.
HMM... BUT IF NO ONE'S ANSWERING...
... MAYBE THEY EVACUATED SOMEWHERE.
UMM, IF THAT'S THE CASE...
OH YEAH!
SURE! THEY WOULD'VE GONE TO THE ASSOCIATION!
HUNTERS ASSOCIATION

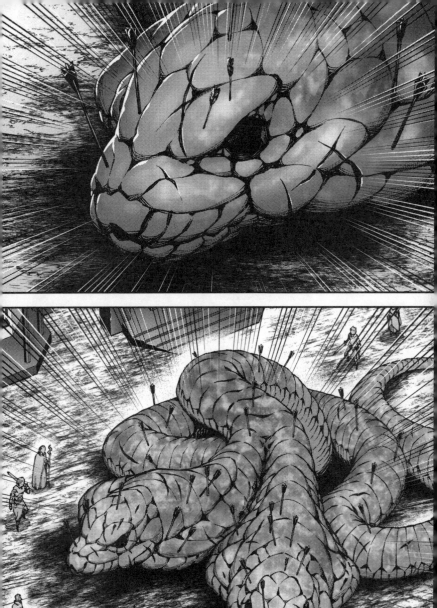

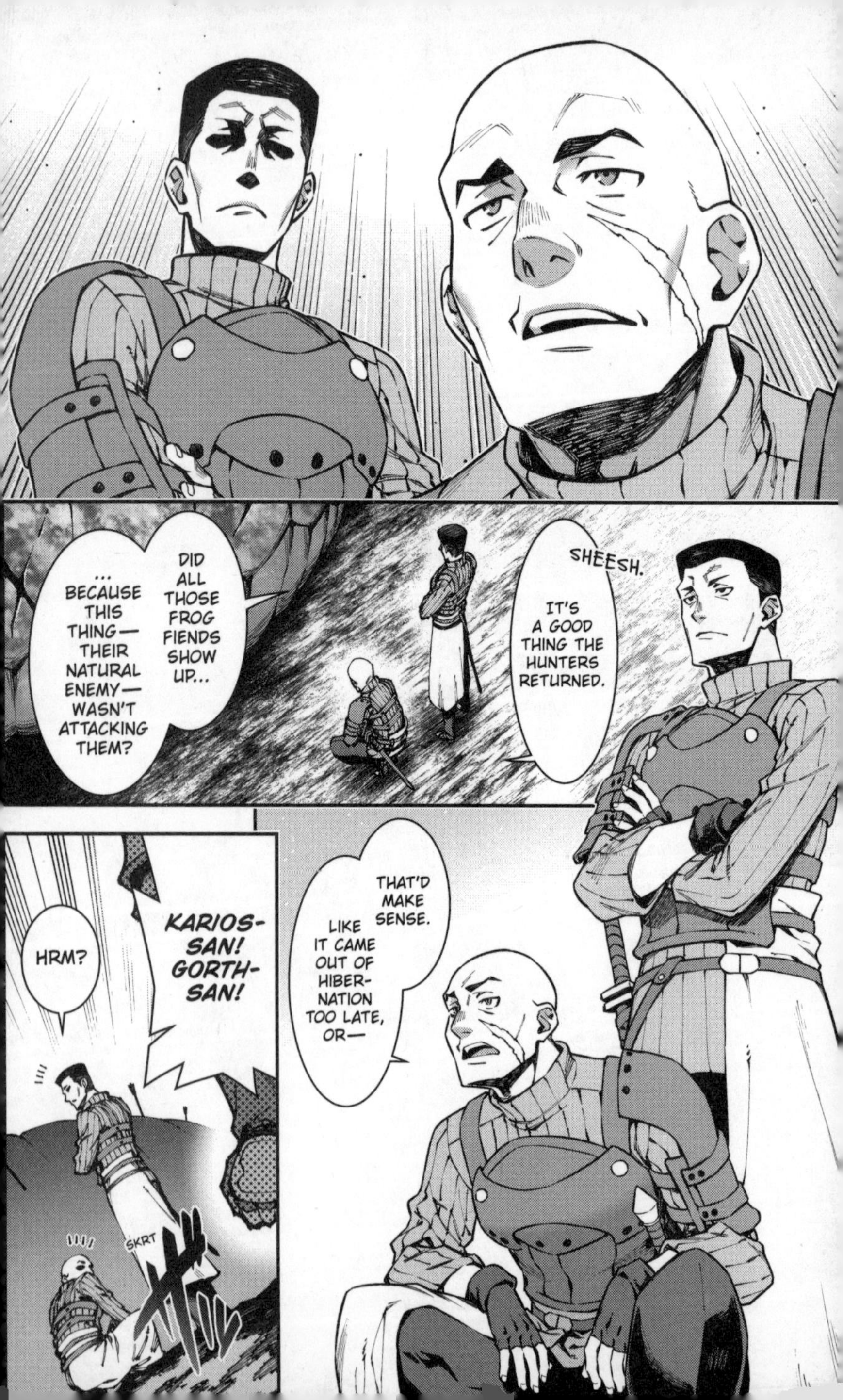
SHEESH.
IT'S A GOOD THING THE HUNTERS RETURNED.
DID ALL THOSE FROG FIENDS SHOW UP...
...BECAUSE THIS THING—THEIR NATURAL ENEMY—WASN'T ATTACKING THEM?
THAT'D MAKE SENSE.
LIKE IT CAME OUT OF HIBER-NATION TOO LATE, OR—
KARIOS-SAN! GORTH-SAN!
HRM?
SKRT

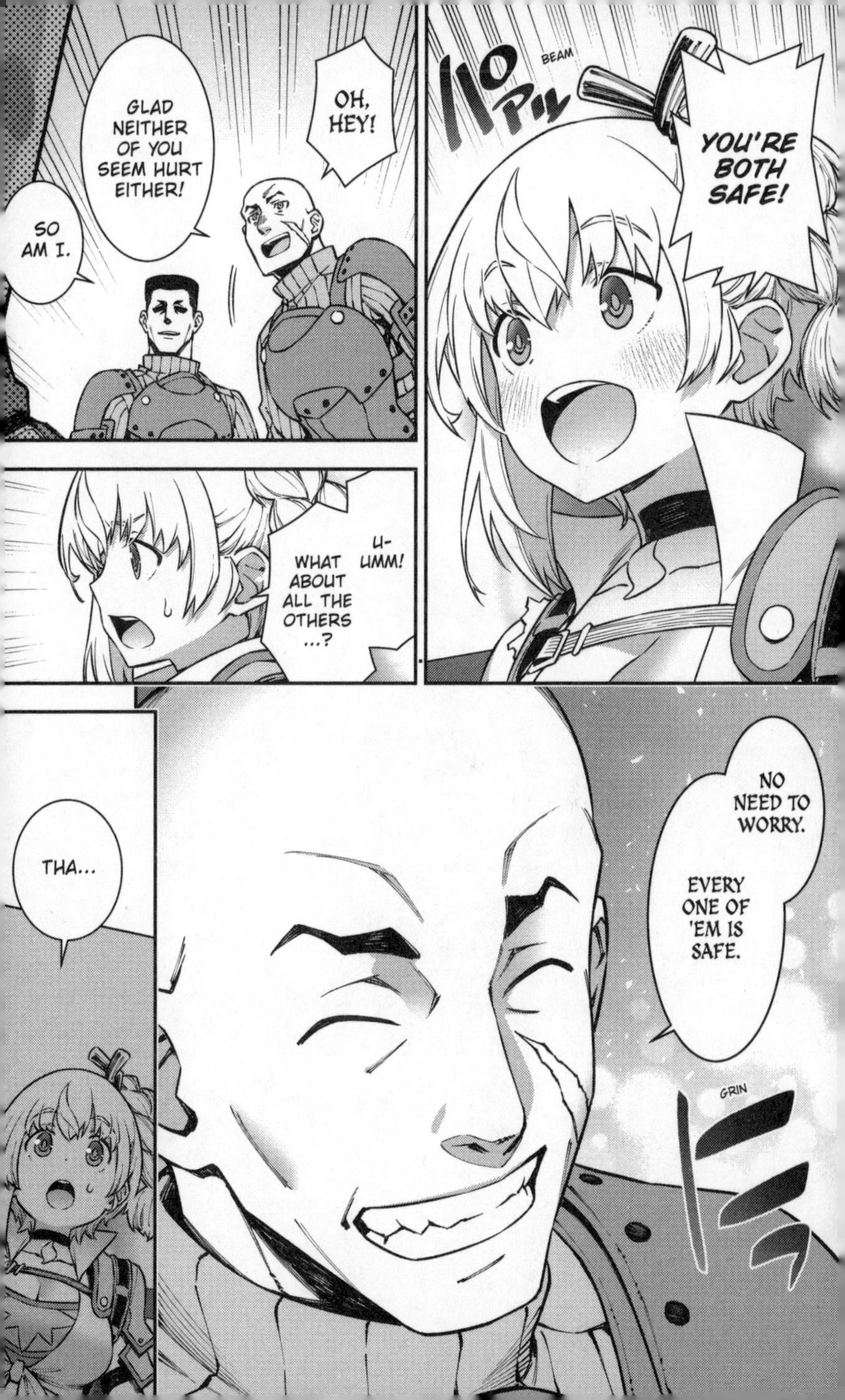
BEAM
YOU'RE BOTH SAFE!
OH, HEY!
GLAD NEITHER OF YOU SEEM HURT EITHER!
SO AM I.
U-UMM!
WHAT ABOUT ALL THE OTHERS ...?
NO NEED TO WORRY.
EVERY ONE OF 'EM IS SAFE.
GRIN
THA...

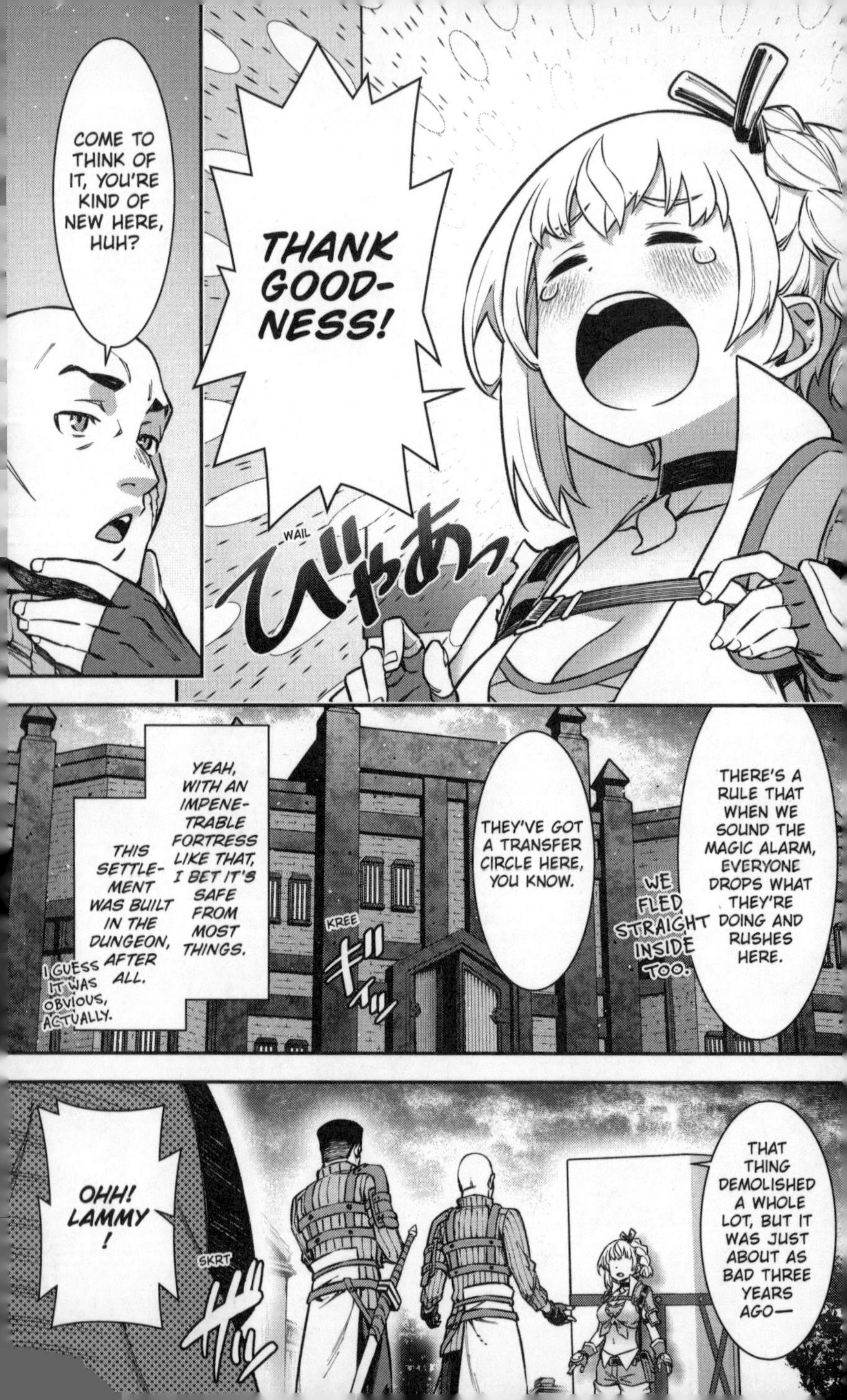
THANK GOOD-NESS!
WAIL
びゃあっ
COME TO THINK OF IT, YOU'RE KIND OF NEW HERE, HUH?
THERE'S A RULE THAT WHEN WE SOUND THE MAGIC ALARM, EVERYONE DROPS WHAT THEY'RE DOING AND RUSHES HERE.
WE FLED STRAIGHT INSIDE TOO.
THEY'VE GOT A TRANSFER CIRCLE HERE, YOU KNOW.
KREE
YEAH, WITH AN IMPENE-TRABLE FORTRESS LIKE THAT, I BET IT'S SAFE FROM MOST THINGS.
THIS SETTLE-MENT WAS BUILT IN THE DUNGEON, AFTER ALL.
I GUESS IT WAS OBVIOUS, ACTUALLY.
THAT THING DEMOLISHED A WHOLE LOT, BUT IT WAS JUST ABOUT AS BAD THREE YEARS AGO—
SKRT
OHH! LAMMY!

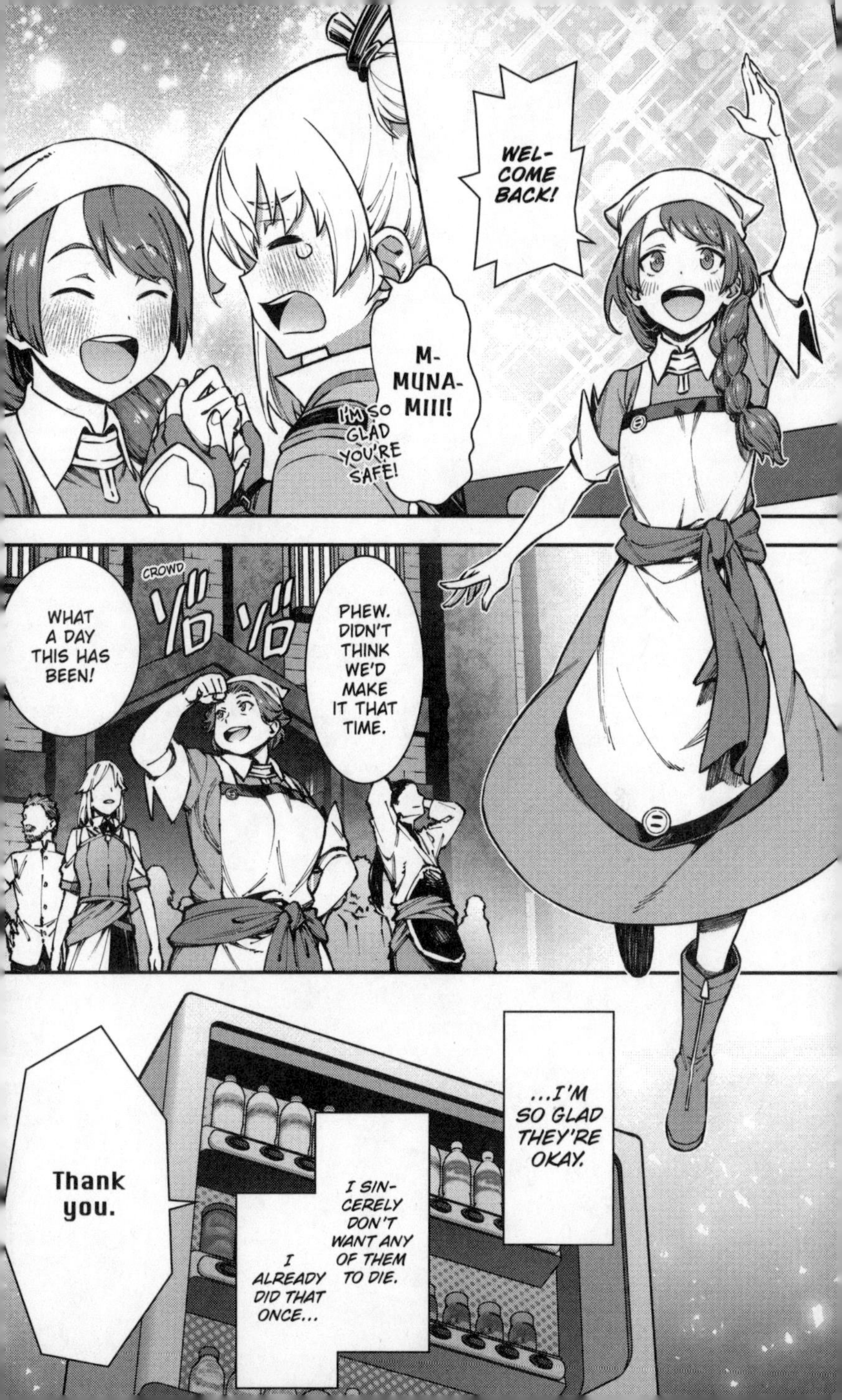
WEL-COME BACK!
M-MUNA-MIII!
I'M SO GLAD YOU'RE SAFE!
PHEW. DIDN'T THINK WE'D MAKE IT THAT TIME.
CROWD
WHAT A DAY THIS HAS BEEN!
...I'M SO GLAD THEY'RE OKAY.
I SIN-CERELY DON'T WANT ANY OF THEM TO DIE.
I ALREADY DID THAT ONCE...
Thank you.

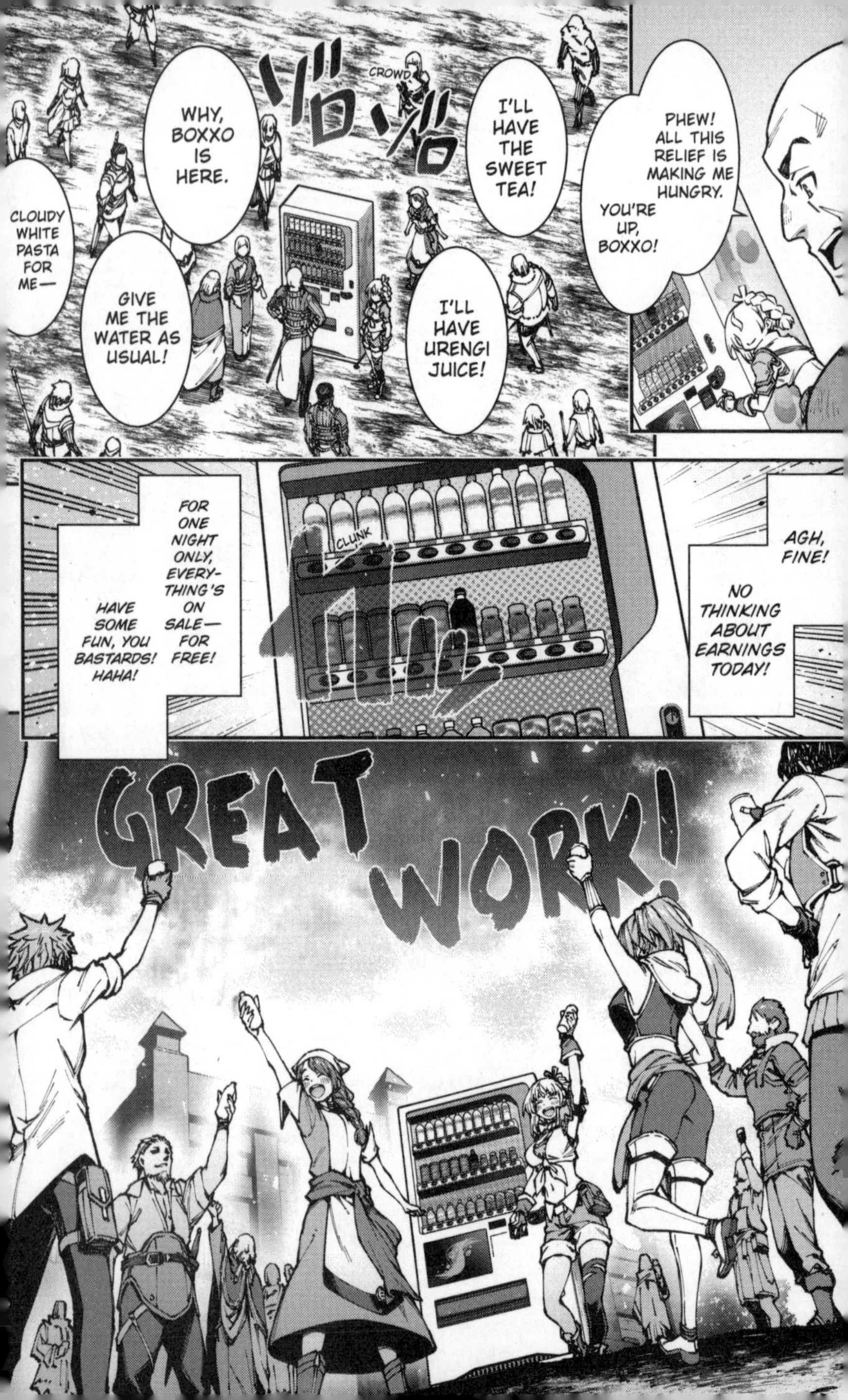
PHEW! ALL THIS RELIEF IS MAKING ME HUNGRY.
YOU'RE UP, BOXXO!
I'LL HAVE THE SWEET TEA!
CROWD
WHY, BOXXO IS HERE.
I'LL HAVE URENGI JUICE!
GIVE ME THE WATER AS USUAL!
CLOUDY WHITE PASTA FOR ME—
AGH, FINE!
NO THINKING ABOUT EARNINGS TODAY!
CLUNK
FOR ONE NIGHT ONLY, EVERYTHING'S ON SALE—FOR FREE!
HAVE SOME FUN, YOU BASTARDS! HAHA!
GREAT WORK!

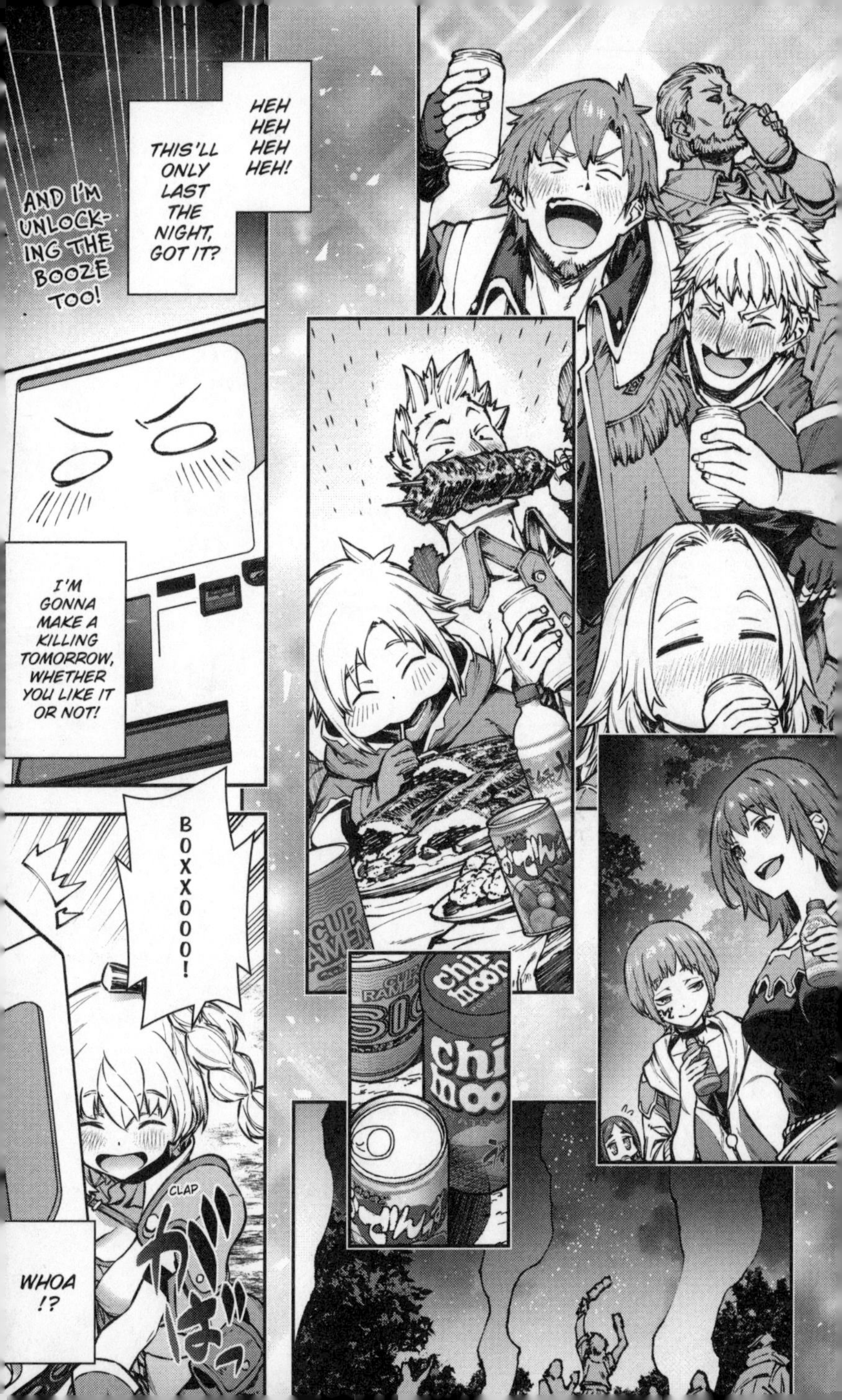
HEH HEH HEH HEH!
THIS'LL ONLY LAST THE NIGHT, GOT IT?
AND I'M UNLOCKING THE BOOZE TOO!
I'M GONNA MAKE A KILLING TOMORROW, WHETHER YOU LIKE IT OR NOT!
BOXXOOOO!
CLAP
WHOA!?

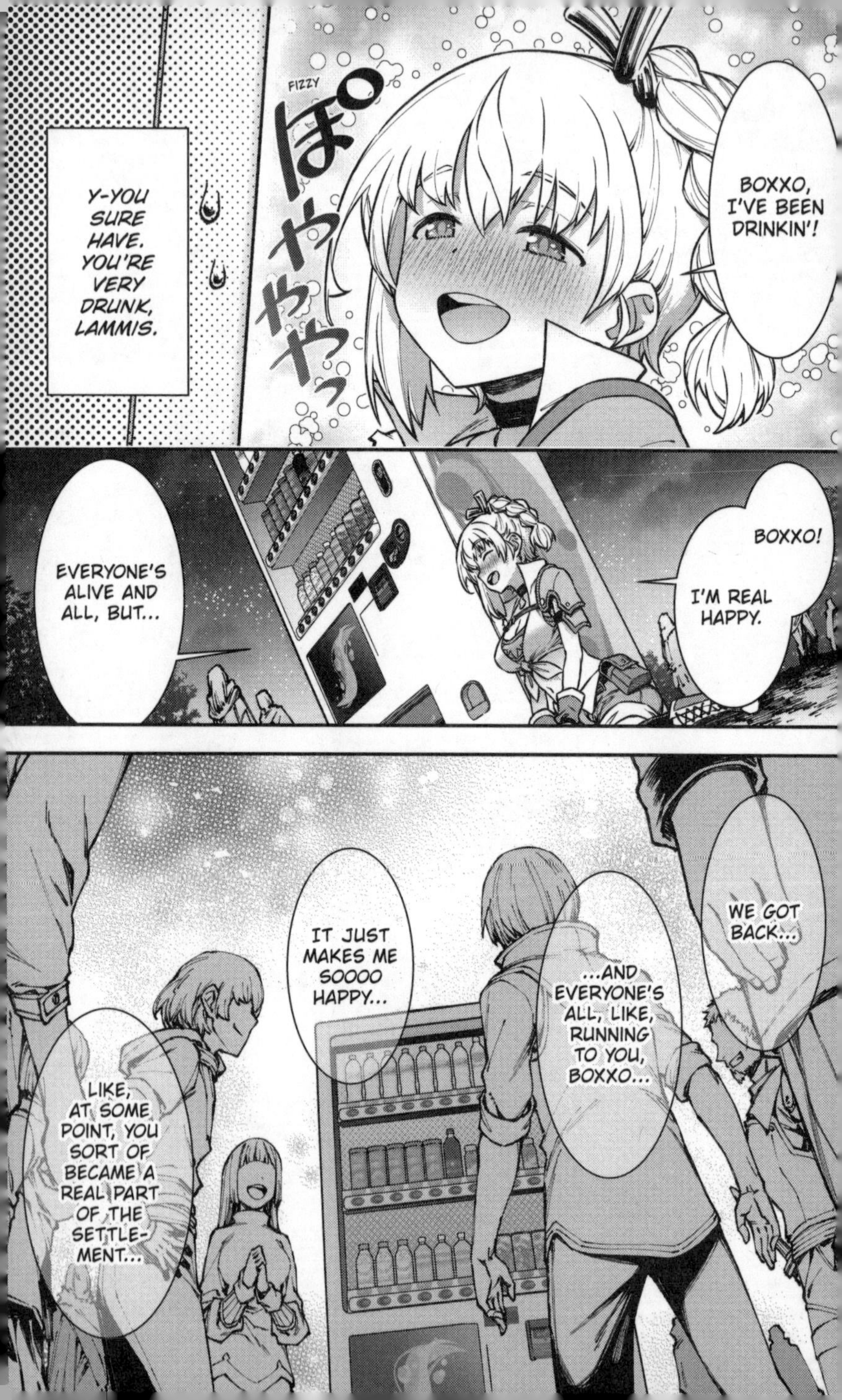
BOXXO, I'VE BEEN DRINKIN'!
FIZZY
ぽやややっ
Y-YOU SURE HAVE. YOU'RE VERY DRUNK, LAMMIS.
BOXXO!
I'M REAL HAPPY.
EVERYONE'S ALIVE AND ALL, BUT...
WE GOT BACK...
...AND EVERYONE'S ALL, LIKE, RUNNING TO YOU, BOXXO...
IT JUST MAKES ME SOOOO HAPPY...
LIKE, AT SOME POINT, YOU SORT OF BECAME A REAL PART OF THE SETTLE-MENT...

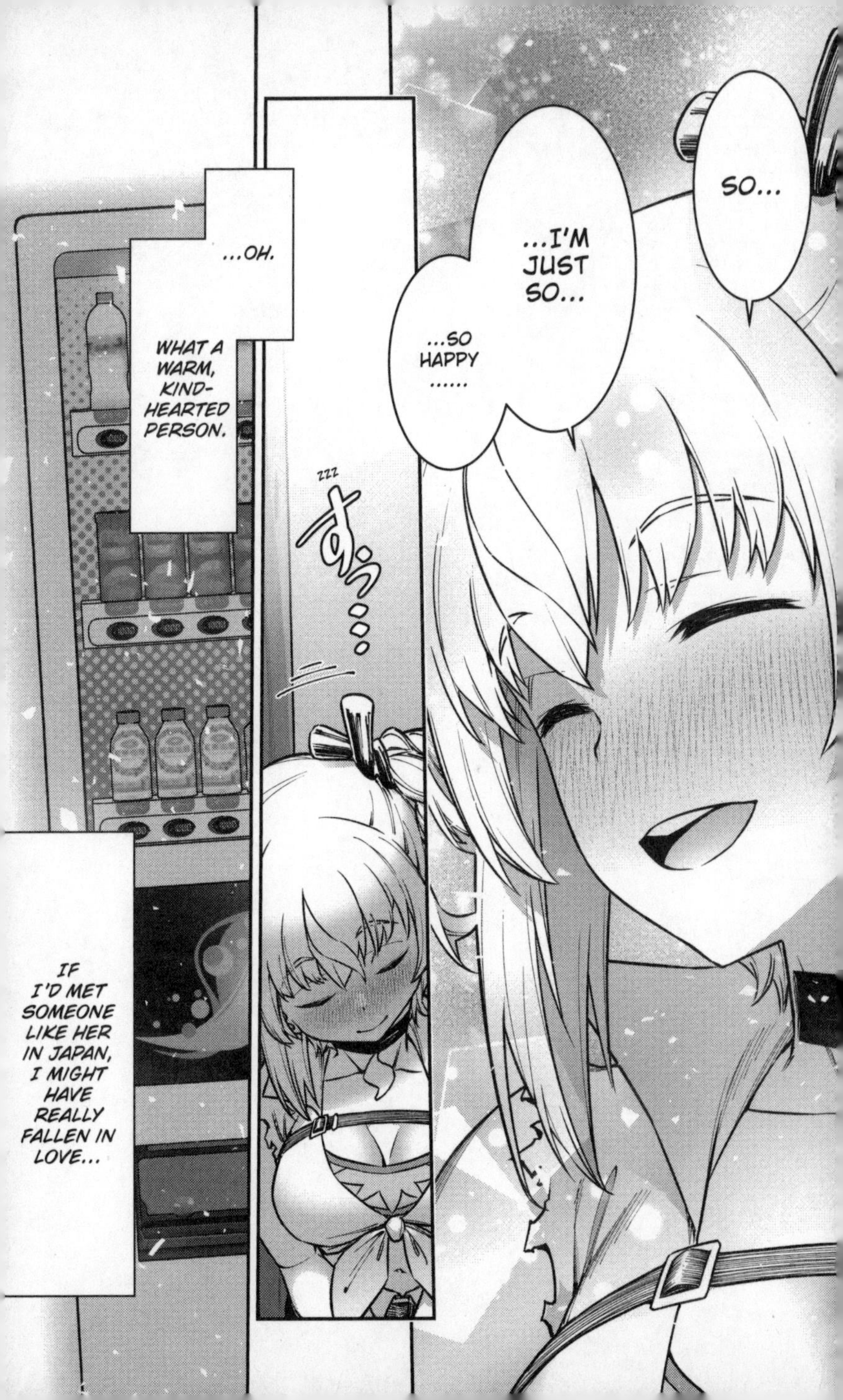
SO...
...I'M JUST SO...
...SO HAPPY ......
zzz
...OH.
WHAT A WARM, KIND-HEARTED PERSON.
IF I'D MET SOMEONE LIKE HER IN JAPAN, I MIGHT HAVE REALLY FALLEN IN LOVE...

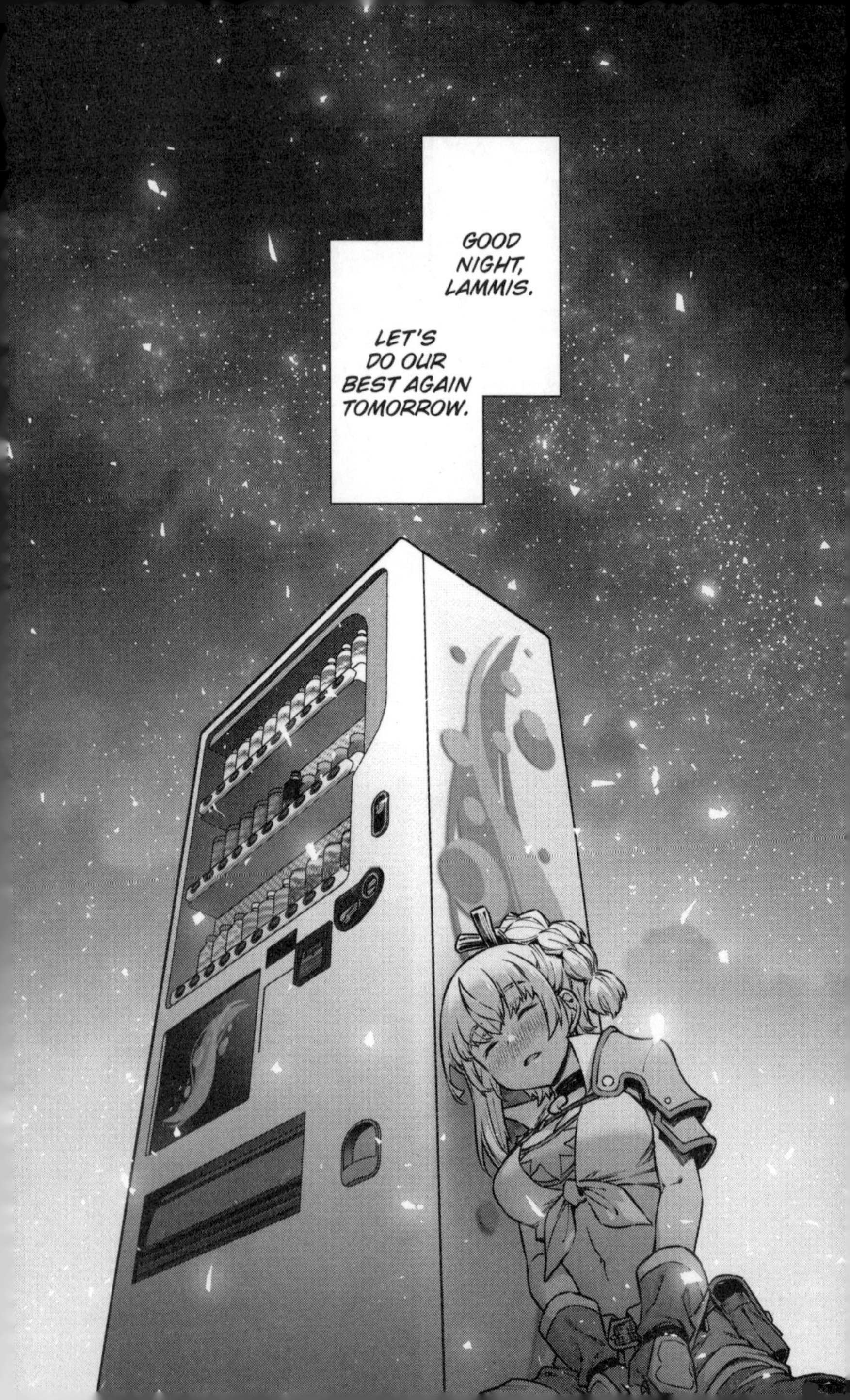
GOOD NIGHT, LAMMIS.
LET'S DO OUR BEST AGAIN TOMORROW.

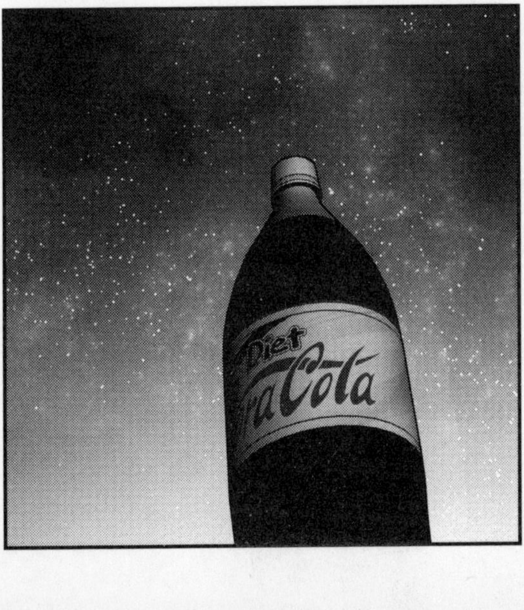
Diet
Cola

Reborn as a Vending Machine, I Now Wander the Dungeon

CHAPTER 10 RECONSTRUCTION WORK

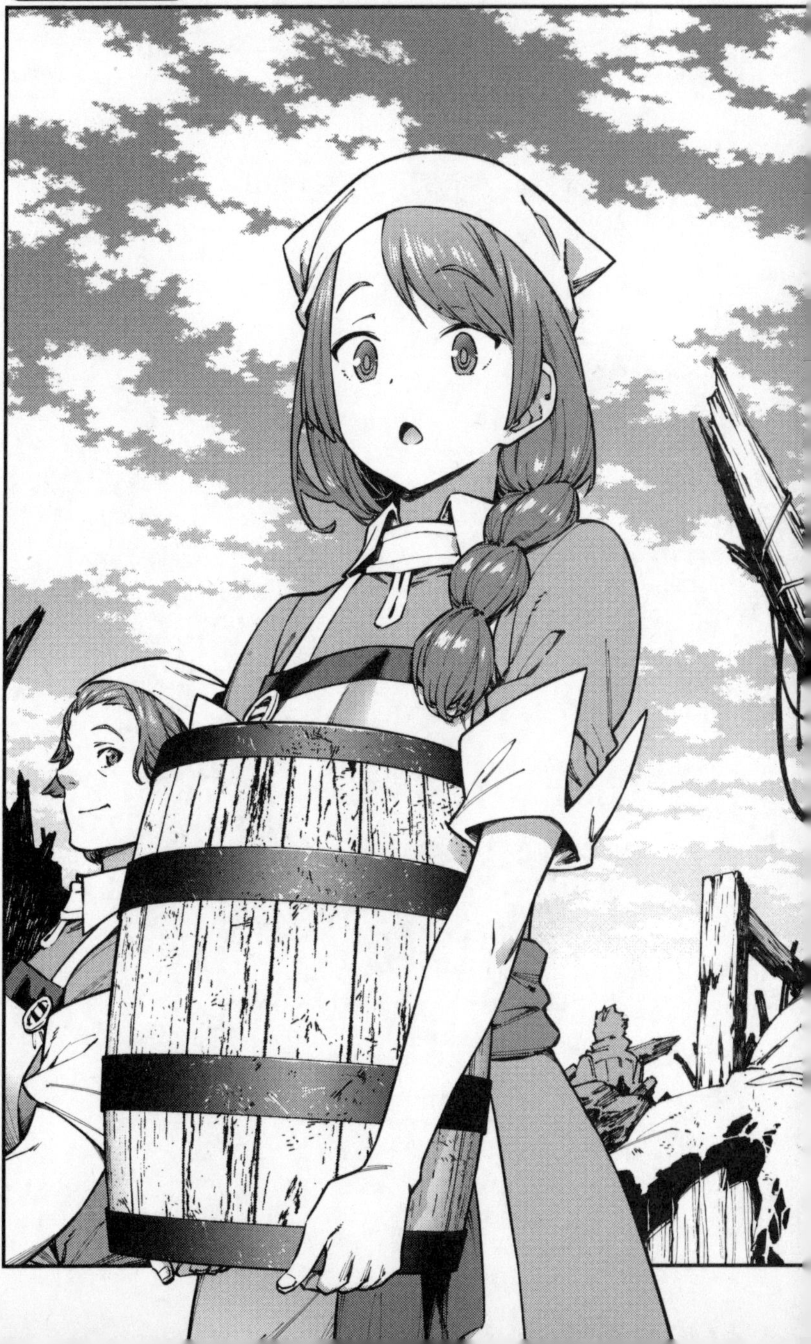

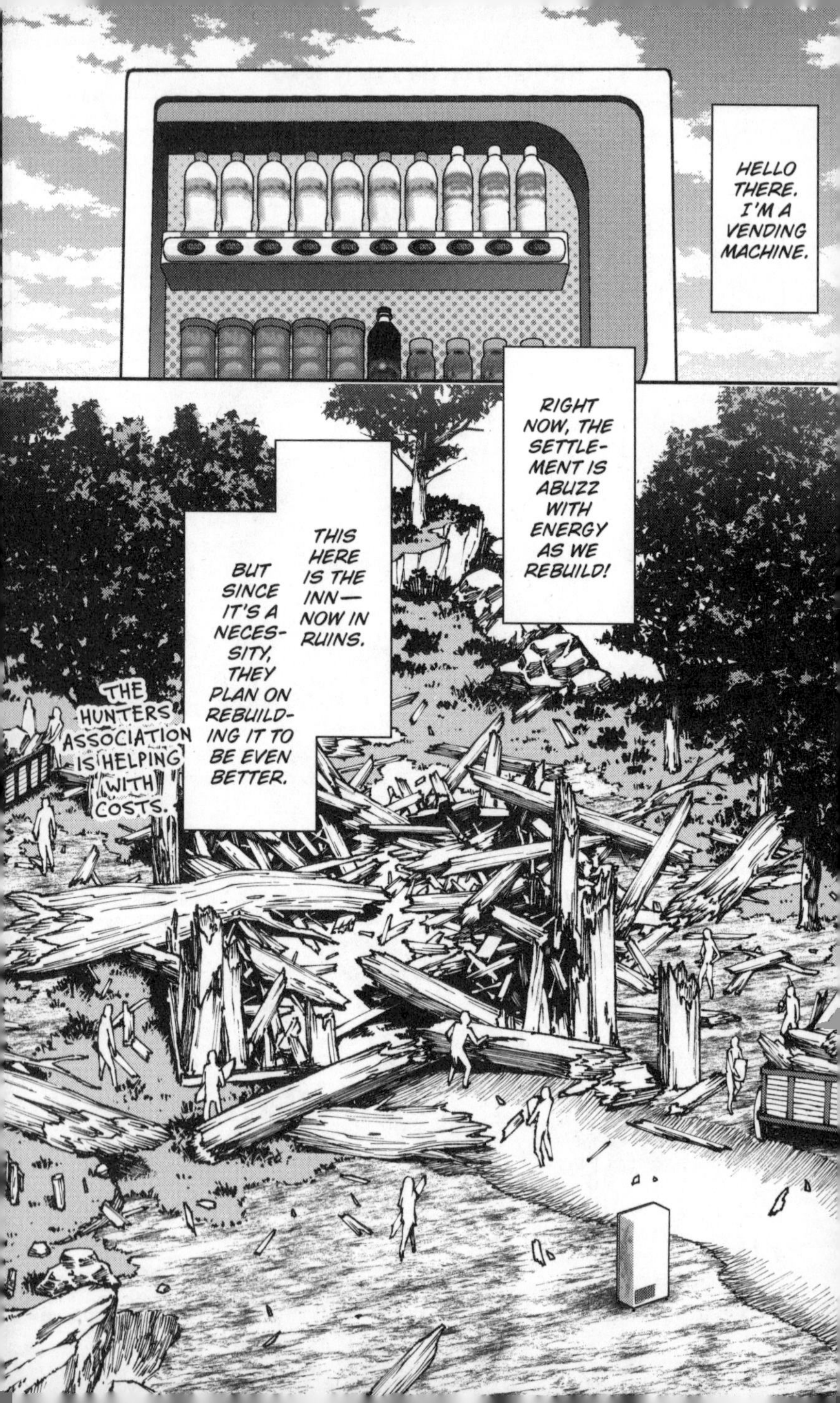
HELLO THERE. I'M A VENDING MACHINE.
RIGHT NOW, THE SETTLE-MENT IS ABUZZ WITH ENERGY AS WE REBUILD!
THIS HERE IS THE INN— NOW IN RUINS.
BUT SINCE IT'S A NECES-SITY, THEY PLAN ON REBUILD-ING IT TO BE EVEN BETTER.
THE HUNTERS ASSOCIATION IS HELPING WITH COSTS.

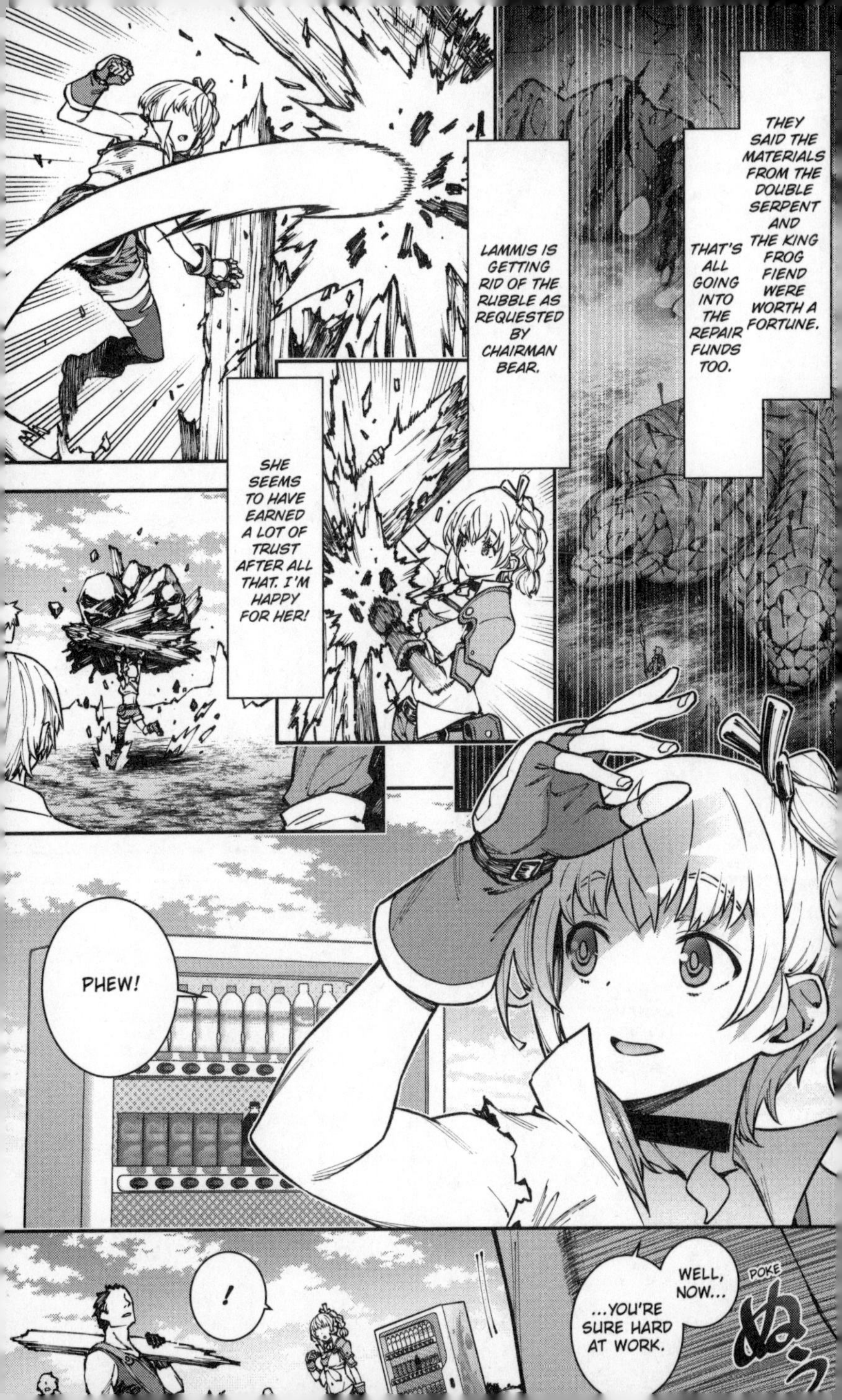

THEY SAID THE MATERIALS FROM THE DOUBLE SERPENT AND THE KING FROG FIEND WERE WORTH A FORTUNE.
THAT'S ALL GOING INTO THE REPAIR FUNDS TOO.
LAMMIS IS GETTING RID OF THE RUBBLE AS REQUESTED BY CHAIRMAN BEAR.
SHE SEEMS TO HAVE EARNED A LOT OF TRUST AFTER ALL THAT. I'M HAPPY FOR HER!
PHEW!
POKE
WELL, NOW...
...YOU'RE SURE HARD AT WORK.
!

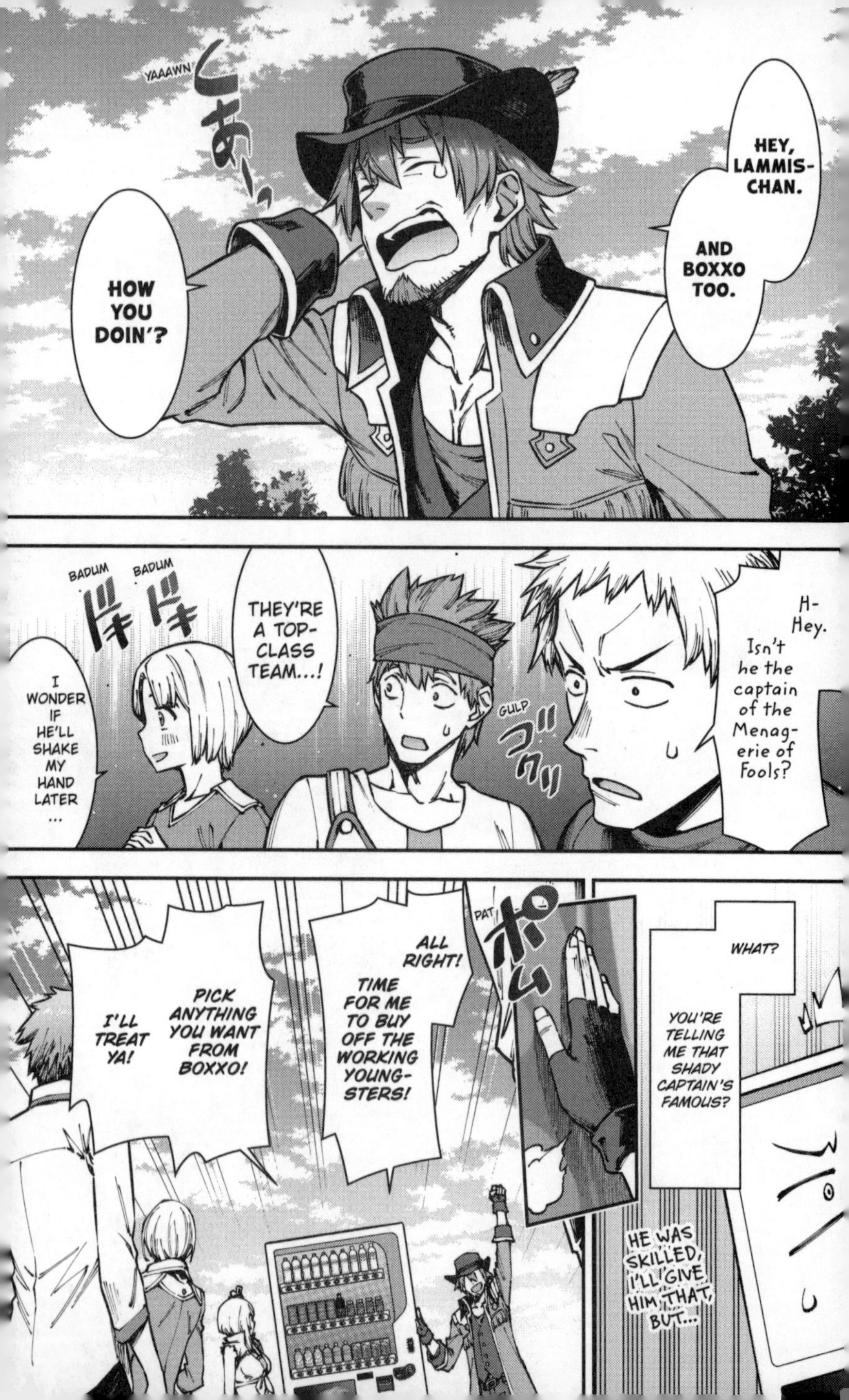
HEY, LAMMIS-CHAN.
AND BOXXO TOO.
YAAAWN
くあ〜
HOW YOU DOIN'?
H-Hey. Isn't he the captain of the Menagerie of Fools?
GULP
ゴクリ
THEY'RE A TOP-CLASS TEAM...!
BADUM BADUM
ドキドキ
I WONDER IF HE'LL SHAKE MY HAND LATER...
WHAT?
YOU'RE TELLING ME THAT SHADY CAPTAIN'S FAMOUS?
HE WAS SKILLED, I'LL GIVE HIM THAT, BUT...
PAT
ポム
ALL RIGHT!
TIME FOR ME TO BUY OFF THE WORKING YOUNGSTERS!
PICK ANYTHING YOU WANT FROM BOXXO!
I'LL TREAT YA!

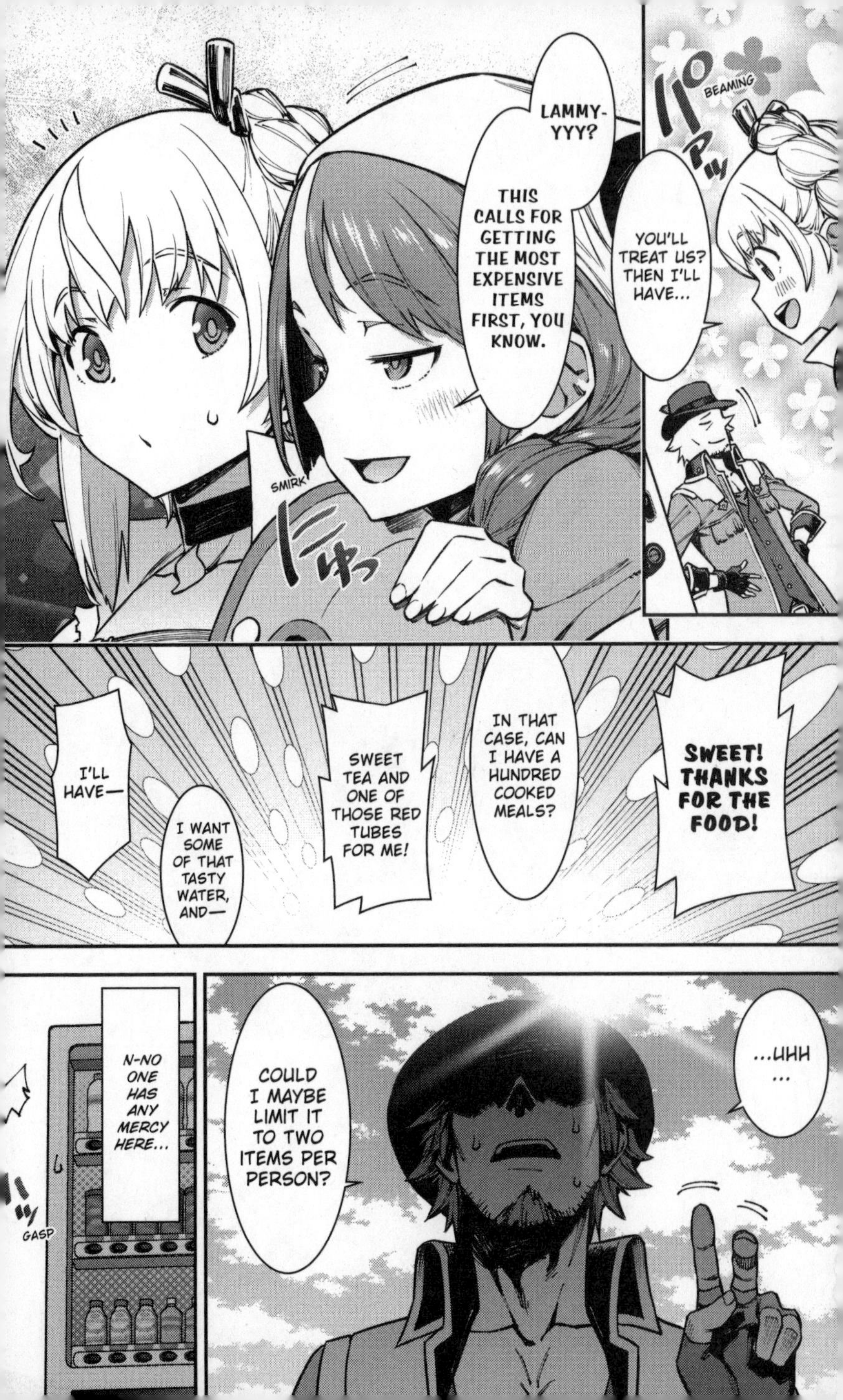
BEAMING
YOU'LL TREAT US? THEN I'LL HAVE...
LAMMY-YYY?
THIS CALLS FOR GETTING THE MOST EXPENSIVE ITEMS FIRST, YOU KNOW.
SMIRK
SWEET! THANKS FOR THE FOOD!
IN THAT CASE, CAN I HAVE A HUNDRED COOKED MEALS?
SWEET TEA AND ONE OF THOSE RED TUBES FOR ME!
I WANT SOME OF THAT TASTY WATER, AND—
I'LL HAVE—
...UHH ...
COULD I MAYBE LIMIT IT TO TWO ITEMS PER PERSON?
N-NO ONE HAS ANY MERCY HERE...
GASP

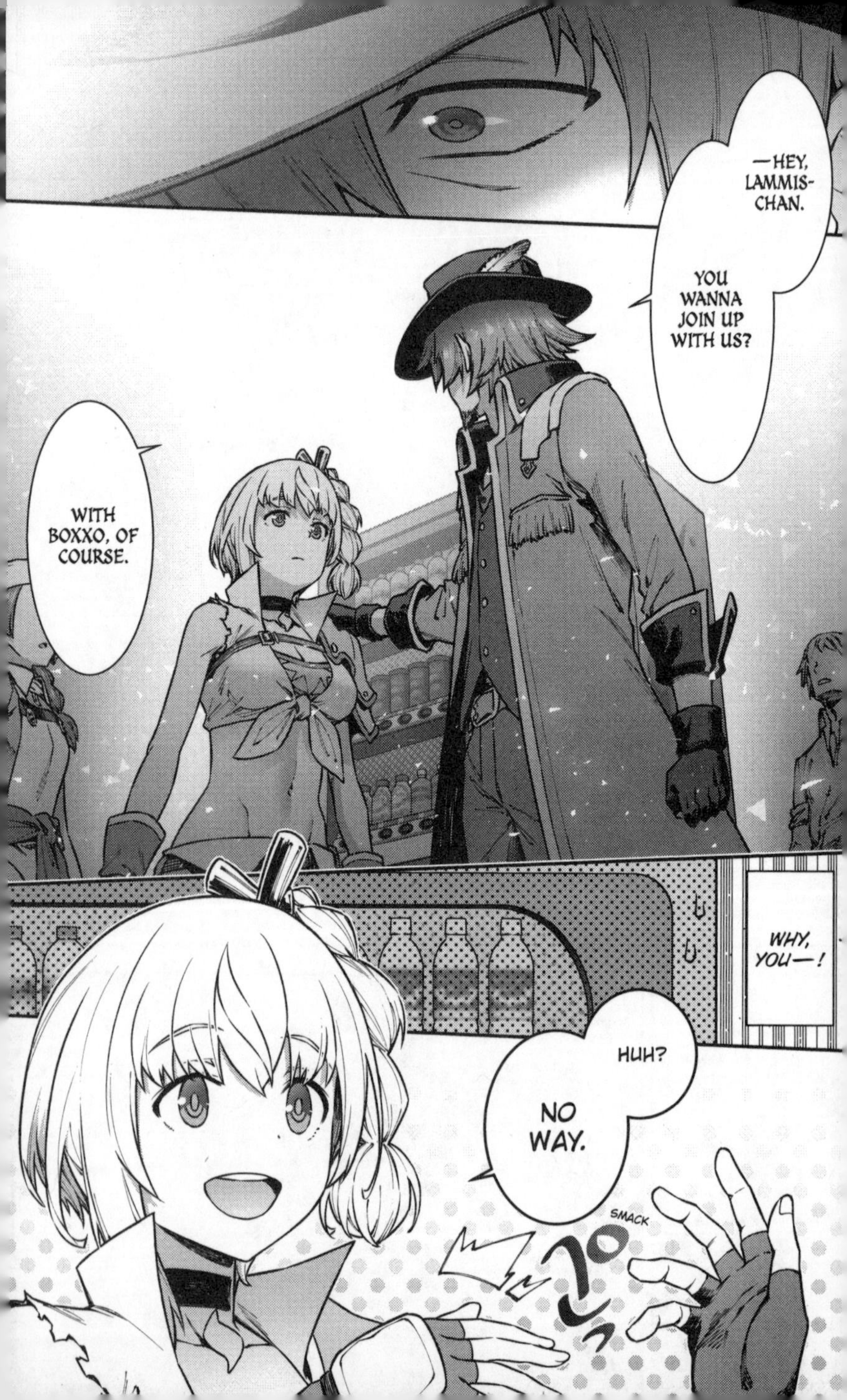
—HEY, LAMMIS-CHAN.
YOU WANNA JOIN UP WITH US?
WITH BOXXO, OF COURSE.
WHY, YOU—!
HUH?
NO WAY.
SMACK

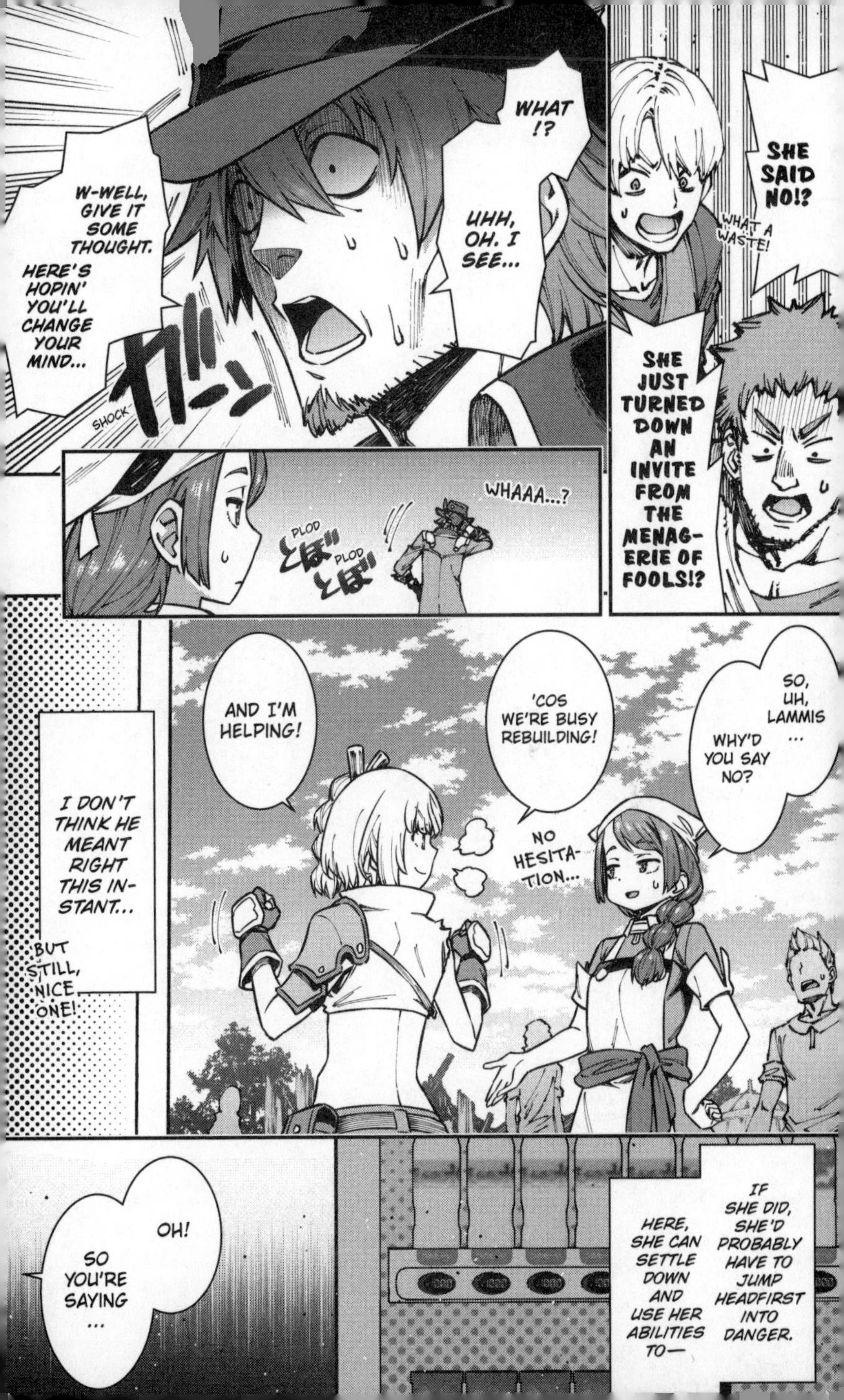
SHE SAID NO!?
WHAT A WASTE!
SHE JUST TURNED DOWN AN INVITE FROM THE MENAGERIE OF FOOLS!?
WHAT!?
UHH, OH. I SEE...
W-WELL, GIVE IT SOME THOUGHT.
HERE'S HOPIN' YOU'LL CHANGE YOUR MIND...
ガーン
SHOCK
WHAAA...?
とぼとぼ
PLOD PLOD
SO, UH, LAMMIS... WHY'D YOU SAY NO?
'COS WE'RE BUSY REBUILDING!
NO HESITATION...
AND I'M HELPING!
I DON'T THINK HE MEANT RIGHT THIS INSTANT...
BUT STILL, NICE ONE!
IF SHE DID, SHE'D PROBABLY HAVE TO JUMP HEADFIRST INTO DANGER.
HERE, SHE CAN SETTLE DOWN AND USE HER ABILITIES TO—
OH!
SO YOU'RE SAYING ...

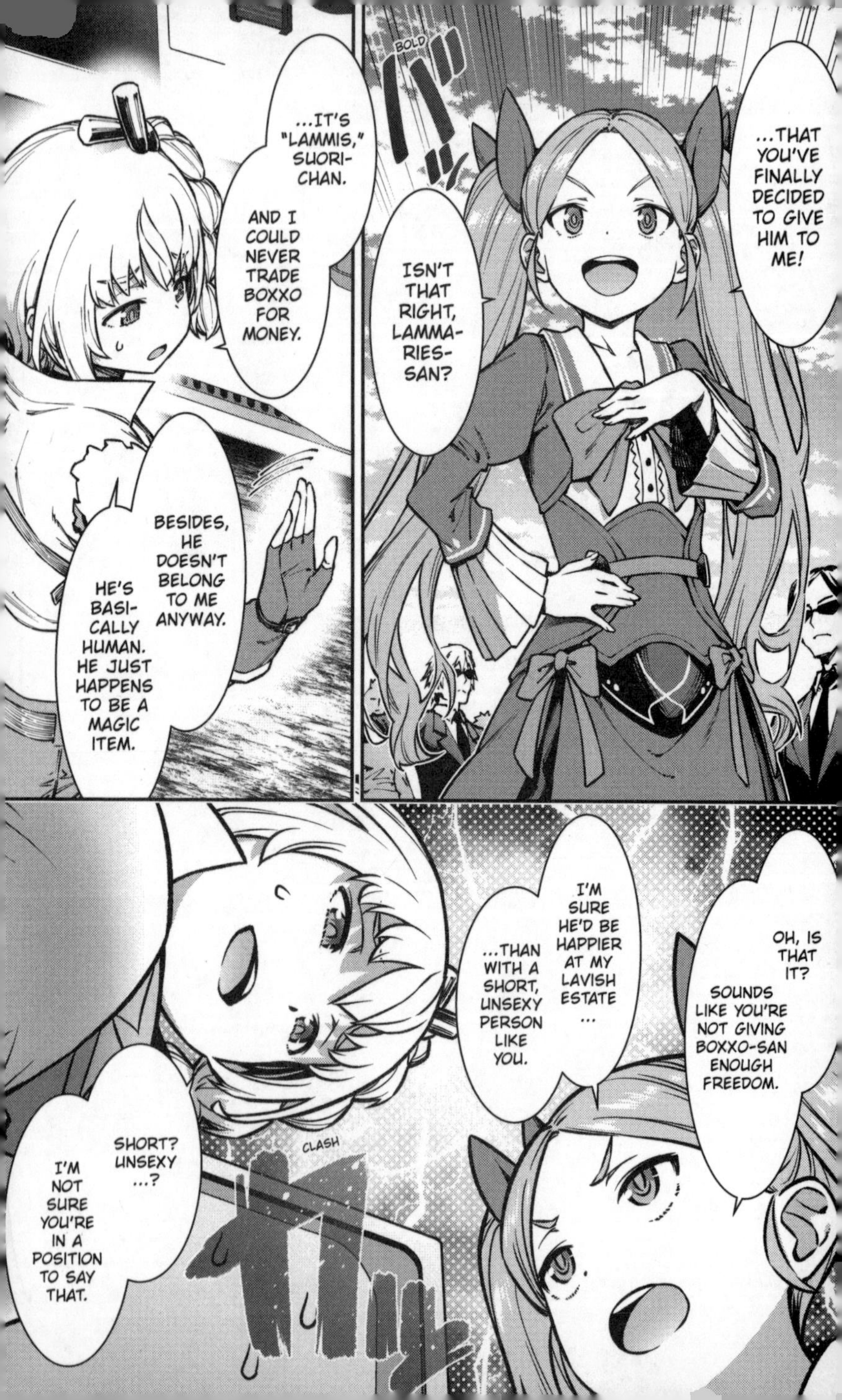
BOLD
...THAT YOU'VE FINALLY DECIDED TO GIVE HIM TO ME!
ISN'T THAT RIGHT, LAMMARIES-SAN?
...IT'S "LAMMIS," SUORI-CHAN.
AND I COULD NEVER TRADE BOXXO FOR MONEY.
BESIDES, HE DOESN'T BELONG TO ME ANYWAY.
HE'S BASICALLY HUMAN. HE JUST HAPPENS TO BE A MAGIC ITEM.
OH, IS THAT IT?
SOUNDS LIKE YOU'RE NOT GIVING BOXXO-SAN ENOUGH FREEDOM.
I'M SURE HE'D BE HAPPIER AT MY LAVISH ESTATE...
...THAN WITH A SHORT, UNSEXY PERSON LIKE YOU.
CLASH
SHORT? UNSEXY...?
I'M NOT SURE YOU'RE IN A POSITION TO SAY THAT.

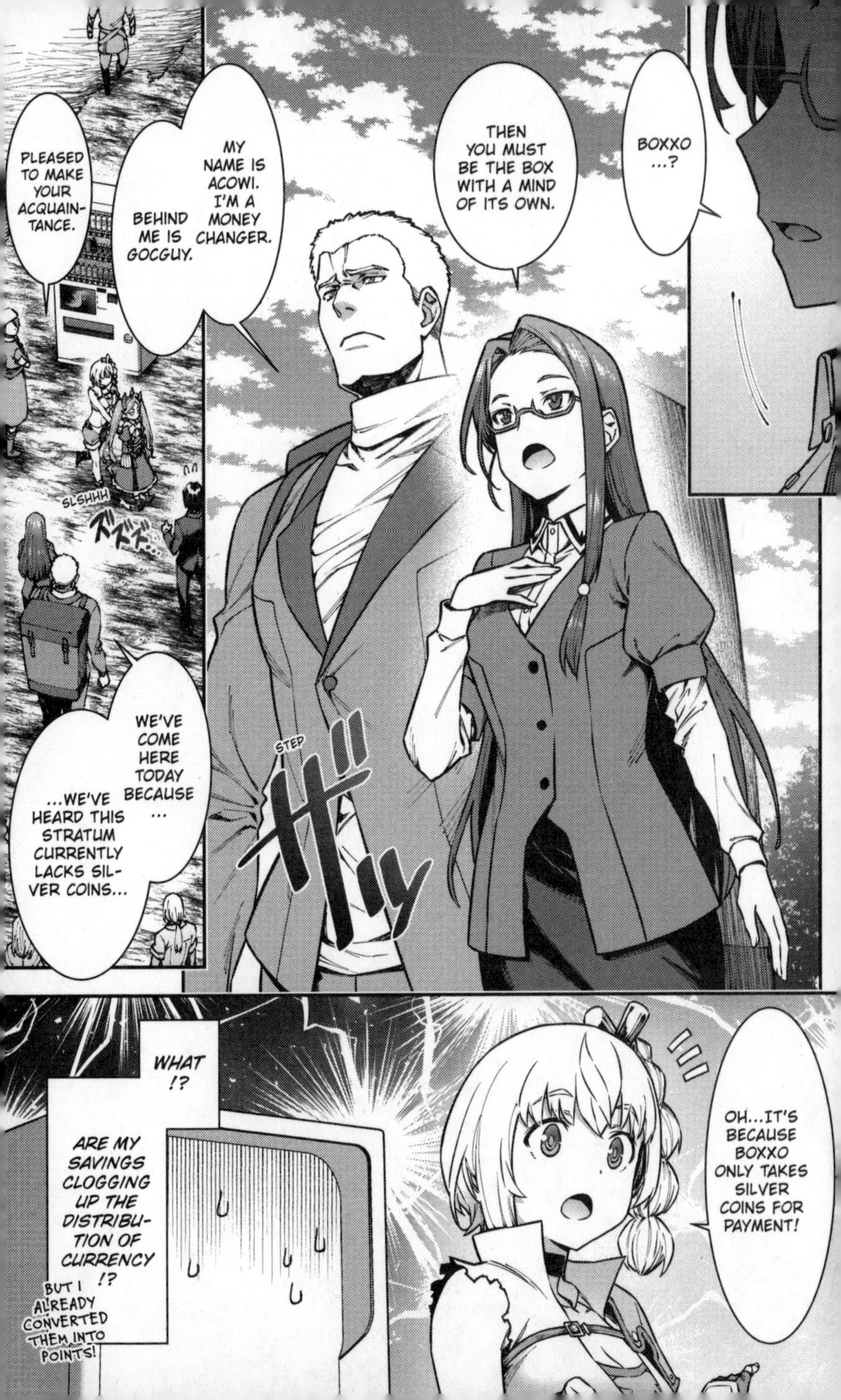
BOXXO ...?
THEN YOU MUST BE THE BOX WITH A MIND OF ITS OWN.
MY NAME IS ACOWI. I'M A MONEY CHANGER.
BEHIND ME IS GOCGUY.
PLEASED TO MAKE YOUR ACQUAIN-TANCE.
SLSHHH
WE'VE COME HERE TODAY BECAUSE ...
...WE'VE HEARD THIS STRATUM CURRENTLY LACKS SIL-VER COINS...
STEP
OH...IT'S BECAUSE BOXXO ONLY TAKES SILVER COINS FOR PAYMENT!
WHAT !?
ARE MY SAVINGS CLOGGING UP THE DISTRIBU-TION OF CURRENCY !?
BUT I ALREADY CONVERTED THEM INTO POINTS!

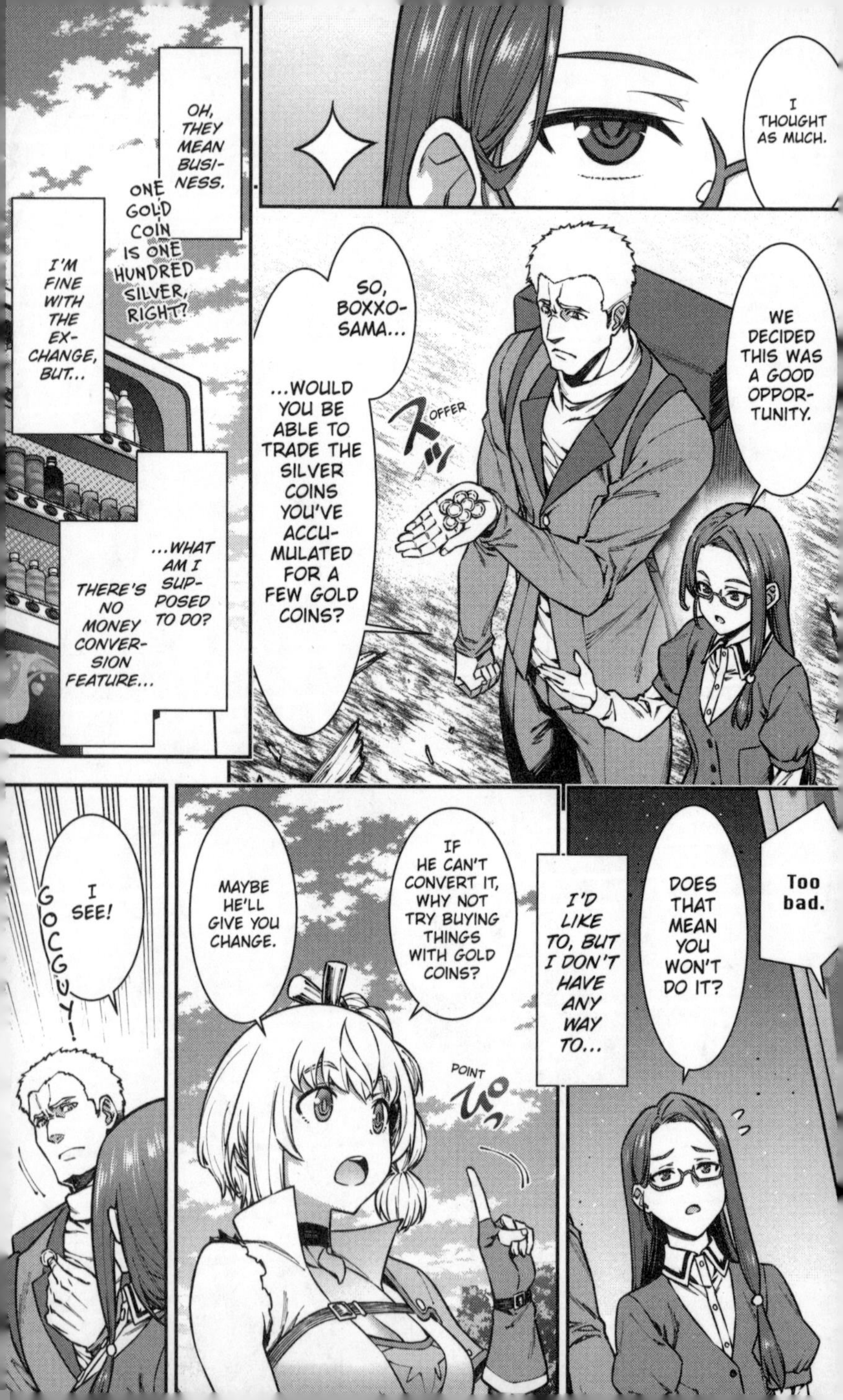
I THOUGHT AS MUCH.
WE DECIDED THIS WAS A GOOD OPPORTUNITY.
SO, BOXXO-SAMA...
...WOULD YOU BE ABLE TO TRADE THE SILVER COINS YOU'VE ACCUMULATED FOR A FEW GOLD COINS?
OFFER
OH, THEY MEAN BUSINESS.
ONE GOLD COIN IS ONE HUNDRED SILVER, RIGHT?
I'M FINE WITH THE EXCHANGE, BUT...
THERE'S NO MONEY CONVERSION FEATURE...
...WHAT AM I SUPPOSED TO DO?
Too bad.
DOES THAT MEAN YOU WON'T DO IT?
I'D LIKE TO, BUT I DON'T HAVE ANY WAY TO...
IF HE CAN'T CONVERT IT, WHY NOT TRY BUYING THINGS WITH GOLD COINS?
MAYBE HE'LL GIVE YOU CHANGE.
POINT
I SEE!
GOCGUY!

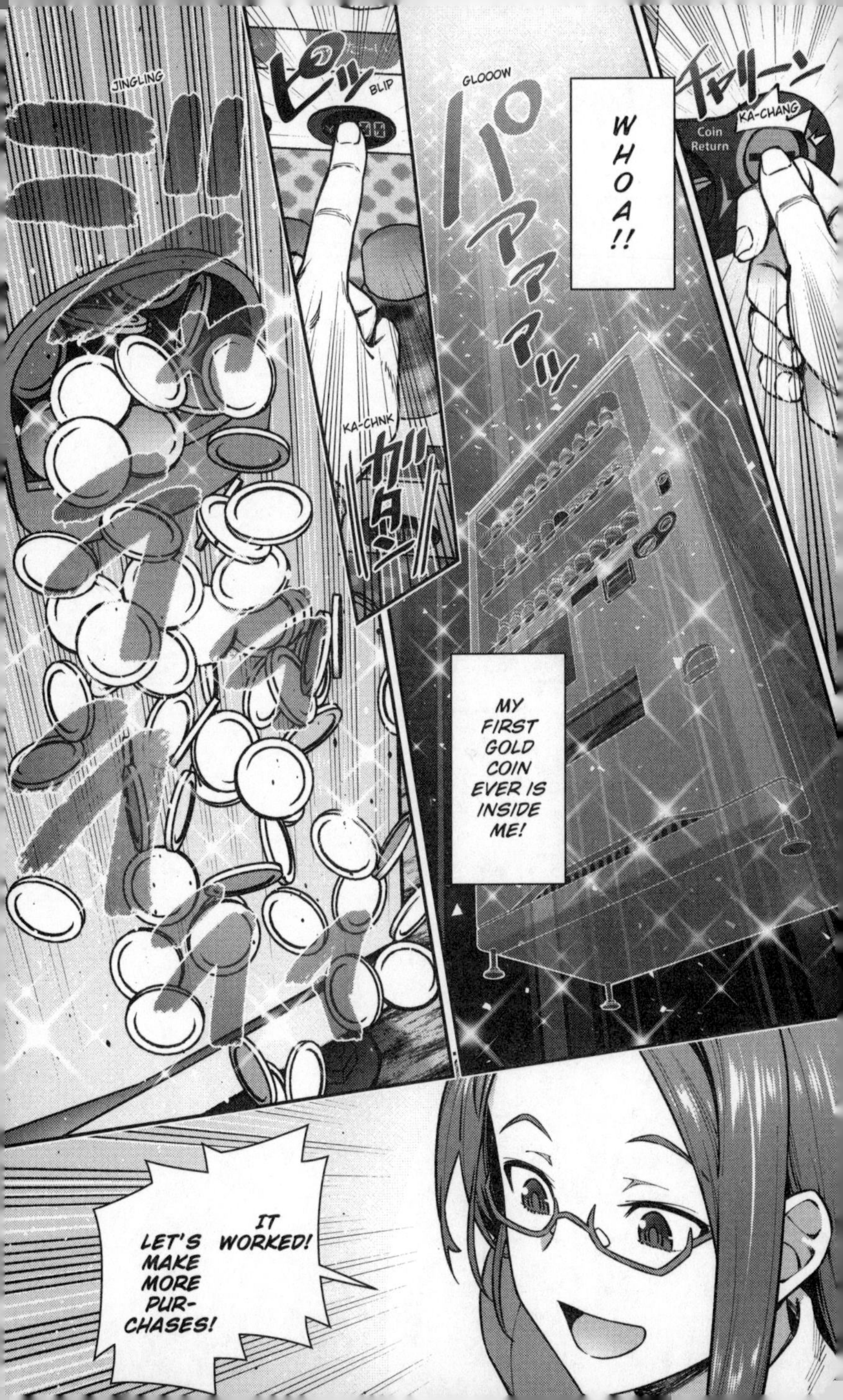
チャリーン
KA-CHANG
Coin Return
GLOOOW
パアアアッ
WHOA!!
MY FIRST GOLD COIN EVER IS INSIDE ME!
ピッ
BLIP
KA-CHNK
ガタン
JINGLING
IT WORKED!
LET'S MAKE MORE PUR-CHASES!

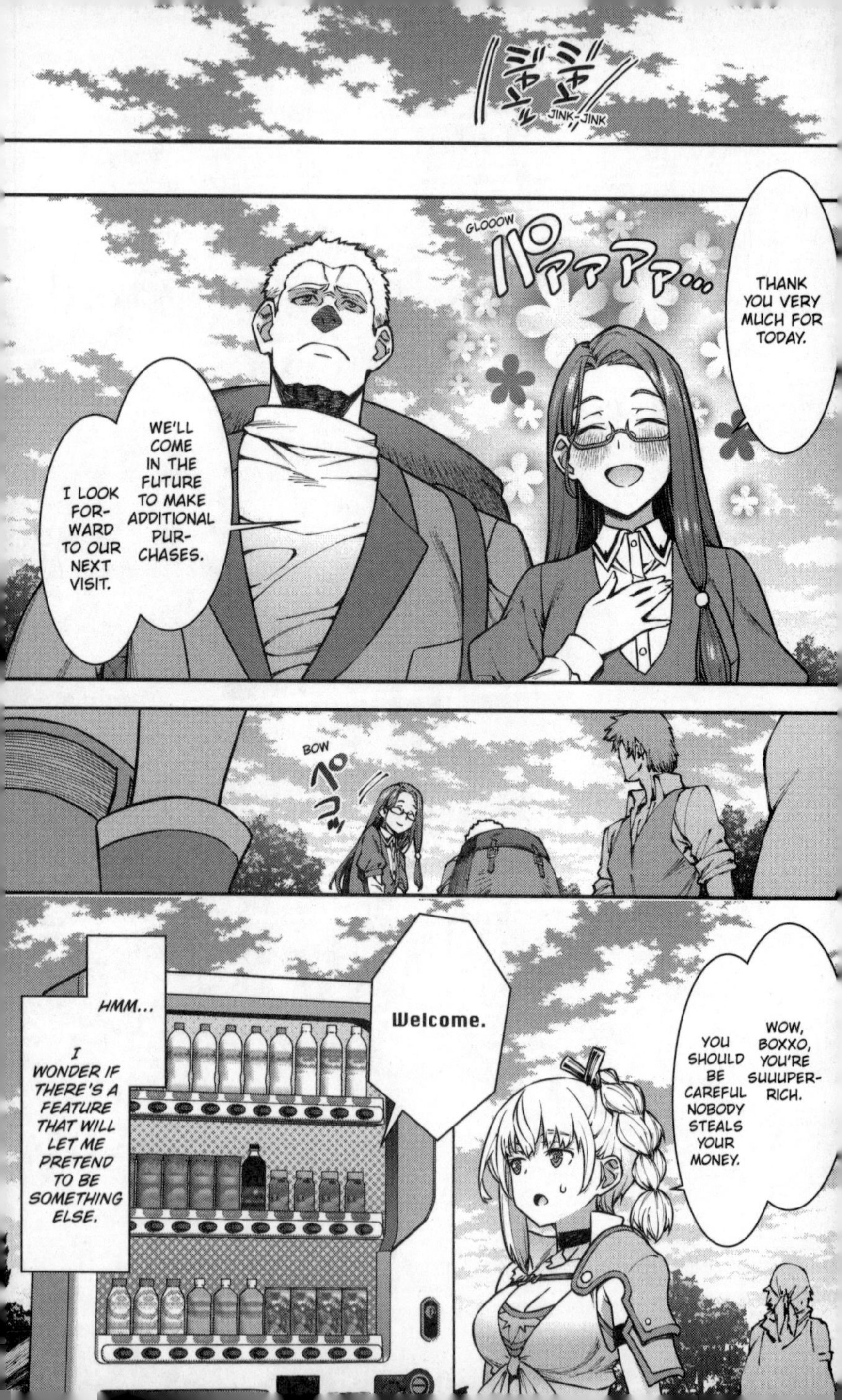
JINK-JINK
THANK YOU VERY MUCH FOR TODAY.
GLOOOW
パァァァァ…
WE'LL COME IN THE FUTURE TO MAKE ADDITIONAL PUR- CHASES.
I LOOK FOR- WARD TO OUR NEXT VISIT.
BOW
ペコッ
WOW, BOXXO, YOU'RE SUUUPER-RICH.
YOU SHOULD BE CAREFUL NOBODY STEALS YOUR MONEY.
Welcome.
HMM...
I WONDER IF THERE'S A FEATURE THAT WILL LET ME PRETEND TO BE SOMETHING ELSE.

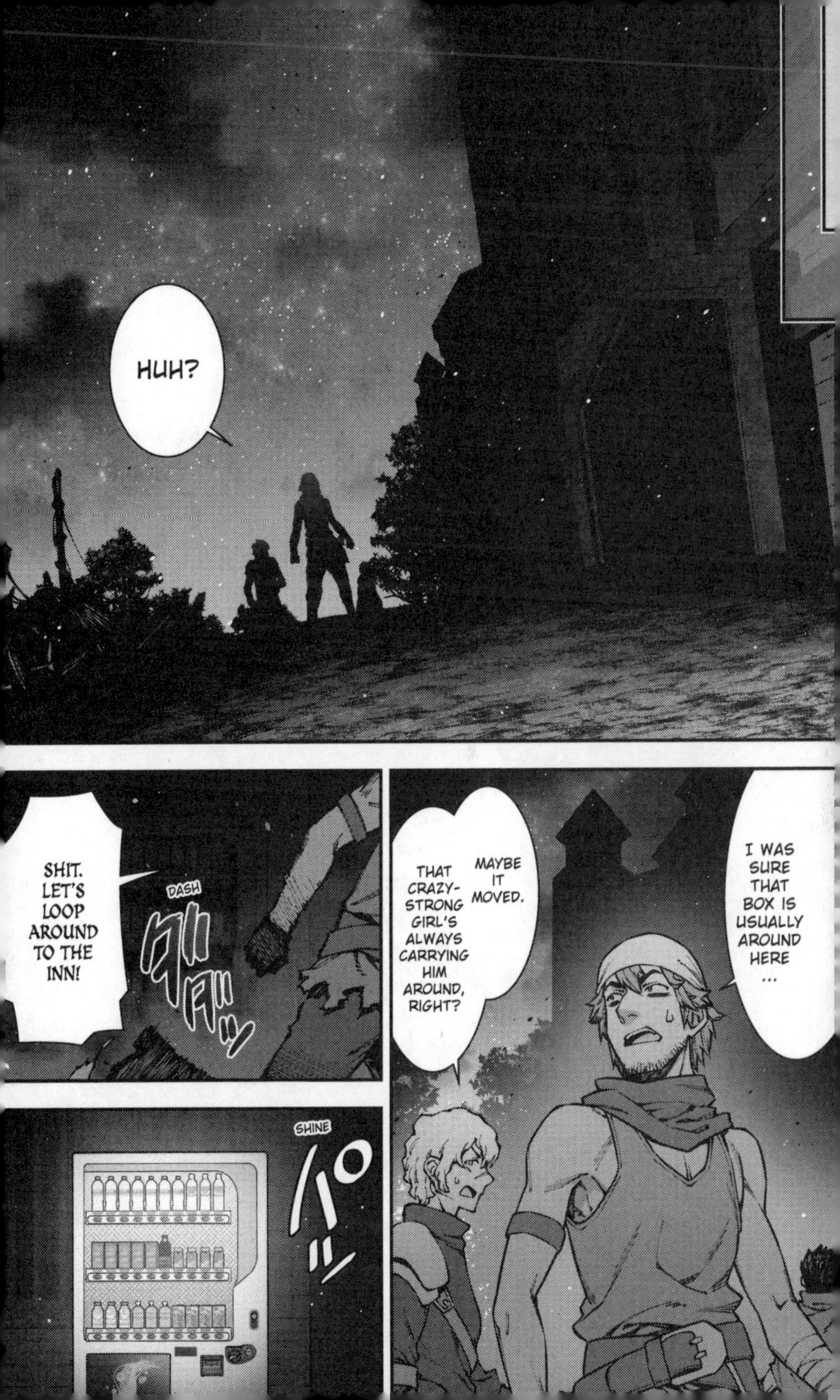
HUH?
I WAS SURE THAT BOX IS USUALLY AROUND HERE...
MAYBE IT MOVED.
THAT CRAZY-STRONG GIRL'S ALWAYS CARRYING HIM AROUND, RIGHT?
SHIT. LET'S LOOP AROUND TO THE INN!
DASH
SHINE

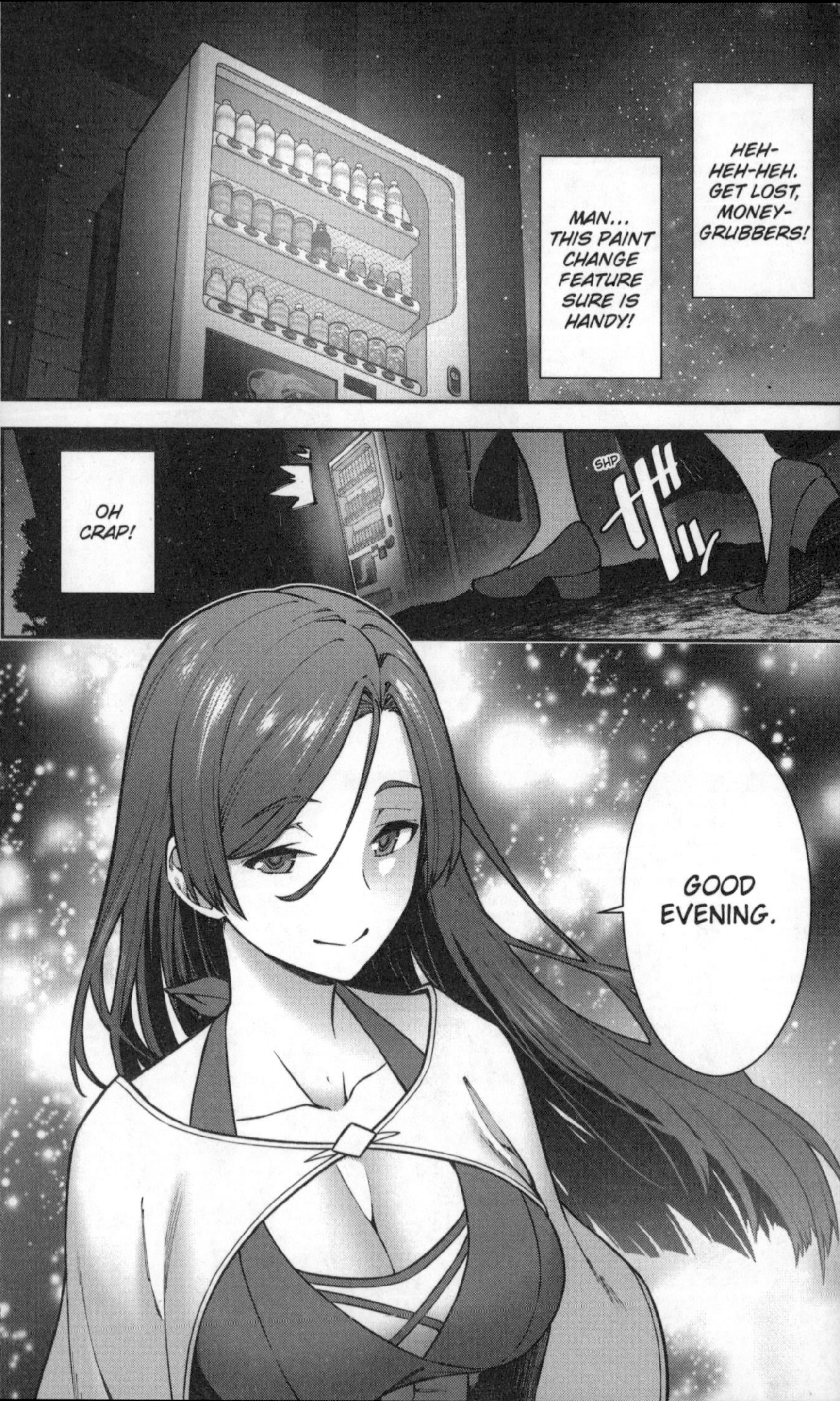
HEH-HEH-HEH. GET LOST, MONEY-GRUBBERS!
MAN... THIS PAINT CHANGE FEATURE SURE IS HANDY!
SHP
OH CRAP!
GOOD EVENING.

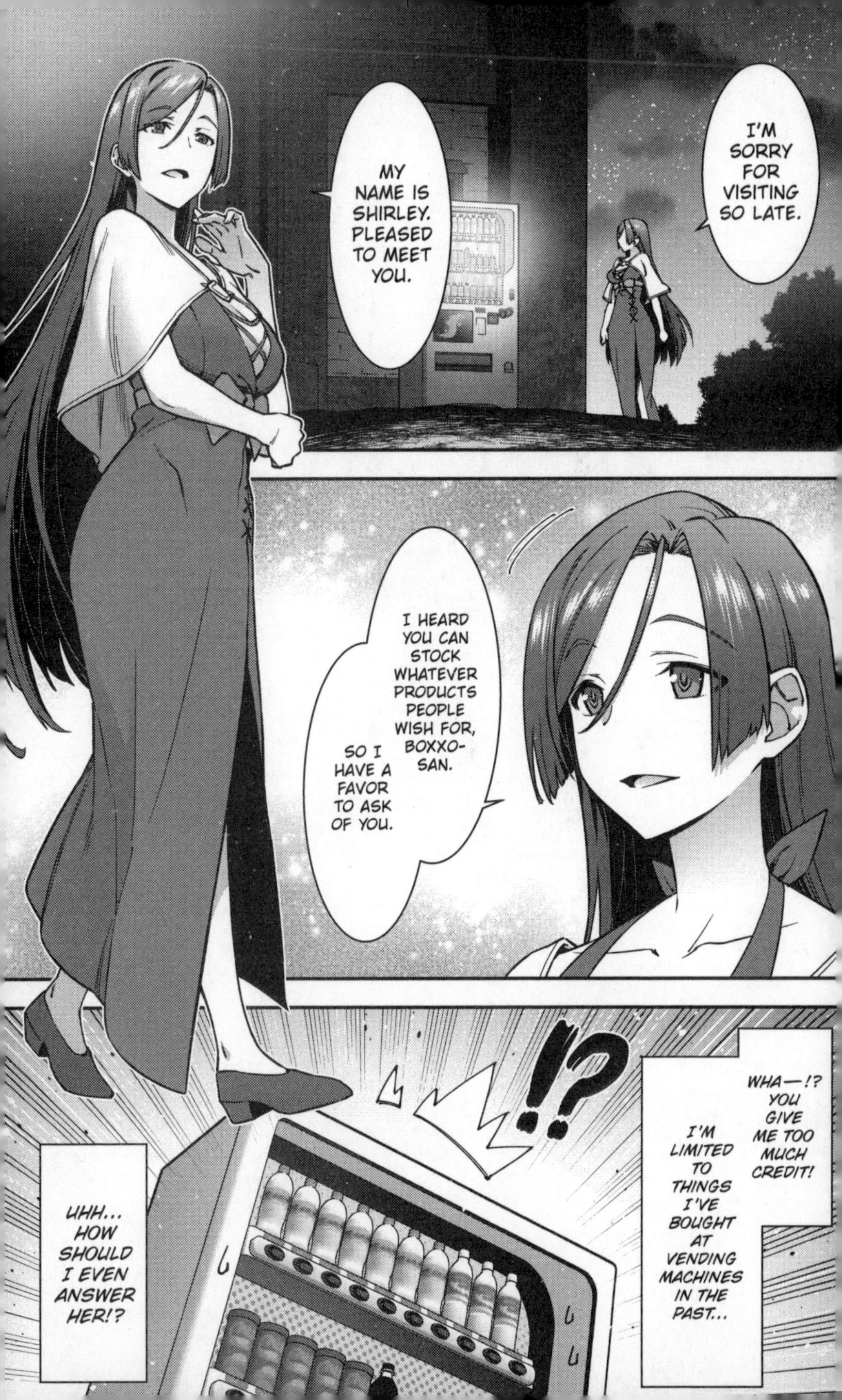

I'M SORRY FOR VISITING SO LATE.
MY NAME IS SHIRLEY. PLEASED TO MEET YOU.
I HEARD YOU CAN STOCK WHATEVER PRODUCTS PEOPLE WISH FOR, BOXXO-SAN.
SO I HAVE A FAVOR TO ASK OF YOU.
!?
WHA—!? YOU GIVE ME TOO MUCH CREDIT!
I'M LIMITED TO THINGS I'VE BOUGHT AT VENDING MACHINES IN THE PAST...
UHH... HOW SHOULD I EVEN ANSWER HER!?

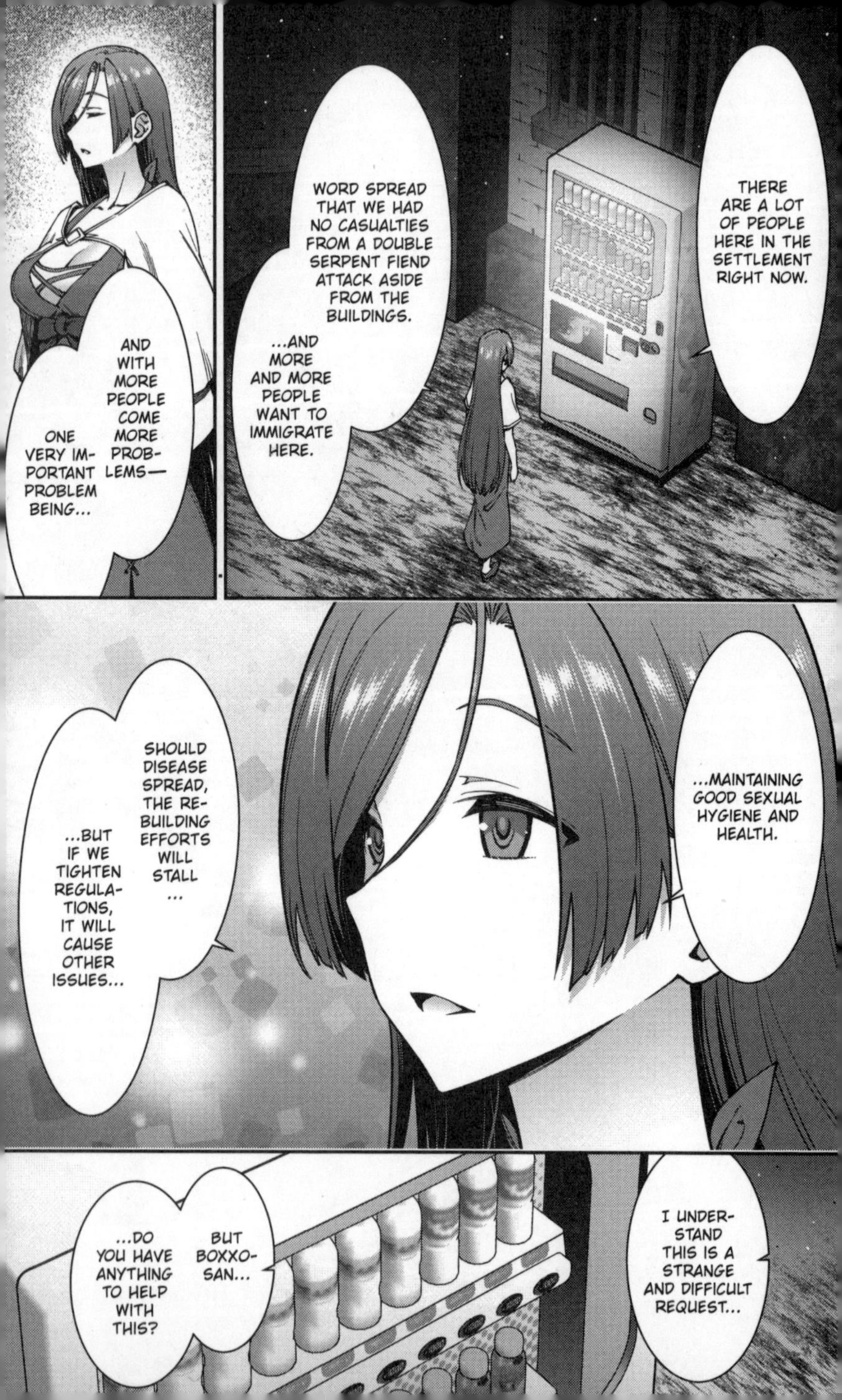
THERE ARE A LOT OF PEOPLE HERE IN THE SETTLEMENT RIGHT NOW.
WORD SPREAD THAT WE HAD NO CASUALTIES FROM A DOUBLE SERPENT FIEND ATTACK ASIDE FROM THE BUILDINGS.
...AND MORE AND MORE PEOPLE WANT TO IMMIGRATE HERE.
AND WITH MORE PEOPLE COME MORE PROBLEMS—
ONE VERY IMPORTANT PROBLEM BEING...
...MAINTAINING GOOD SEXUAL HYGIENE AND HEALTH.
SHOULD DISEASE SPREAD, THE REBUILDING EFFORTS WILL STALL...
...BUT IF WE TIGHTEN REGULATIONS, IT WILL CAUSE OTHER ISSUES...
I UNDERSTAND THIS IS A STRANGE AND DIFFICULT REQUEST...
BUT BOXXO-SAN...
...DO YOU HAVE ANYTHING TO HELP WITH THIS?

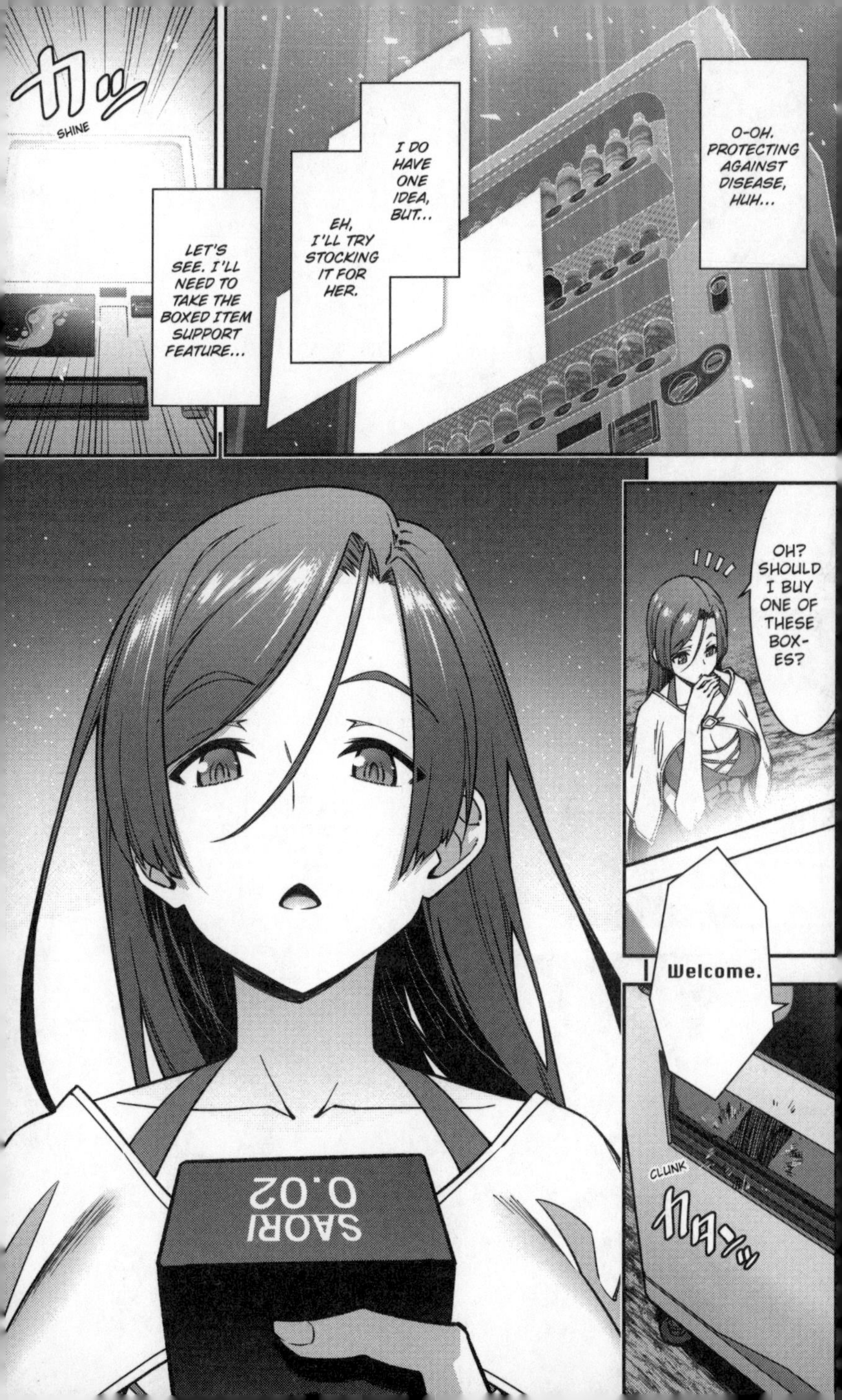
O-OH. PROTECTING AGAINST DISEASE, HUH...
I DO HAVE ONE IDEA, BUT...
EH, I'LL TRY STOCKING IT FOR HER.
SHINE
LET'S SEE. I'LL NEED TO TAKE THE BOXED ITEM SUPPORT FEATURE...
OH? SHOULD I BUY ONE OF THESE BOX-ES?
Welcome.
CLUNK
SAORI 0.02

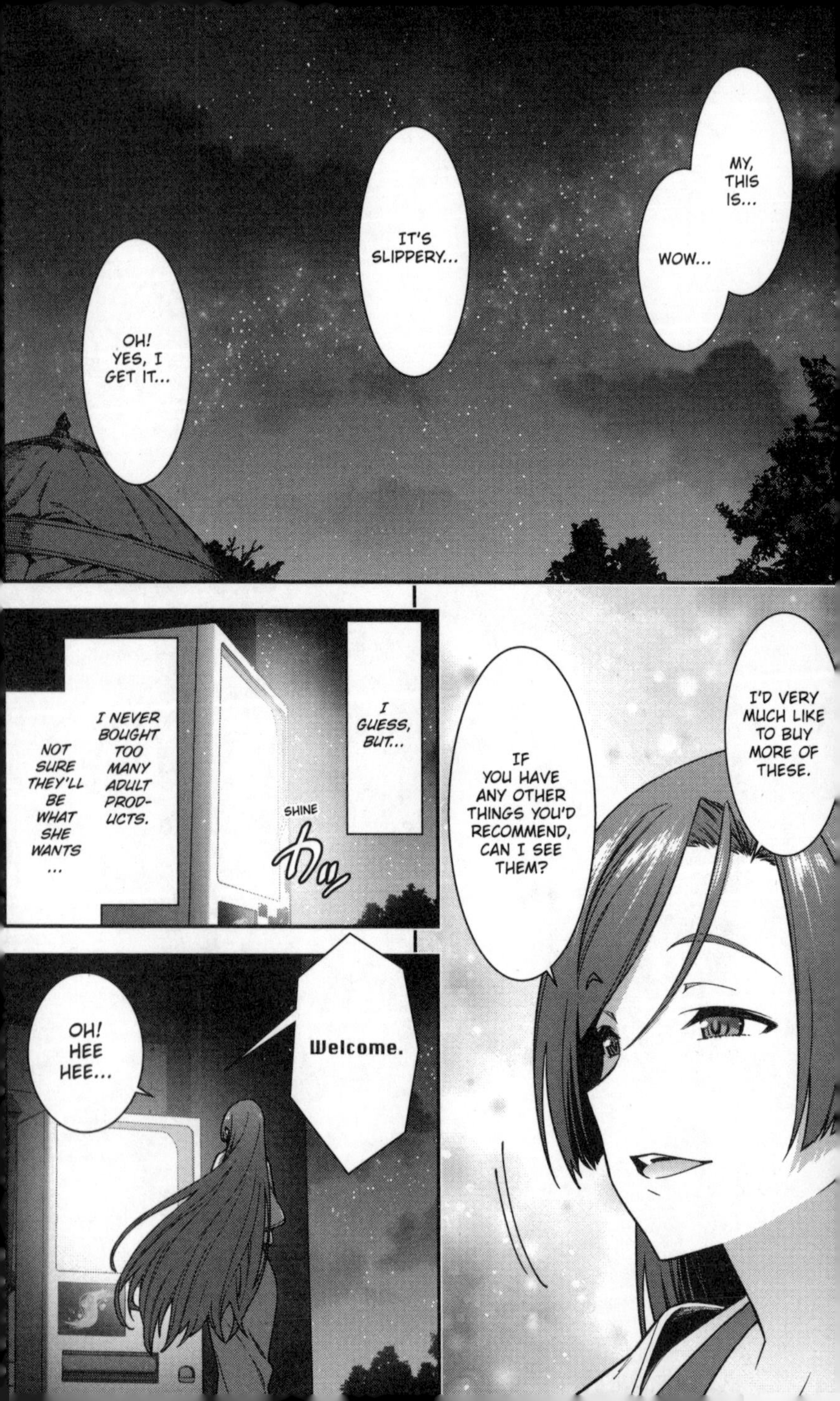
MY, THIS IS...
WOW...
IT'S SLIPPERY...
OH! YES, I GET IT...
I'D VERY MUCH LIKE TO BUY MORE OF THESE.
IF YOU HAVE ANY OTHER THINGS YOU'D RECOMMEND, CAN I SEE THEM?
I GUESS, BUT...
SHINE
I NEVER BOUGHT TOO MANY ADULT PRODUCTS.
NOT SURE THEY'LL BE WHAT SHE WANTS ...
Welcome.
OH! HEE HEE...

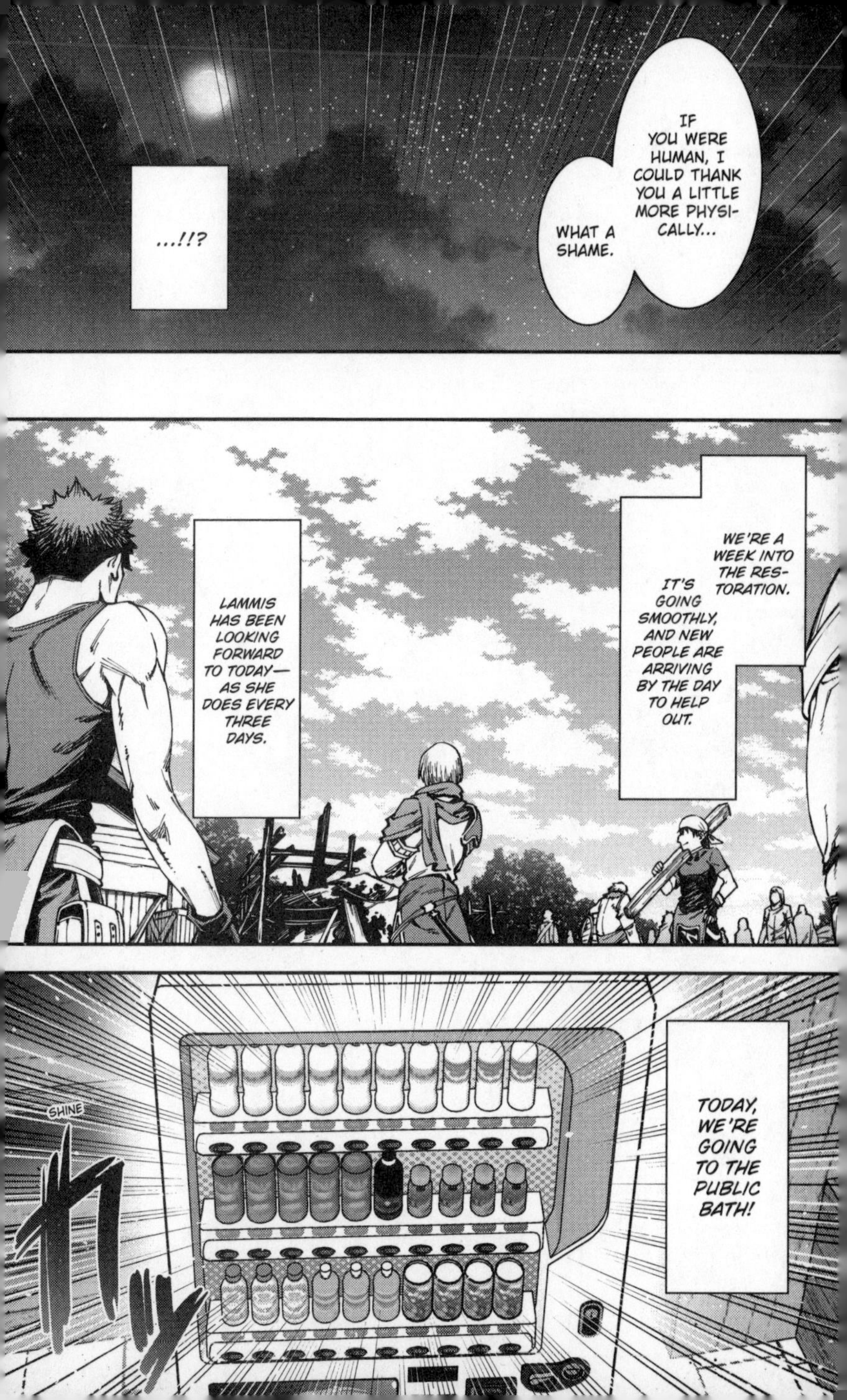
IF YOU WERE HUMAN, I COULD THANK YOU A LITTLE MORE PHYSI-CALLY...
WHAT A SHAME.
...!!?
WE'RE A WEEK INTO THE RES-TORATION.
IT'S GOING SMOOTHLY, AND NEW PEOPLE ARE ARRIVING BY THE DAY TO HELP OUT.
LAMMIS HAS BEEN LOOKING FORWARD TO TODAY—AS SHE DOES EVERY THREE DAYS.
TODAY, WE'RE GOING TO THE PUBLIC BATH!
SHINE

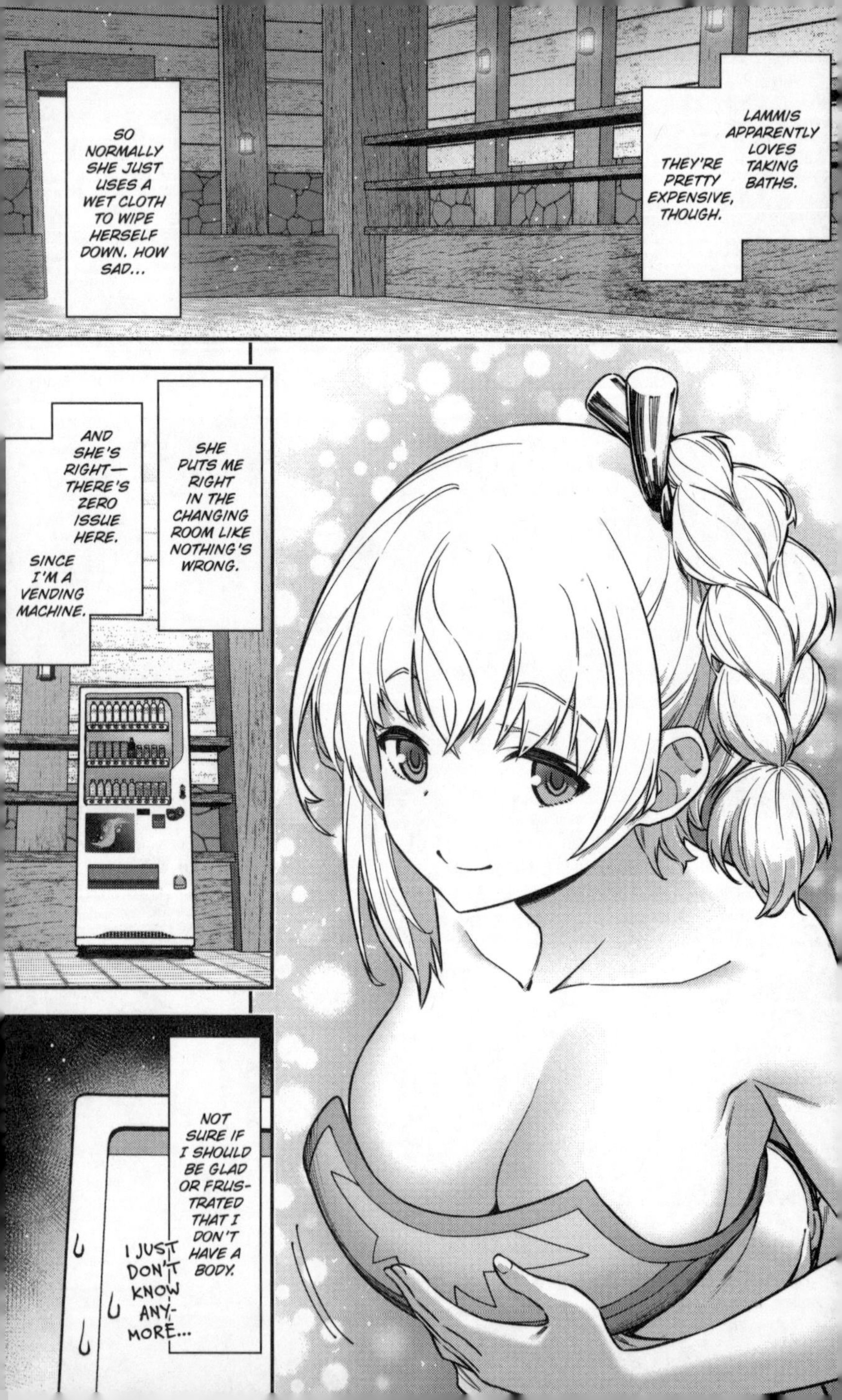
LAMMIS APPARENTLY LOVES TAKING BATHS.
THEY'RE PRETTY EXPENSIVE, THOUGH.
SO NORMALLY SHE JUST USES A WET CLOTH TO WIPE HERSELF DOWN. HOW SAD...
SHE PUTS ME RIGHT IN THE CHANGING ROOM LIKE NOTHING'S WRONG.
AND SHE'S RIGHT— THERE'S ZERO ISSUE HERE.
SINCE I'M A VENDING MACHINE.
NOT SURE IF I SHOULD BE GLAD OR FRUS-TRATED THAT I DON'T HAVE A BODY.
I JUST DON'T KNOW ANY-MORE...

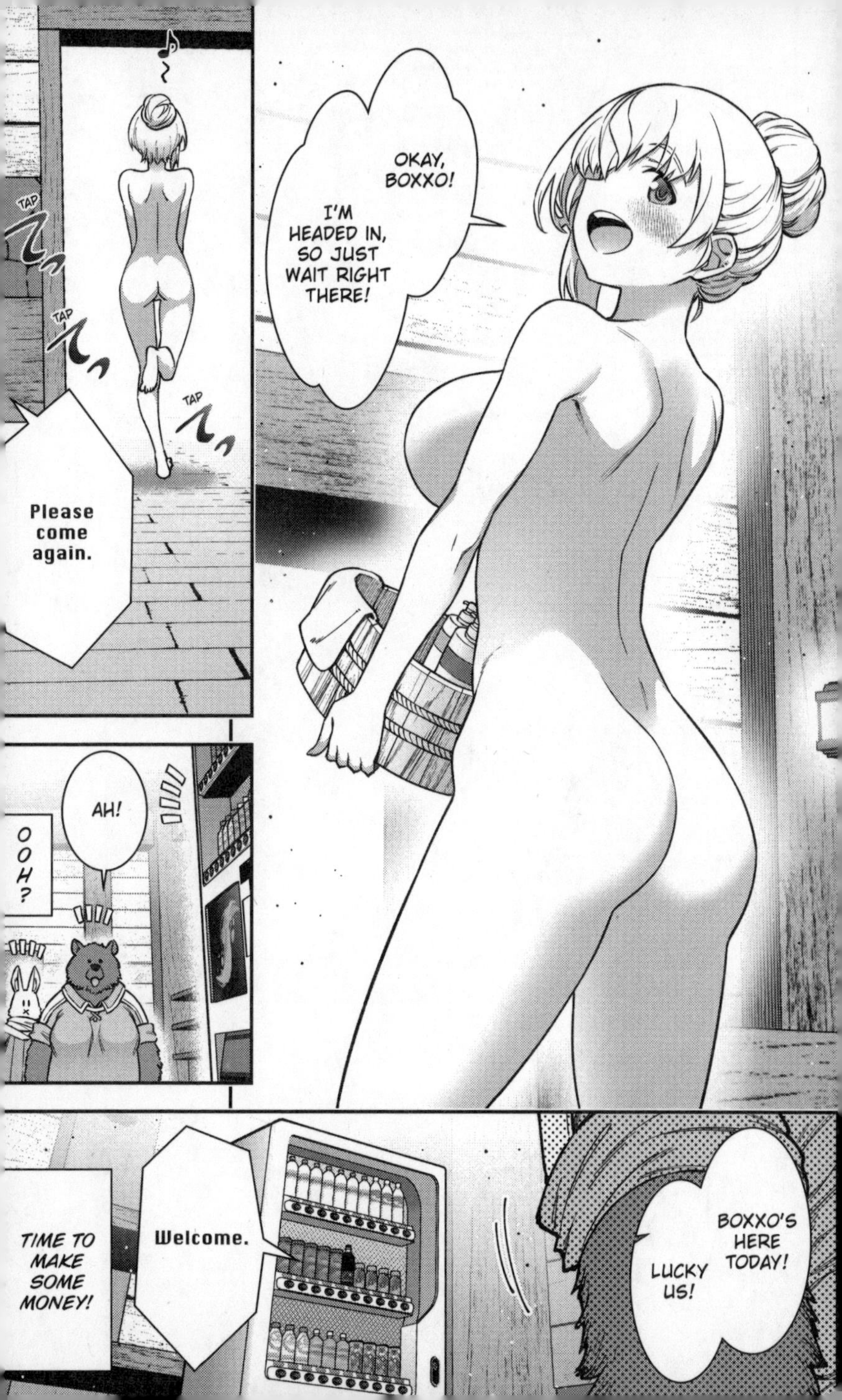

OKAY, BOXXO!
I'M HEADED IN, SO JUST WAIT RIGHT THERE!
TAP
TAP
TAP
Please come again.
AH!
OOH?
BOXXO'S HERE TODAY!
LUCKY US!
Welcome.
TIME TO MAKE SOME MONEY!

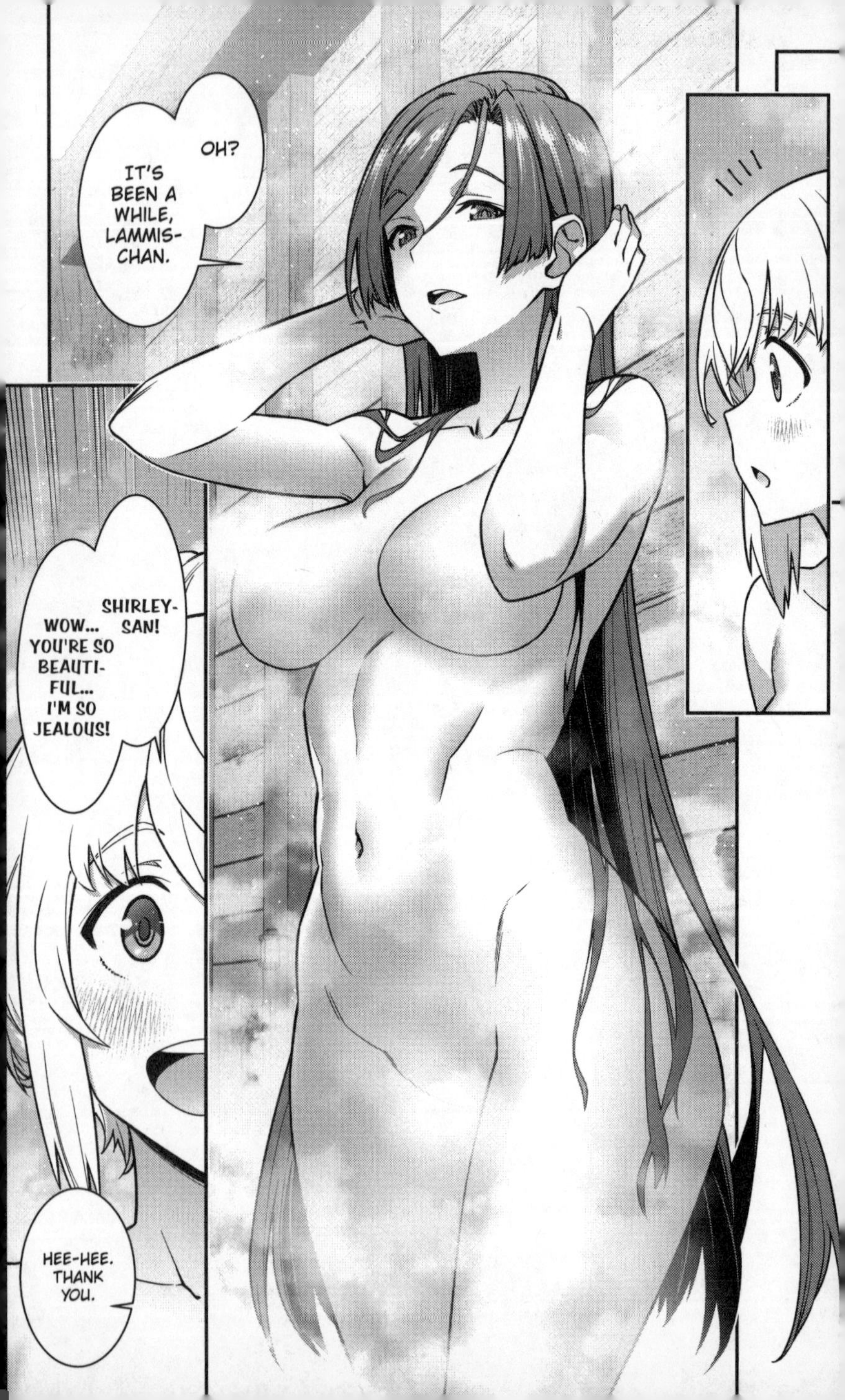
OH? IT'S BEEN A WHILE, LAMMIS-CHAN.
SHIRLEY-SAN! WOW... YOU'RE SO BEAUTIFUL... I'M SO JEALOUS!
HEE-HEE. THANK YOU.

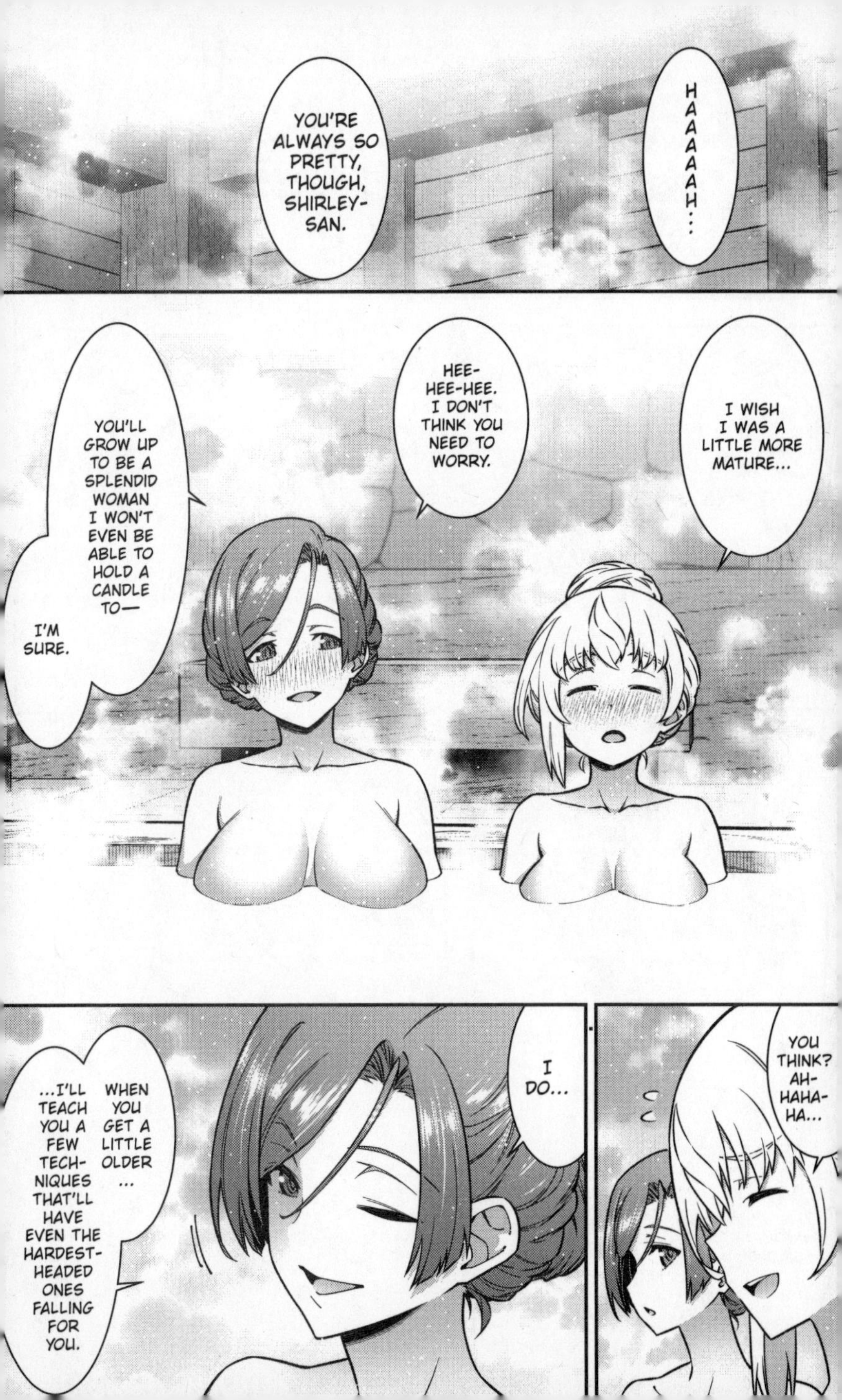
HAAAAAH...
YOU'RE ALWAYS SO PRETTY, THOUGH, SHIRLEY-SAN.
I WISH I WAS A LITTLE MORE MATURE...
HEE-HEE-HEE. I DON'T THINK YOU NEED TO WORRY.
YOU'LL GROW UP TO BE A SPLENDID WOMAN I WON'T EVEN BE ABLE TO HOLD A CANDLE TO—
I'M SURE.
YOU THINK? AH-HAHAHA...
I DO...
WHEN YOU GET A LITTLE OLDER...
...I'LL TEACH YOU A FEW TECHNIQUES THAT'LL HAVE EVEN THE HARDEST-HEADED ONES FALLING FOR YOU.

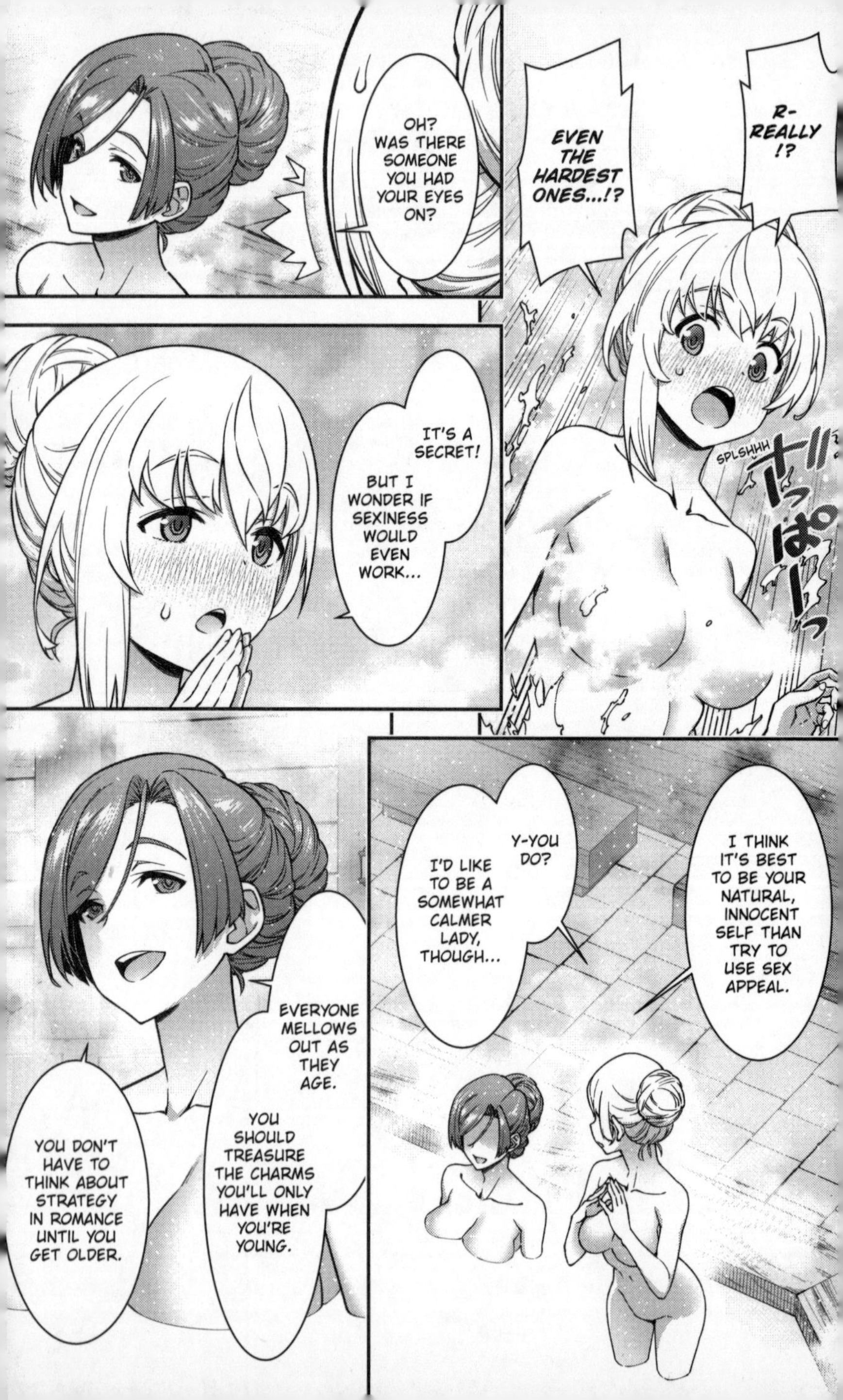
R-REALLY!?
EVEN THE HARDEST ONES...!?
SPLSHHH
ざっぱーっ
OH? WAS THERE SOMEONE YOU HAD YOUR EYES ON?
IT'S A SECRET!
BUT I WONDER IF SEXINESS WOULD EVEN WORK...
I THINK IT'S BEST TO BE YOUR NATURAL, INNOCENT SELF THAN TRY TO USE SEX APPEAL.
Y-YOU DO?
I'D LIKE TO BE A SOMEWHAT CALMER LADY, THOUGH...
EVERYONE MELLOWS OUT AS THEY AGE.
YOU SHOULD TREASURE THE CHARMS YOU'LL ONLY HAVE WHEN YOU'RE YOUNG.
YOU DON'T HAVE TO THINK ABOUT STRATEGY IN ROMANCE UNTIL YOU GET OLDER.

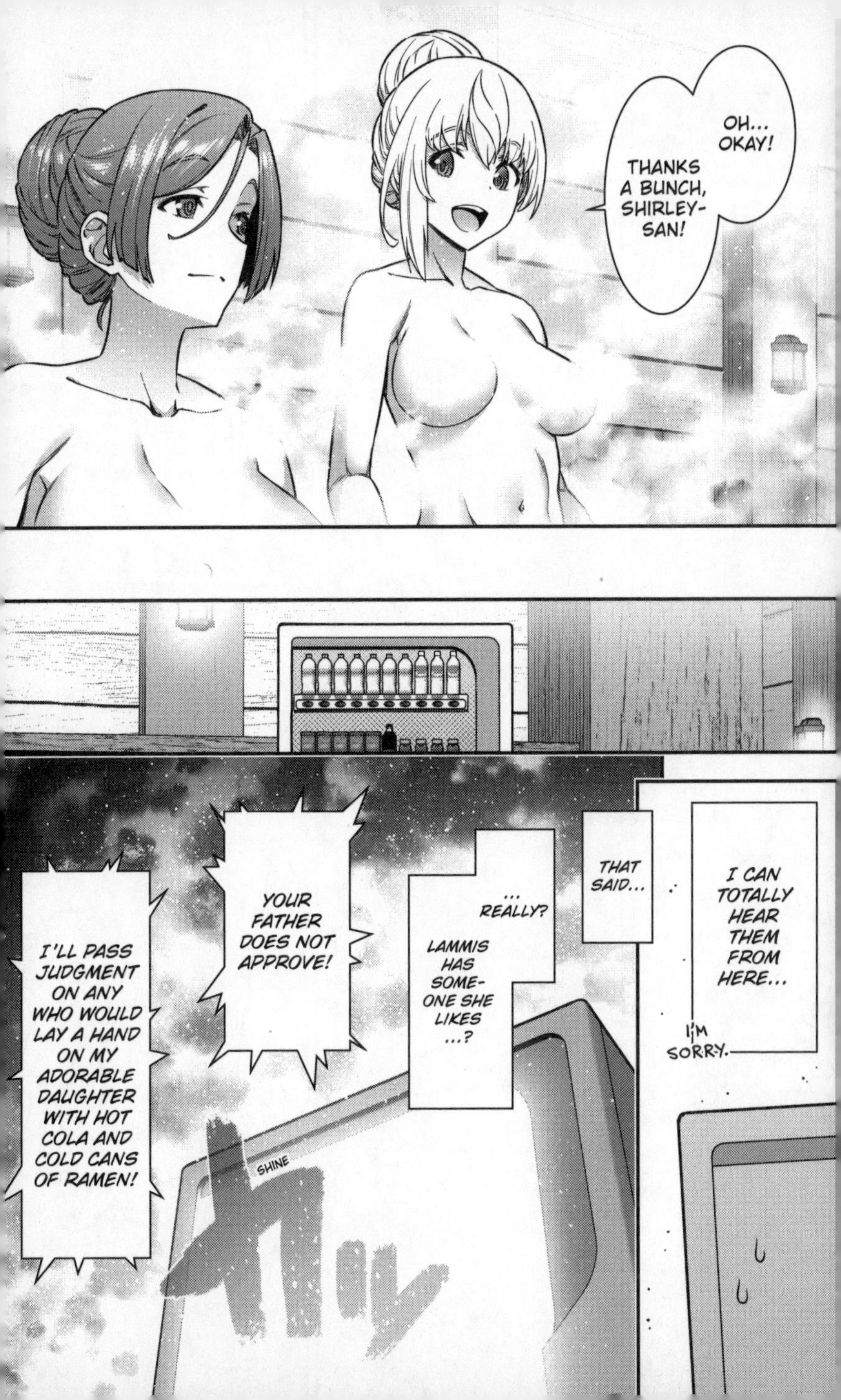
OH... OKAY!
THANKS A BUNCH, SHIRLEY-SAN!
I CAN TOTALLY HEAR THEM FROM HERE...
I'M SORRY.
THAT SAID...
... REALLY?
LAMMIS HAS SOME-ONE SHE LIKES ...?
YOUR FATHER DOES NOT APPROVE!
SHINE
I'LL PASS JUDGMENT ON ANY WHO WOULD LAY A HAND ON MY ADORABLE DAUGHTER WITH HOT COLA AND COLD CANS OF RAMEN!

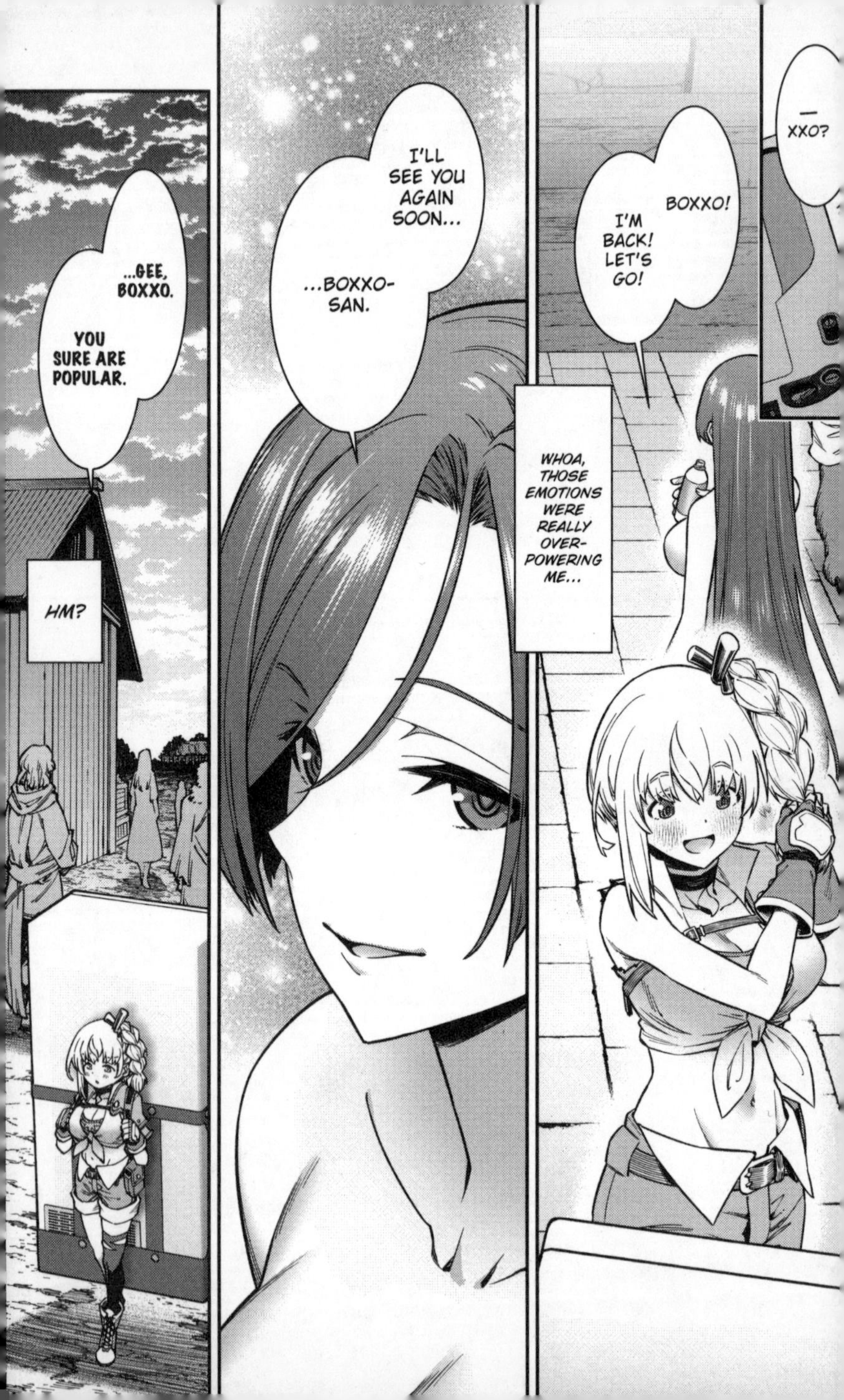
—XXO?
BOXXO! I'M BACK! LET'S GO!
WHOA, THOSE EMOTIONS WERE REALLY OVER-POWERING ME...
I'LL SEE YOU AGAIN SOON... ...BOXXO-SAN.
...GEE, BOXXO. YOU SURE ARE POPULAR.
HM?

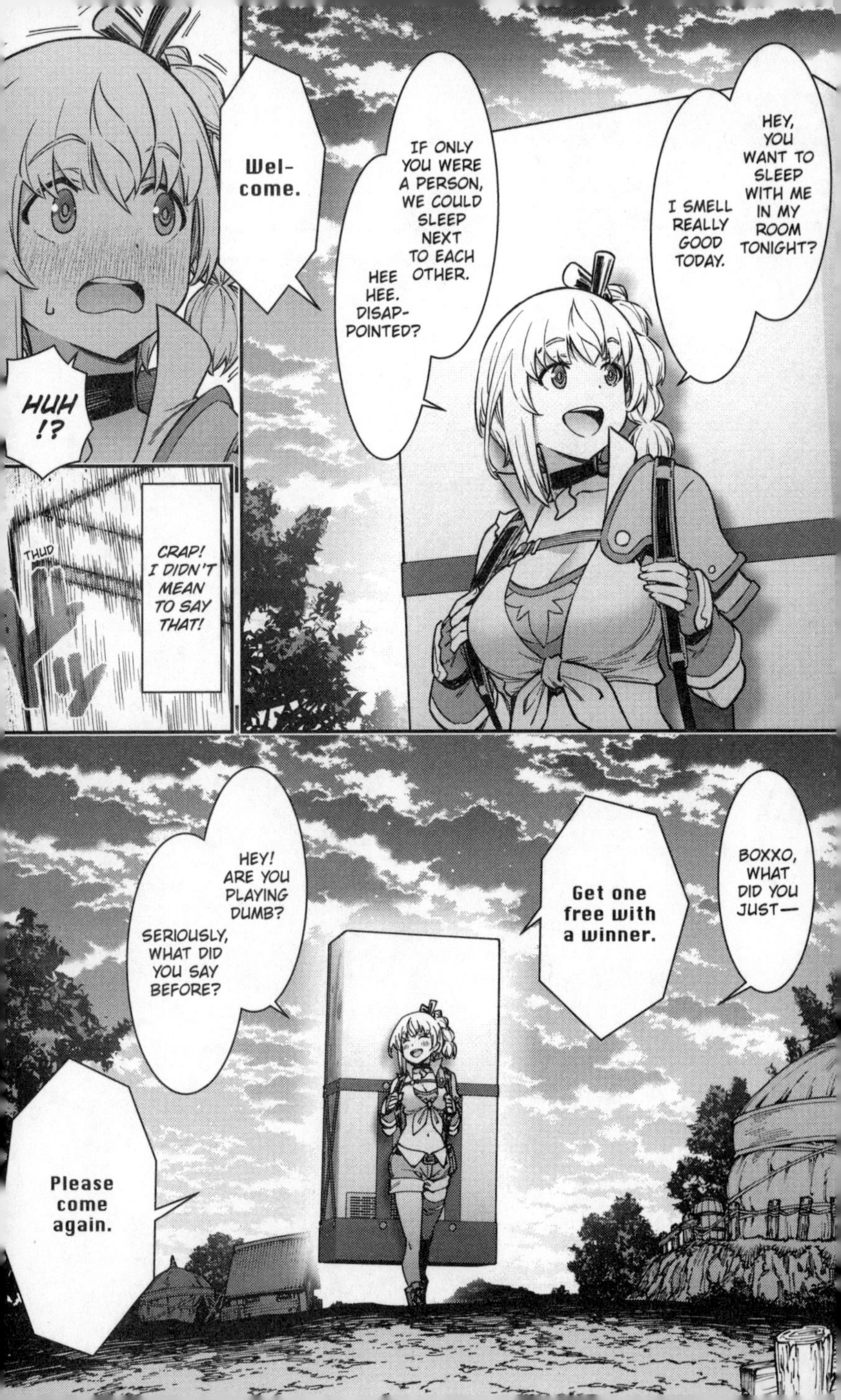
HEY, YOU WANT TO SLEEP WITH ME IN MY ROOM TONIGHT?
I SMELL REALLY GOOD TODAY.
IF ONLY YOU WERE A PERSON, WE COULD SLEEP NEXT TO EACH OTHER.
HEE HEE. DISAP-POINTED?
Wel-come.
HUH!?
THUD
CRAP! I DIDN'T MEAN TO SAY THAT!
BOXXO, WHAT DID YOU JUST—
Get one free with a winner.
HEY! ARE YOU PLAYING DUMB?
SERIOUSLY, WHAT DID YOU SAY BEFORE?
Please come again.

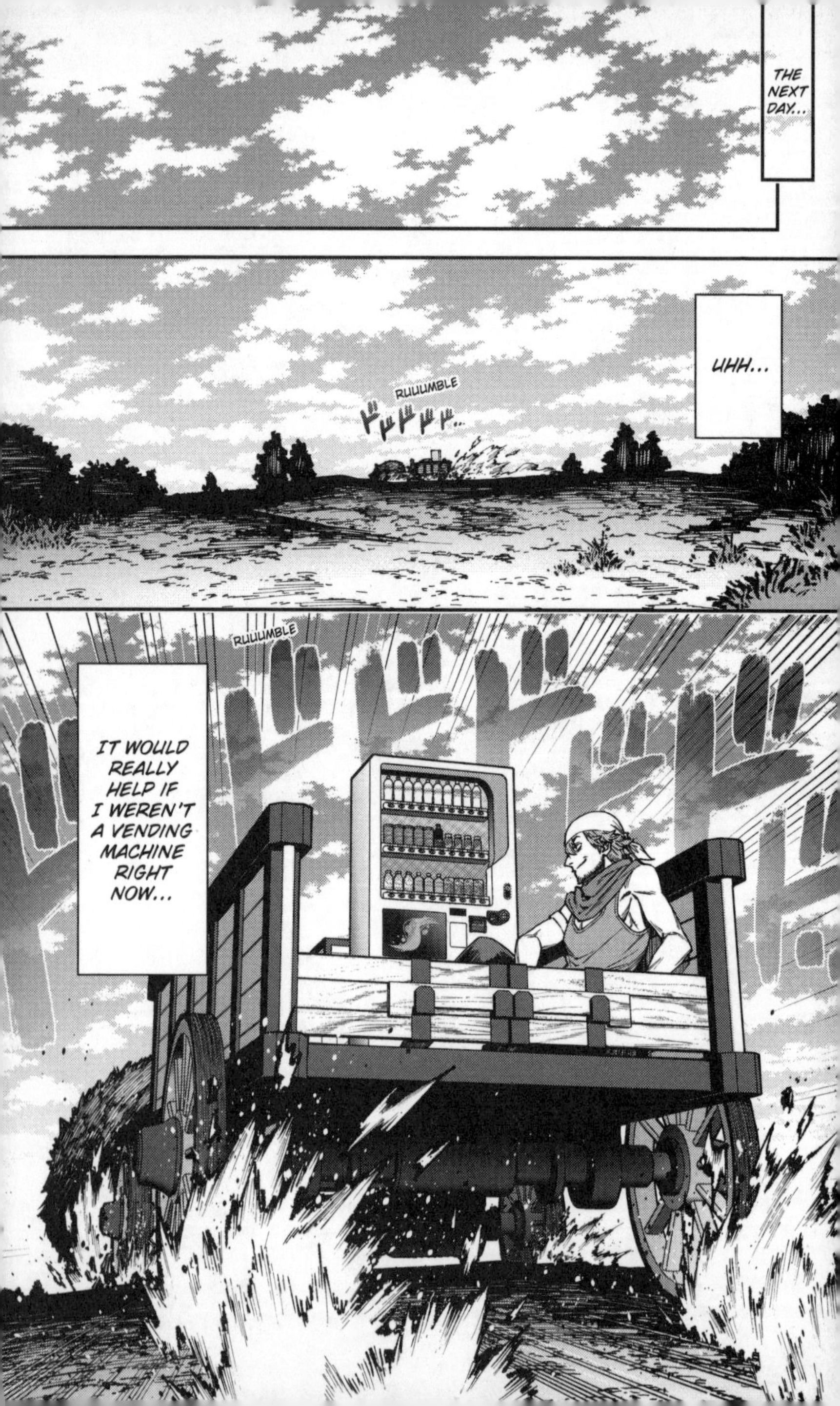
THE NEXT DAY...
UHH...
RUUUMBLE
RUUUMBLE
IT WOULD REALLY HELP IF I WEREN'T A VENDING MACHINE RIGHT NOW...

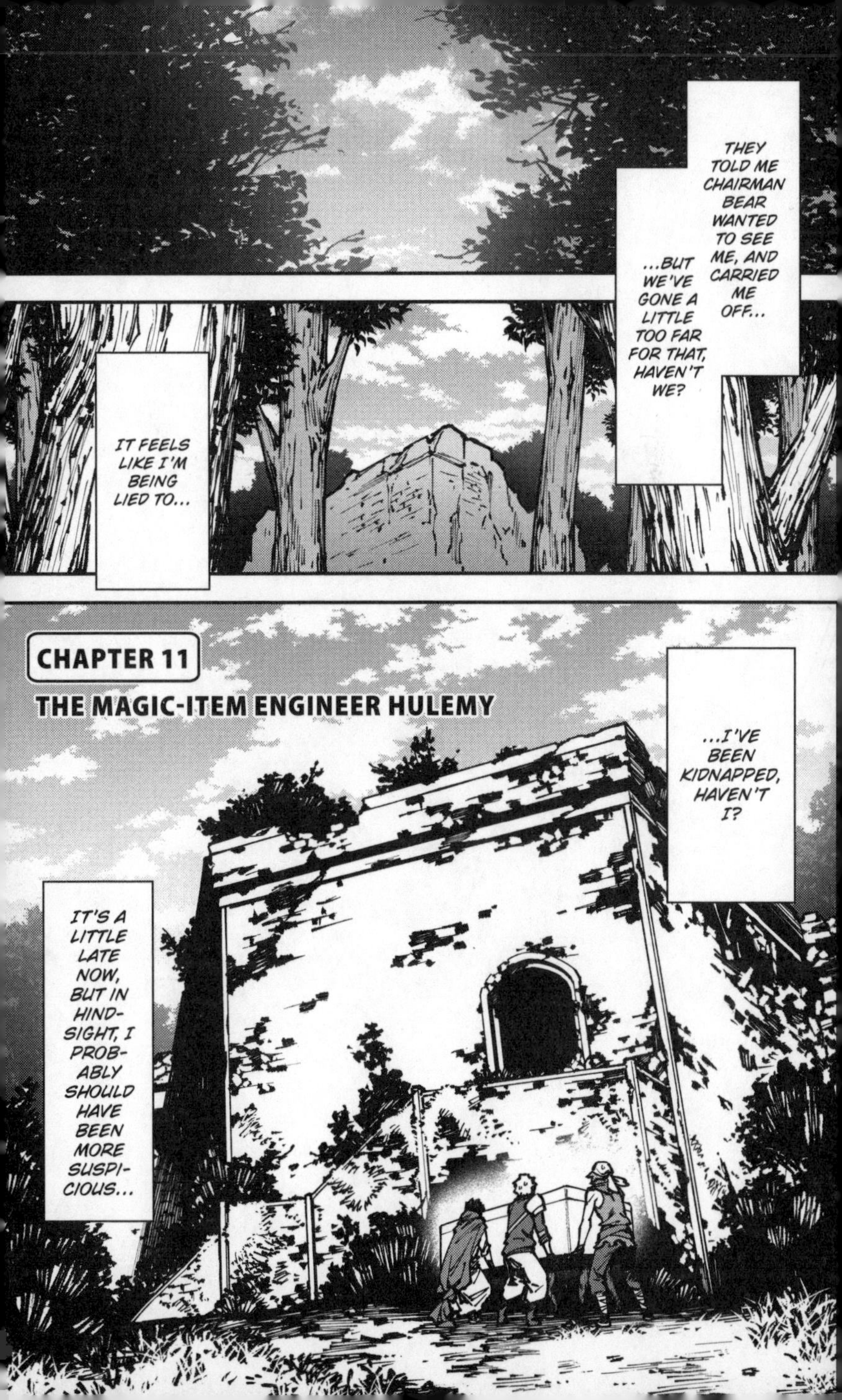
THEY TOLD ME CHAIRMAN BEAR WANTED TO SEE ME, AND CARRIED ME OFF...
...BUT WE'VE GONE A LITTLE TOO FAR FOR THAT, HAVEN'T WE?
IT FEELS LIKE I'M BEING LIED TO...
CHAPTER 11
THE MAGIC-ITEM ENGINEER HULEMY
...I'VE BEEN KIDNAPPED, HAVEN'T I?
IT'S A LITTLE LATE NOW, BUT IN HIND-SIGHT, I PROB-ABLY SHOULD HAVE BEEN MORE SUSPI-CIOUS...

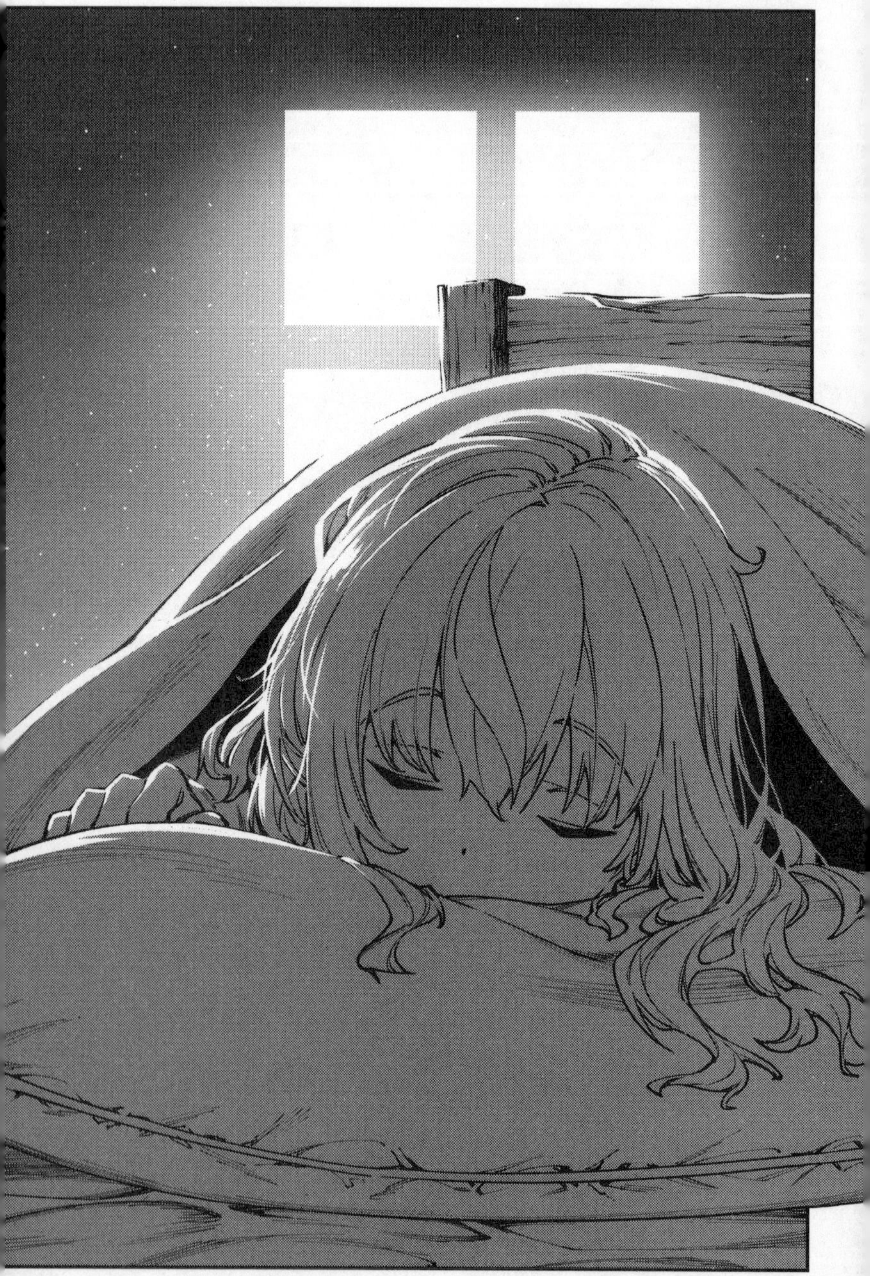

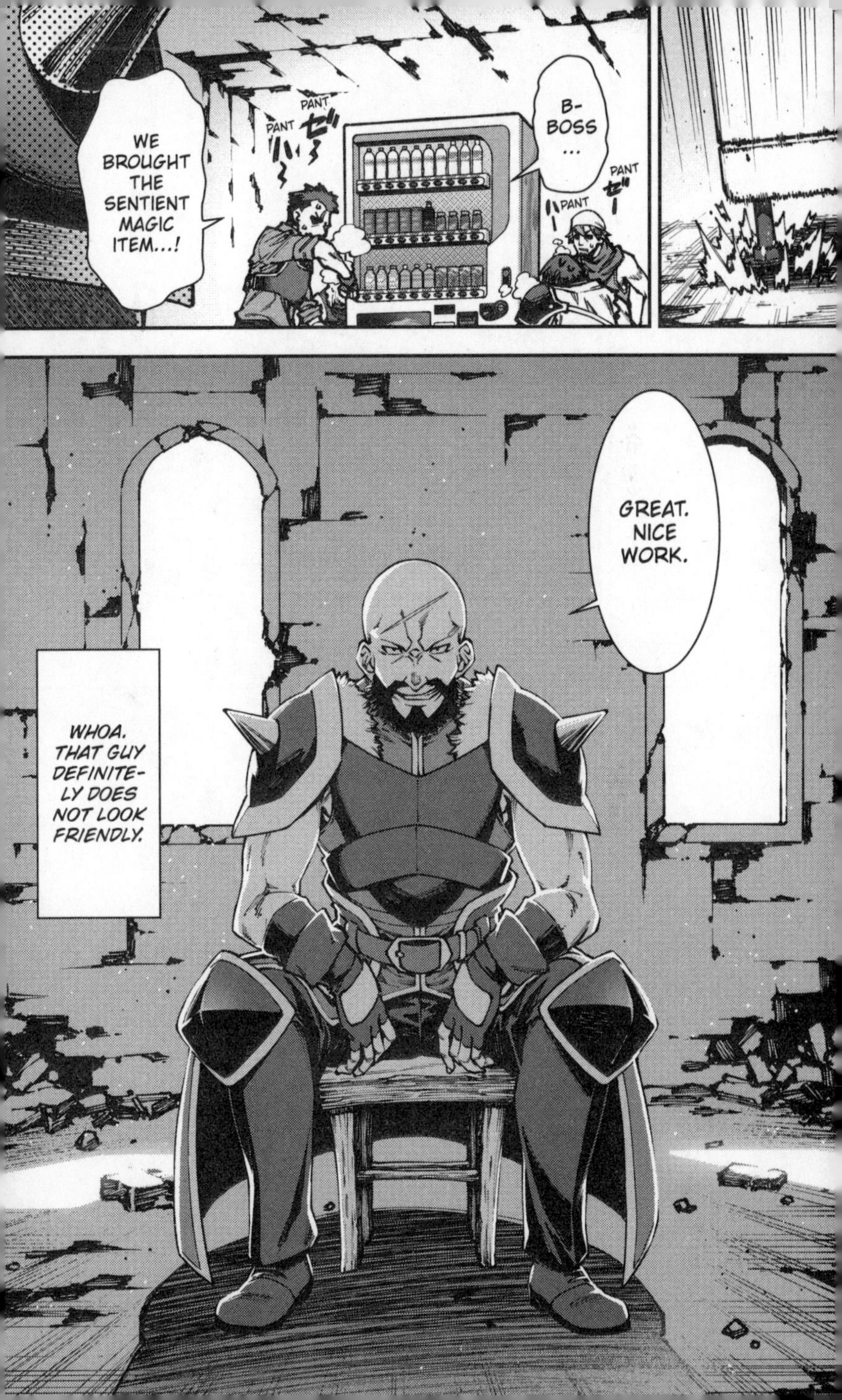
B-BOSS ...
PANT
PANT
PANT
PANT
WE BROUGHT THE SENTIENT MAGIC ITEM...!
GREAT. NICE WORK.
WHOA. THAT GUY DEFINITE-LY DOES NOT LOOK FRIENDLY.

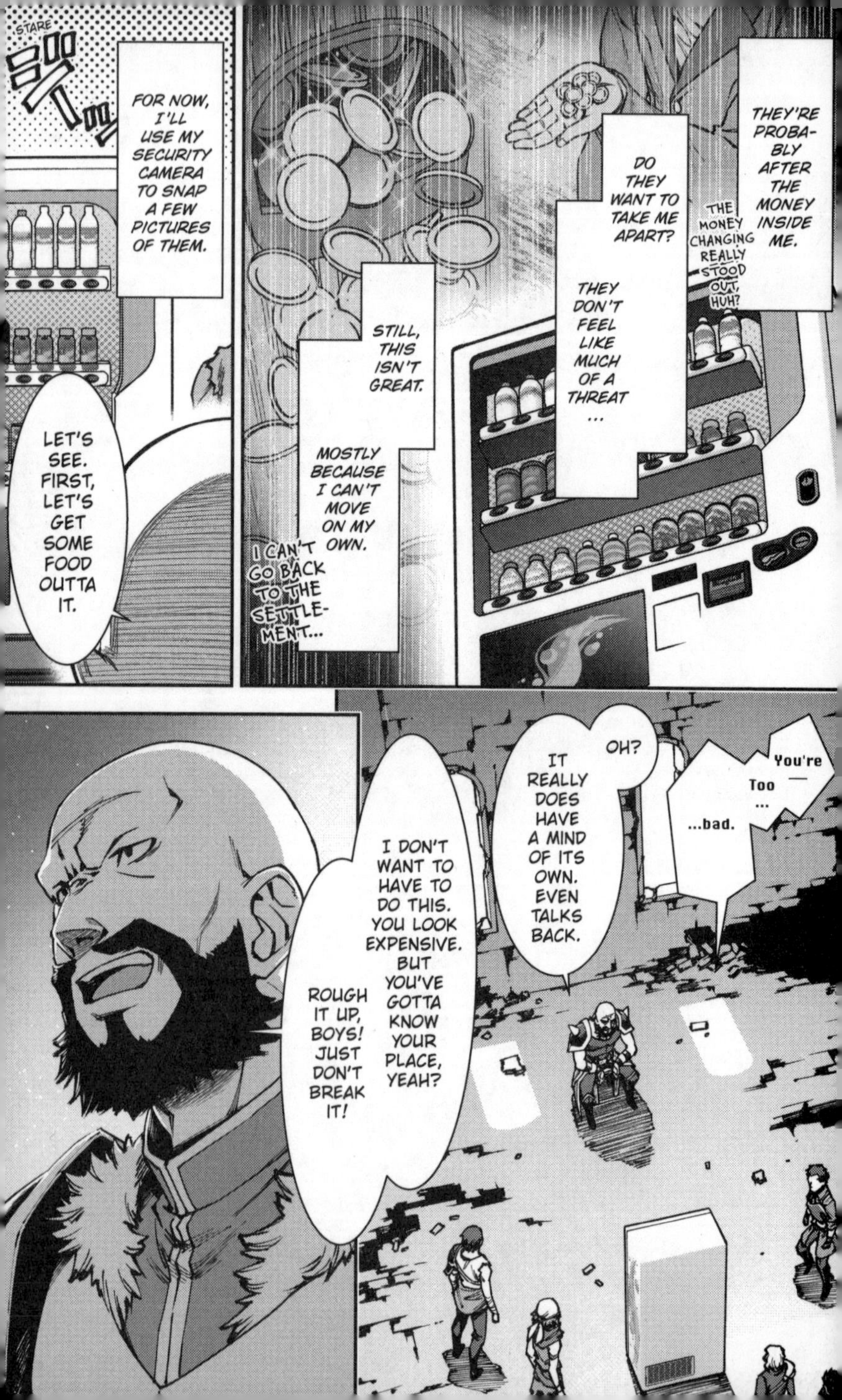
THEY'RE PROBA-BLY AFTER THE MONEY INSIDE ME.
THE MONEY CHANGING REALLY STOOD OUT, HUH?
DO THEY WANT TO TAKE ME APART?
THEY DON'T FEEL LIKE MUCH OF A THREAT...
STILL, THIS ISN'T GREAT.
MOSTLY BECAUSE I CAN'T MOVE ON MY OWN.
I CAN'T GO BACK TO THE SETTLE-MENT...
STARE
FOR NOW, I'LL USE MY SECURITY CAMERA TO SNAP A FEW PICTURES OF THEM.
LET'S SEE. FIRST, LET'S GET SOME FOOD OUTTA IT.
You're — Too ... ...bad.
OH?
IT REALLY DOES HAVE A MIND OF ITS OWN. EVEN TALKS BACK.
I DON'T WANT TO HAVE TO DO THIS. YOU LOOK EXPENSIVE. BUT YOU'VE GOTTA KNOW YOUR PLACE, YEAH?
ROUGH IT UP, BOYS! JUST DON'T BREAK IT!

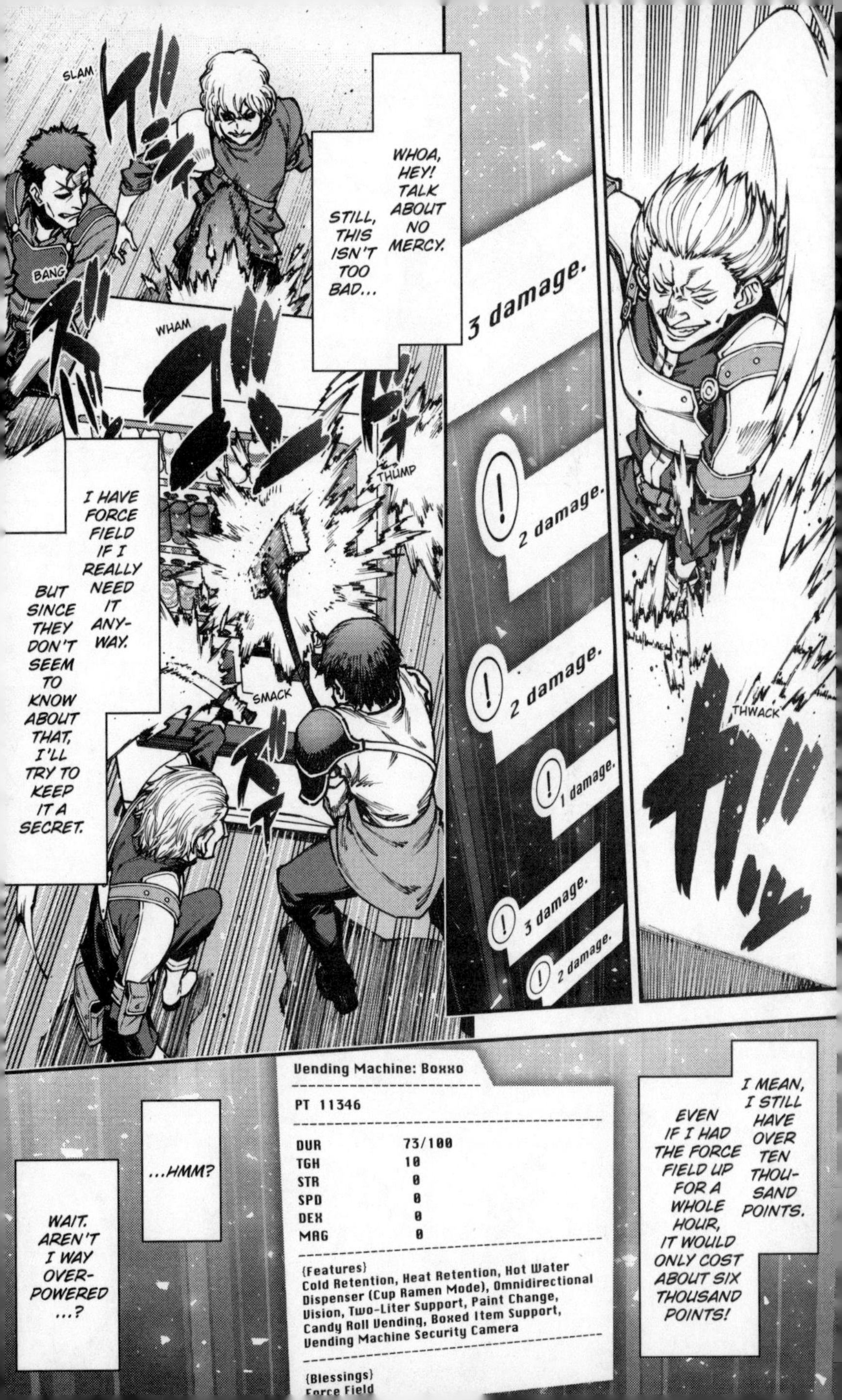
THWACK
3 damage.
2 damage.
2 damage.
1 damage.
3 damage.
2 damage.
WHOA, HEY! TALK ABOUT NO MERCY.
STILL, THIS ISN'T TOO BAD...
SLAM
BANG
WHAM
THUMP
I HAVE FORCE FIELD IF I REALLY NEED IT ANYWAY.
BUT SINCE THEY DON'T SEEM TO KNOW ABOUT THAT, I'LL TRY TO KEEP IT A SECRET.
SMACK
I MEAN, I STILL HAVE OVER TEN THOUSAND POINTS.
EVEN IF I HAD THE FORCE FIELD UP FOR A WHOLE HOUR, IT WOULD ONLY COST ABOUT SIX THOUSAND POINTS!
Vending Machine: Boxxo
PT 11346
DUR 73/100
TGH 10
STR 0
SPD 0
DEX 0
MAG 0
{Features}
Cold Retention, Heat Retention, Hot Water Dispenser (Cup Ramen Mode), Omnidirectional Vision, Two-Liter Support, Paint Change, Candy Roll Vending, Boxed Item Support, Vending Machine Security Camera
{Blessings}
Force Field
...HMM?
WAIT. AREN'T I WAY OVER-POWERED ...?

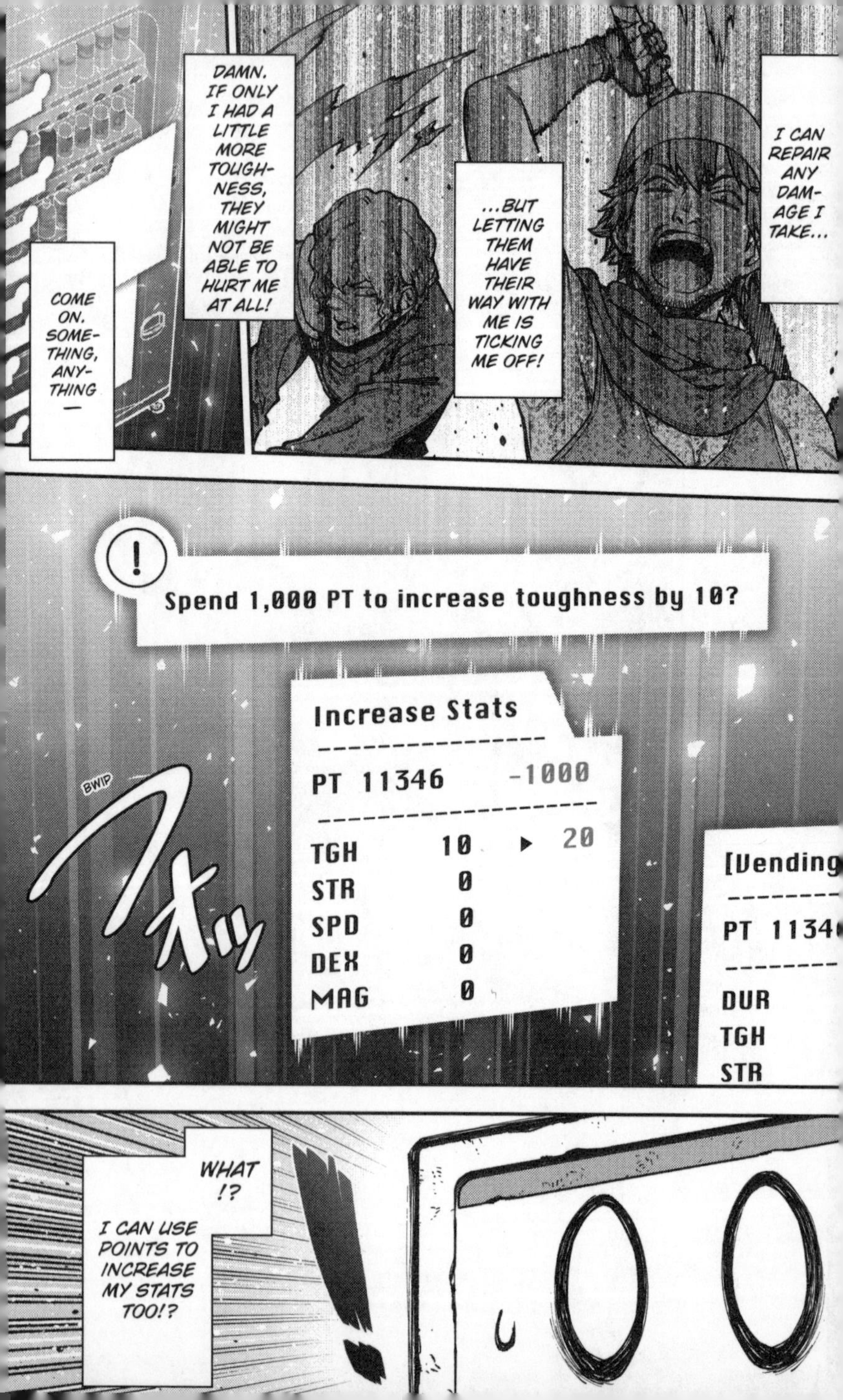
I CAN REPAIR ANY DAMAGE I TAKE...
...BUT LETTING THEM HAVE THEIR WAY WITH ME IS TICKING ME OFF!
DAMN. IF ONLY I HAD A LITTLE MORE TOUGHNESS, THEY MIGHT NOT BE ABLE TO HURT ME AT ALL!
COME ON. SOMETHING, ANYTHING—
Spend 1,000 PT to increase toughness by 10?
[Vending
PT 1134
DUR
TGH
STR
Increase Stats
PT 11346 -1000
TGH 10 ▶ 20
STR 0
SPD 0
DEX 0
MAG 0
BWIP
WHAT!?
I CAN USE POINTS TO INCREASE MY STATS TOO!?

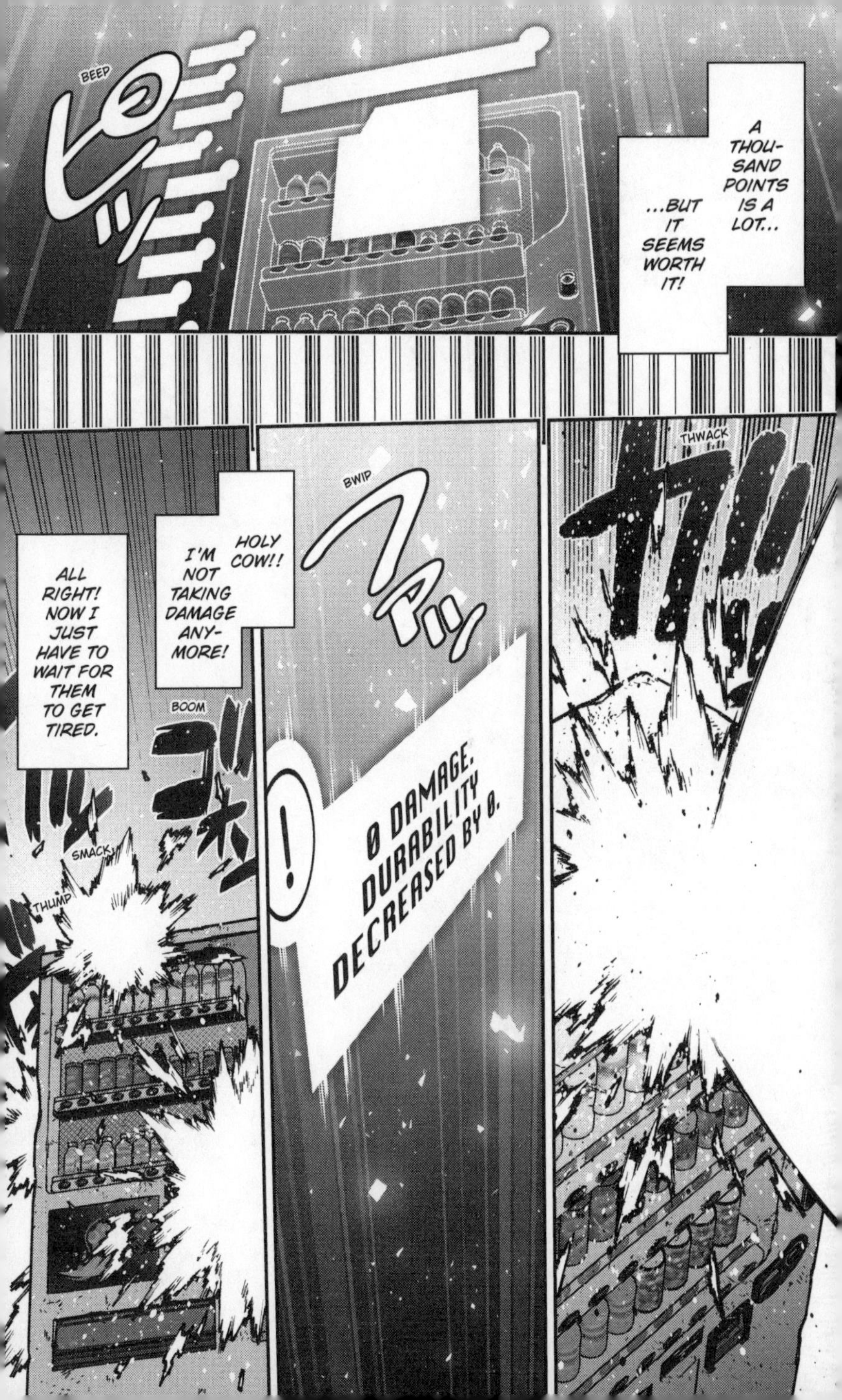
A THOUSAND POINTS IS A LOT...
...BUT IT SEEMS WORTH IT!
BEEP
THWACK
BWIP
!
0 DAMAGE. DURABILITY DECREASED BY 0.
HOLY COW!! I'M NOT TAKING DAMAGE ANYMORE!
ALL RIGHT! NOW I JUST HAVE TO WAIT FOR THEM TO GET TIRED.
BOOM
SMACK
THUMP

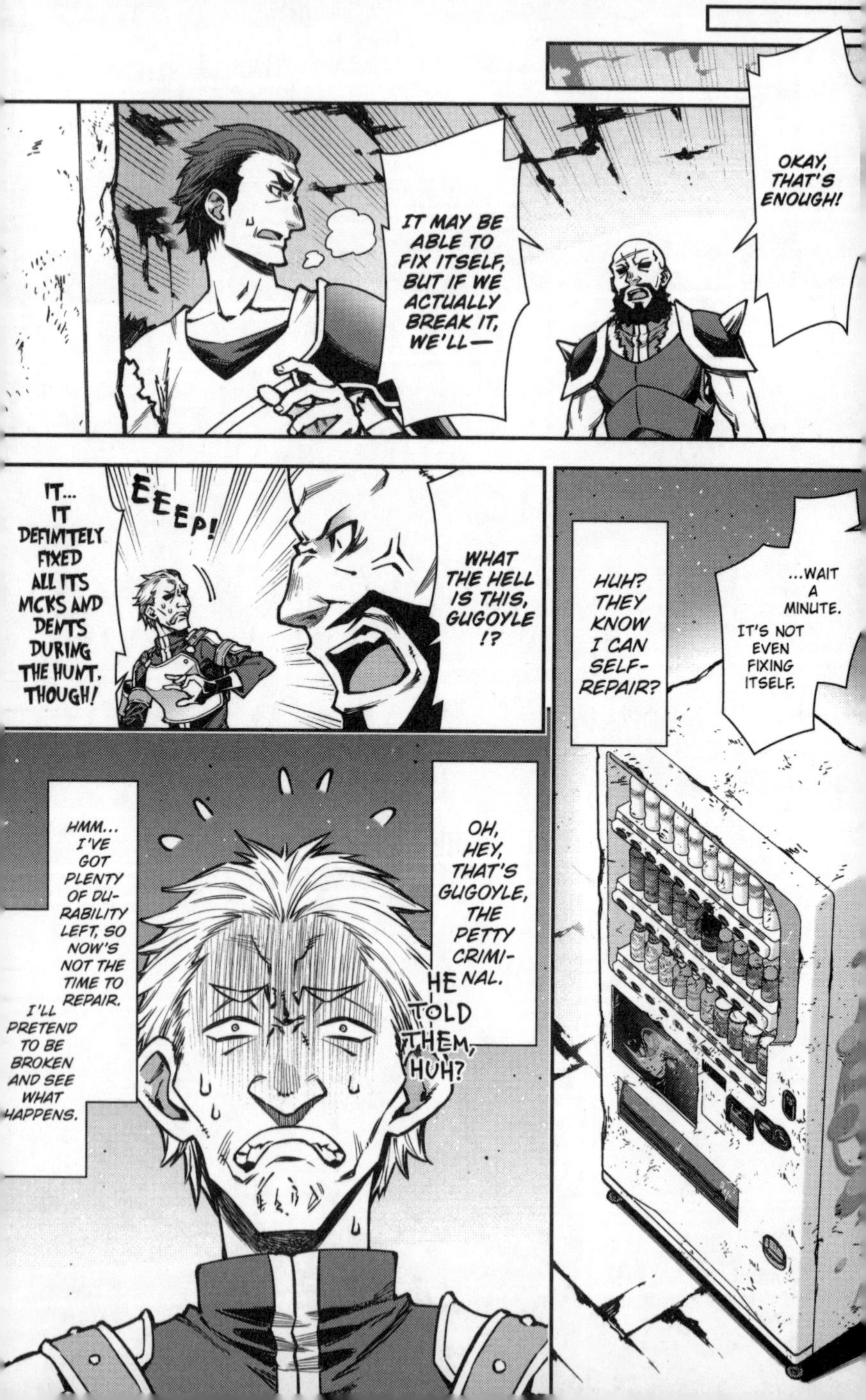
OKAY, THAT'S ENOUGH!
IT MAY BE ABLE TO FIX ITSELF, BUT IF WE ACTUALLY BREAK IT, WE'LL—
...WAIT A MINUTE. IT'S NOT EVEN FIXING ITSELF.
HUH? THEY KNOW I CAN SELF-REPAIR?
WHAT THE HELL IS THIS, GUGOYLE!?
EEEP!
IT... IT DEFINITELY FIXED ALL ITS NICKS AND DENTS DURING THE HUNT, THOUGH!
OH, HEY, THAT'S GUGOYLE, THE PETTY CRIMINAL.
HE TOLD THEM, HUH?
HMM... I'VE GOT PLENTY OF DURABILITY LEFT, SO NOW'S NOT THE TIME TO REPAIR.
I'LL PRETEND TO BE BROKEN AND SEE WHAT HAPPENS.

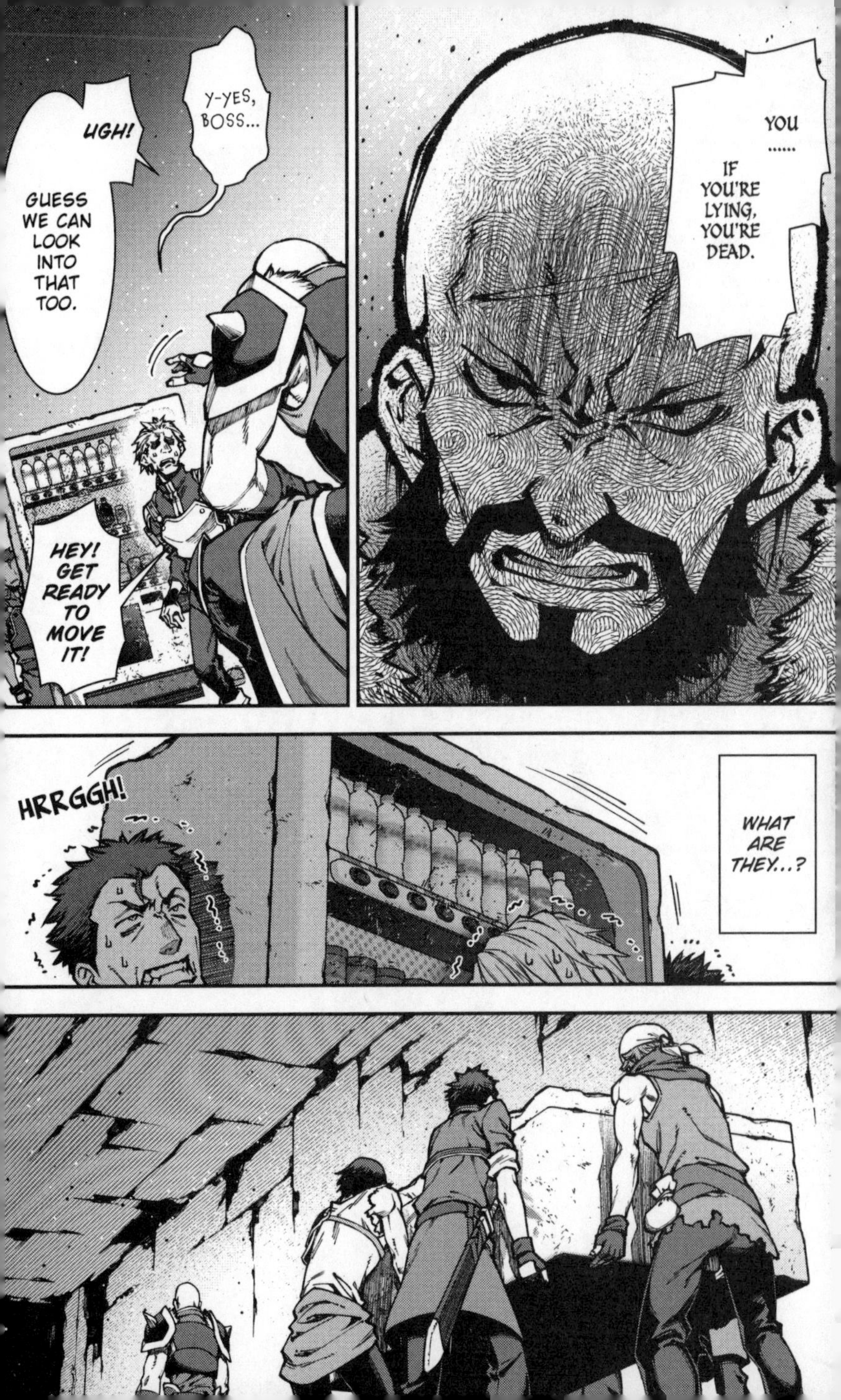

YOU ......
IF YOU'RE LYING, YOU'RE DEAD.
Y-YES, BOSS...
UGH!
GUESS WE CAN LOOK INTO THAT TOO.
HEY! GET READY TO MOVE IT!
WHAT ARE THEY...?
HRRGGH!

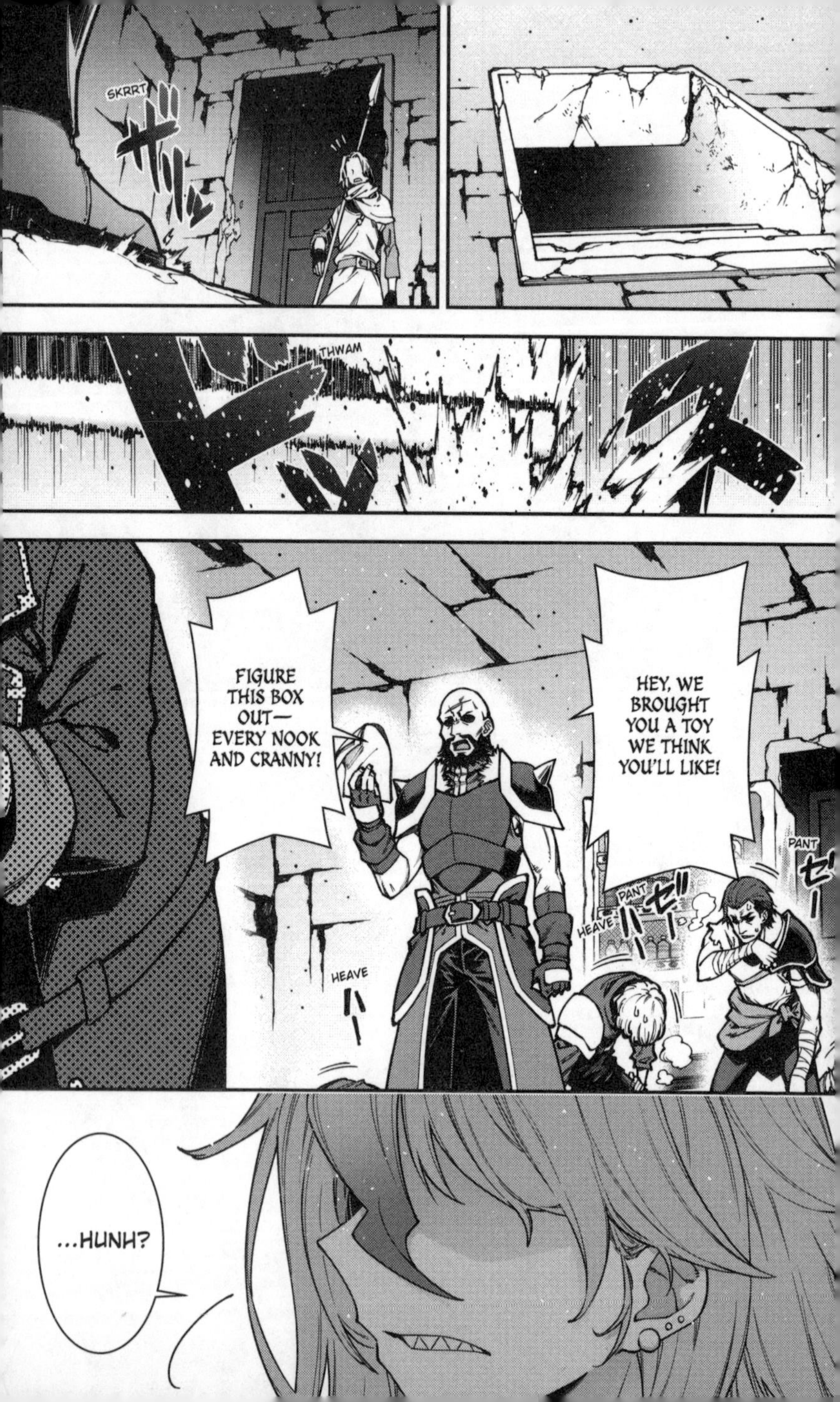
SKRRT
THWAM
HEY, WE BROUGHT YOU A TOY WE THINK YOU'LL LIKE!
FIGURE THIS BOX OUT— EVERY NOOK AND CRANNY!
PANT
PANT
HEAVE
HEAVE
...HUNH?

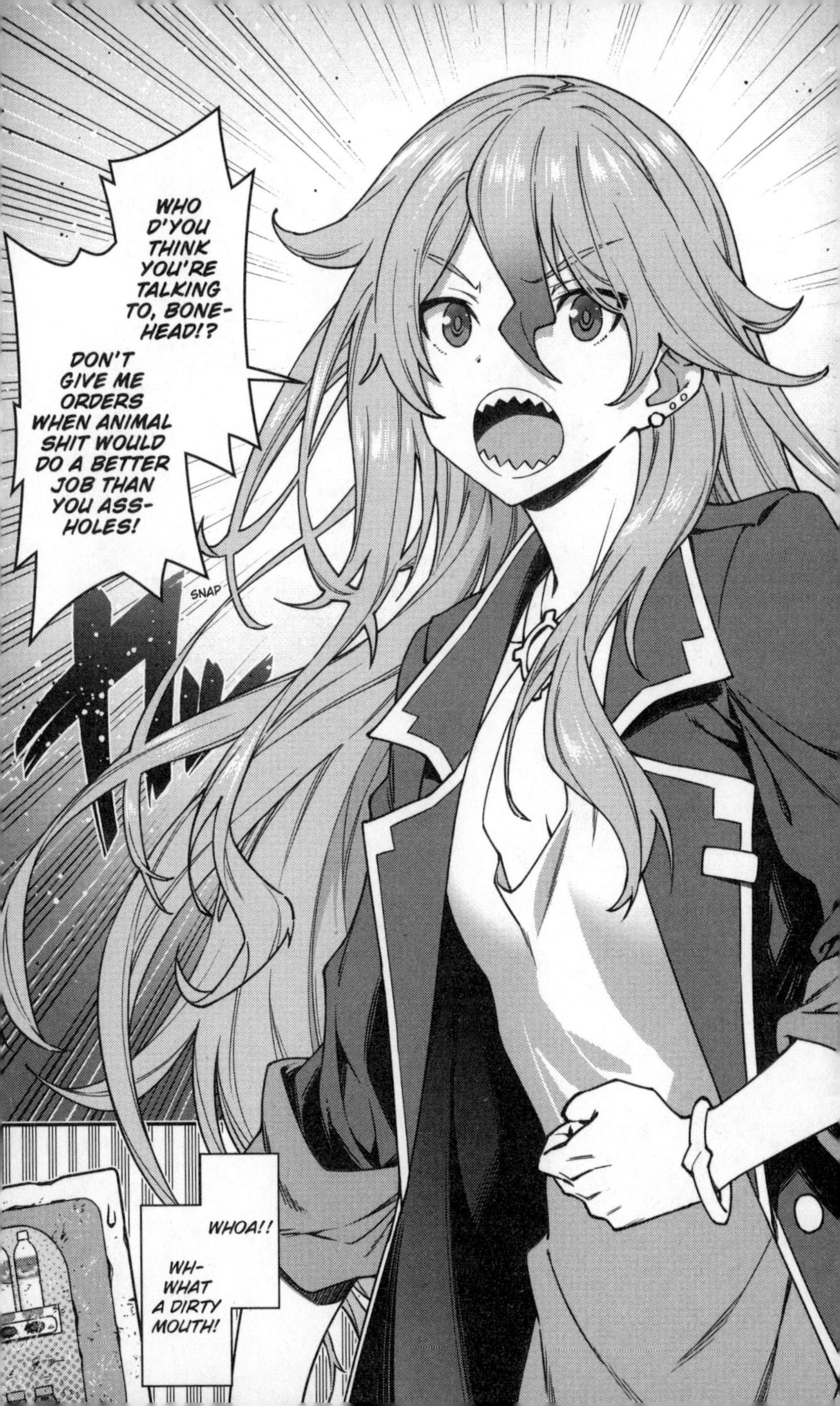
WHO D'YOU THINK YOU'RE TALKING TO, BONE-HEAD!? DON'T GIVE ME ORDERS WHEN ANIMAL SHIT WOULD DO A BETTER JOB THAN YOU ASS-HOLES!
SNAP
WHOA!!
WH-WHAT A DIRTY MOUTH!

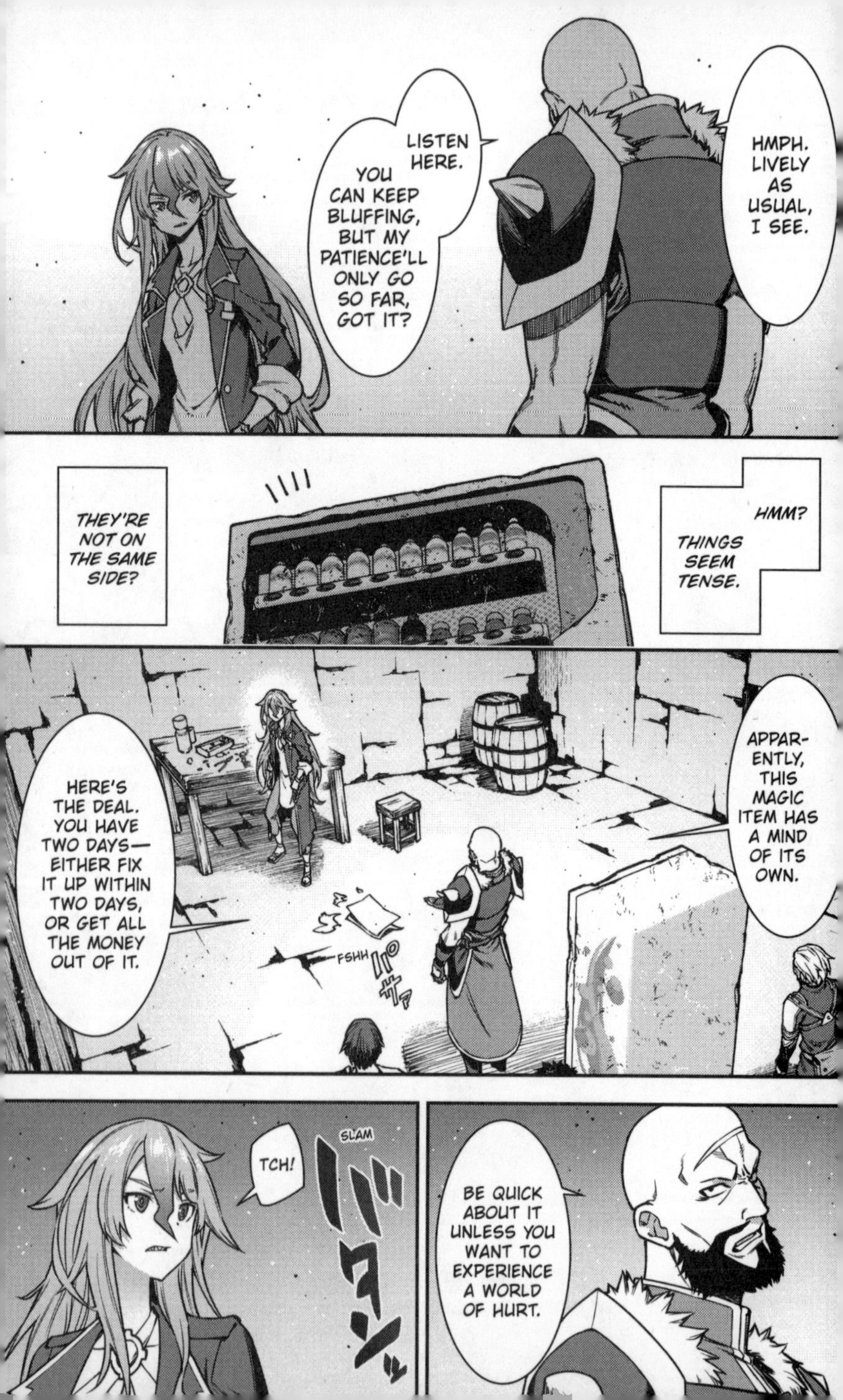
HMPH. LIVELY AS USUAL, I SEE.
LISTEN HERE.
YOU CAN KEEP BLUFFING, BUT MY PATIENCE'LL ONLY GO SO FAR, GOT IT?
HMM?
THINGS SEEM TENSE.
THEY'RE NOT ON THE SAME SIDE?
APPAR-ENTLY, THIS MAGIC ITEM HAS A MIND OF ITS OWN.
HERE'S THE DEAL. YOU HAVE TWO DAYS—EITHER FIX IT UP WITHIN TWO DAYS, OR GET ALL THE MONEY OUT OF IT.
FSHH
BE QUICK ABOUT IT UNLESS YOU WANT TO EXPERIENCE A WORLD OF HURT.
SLAM
TCH!

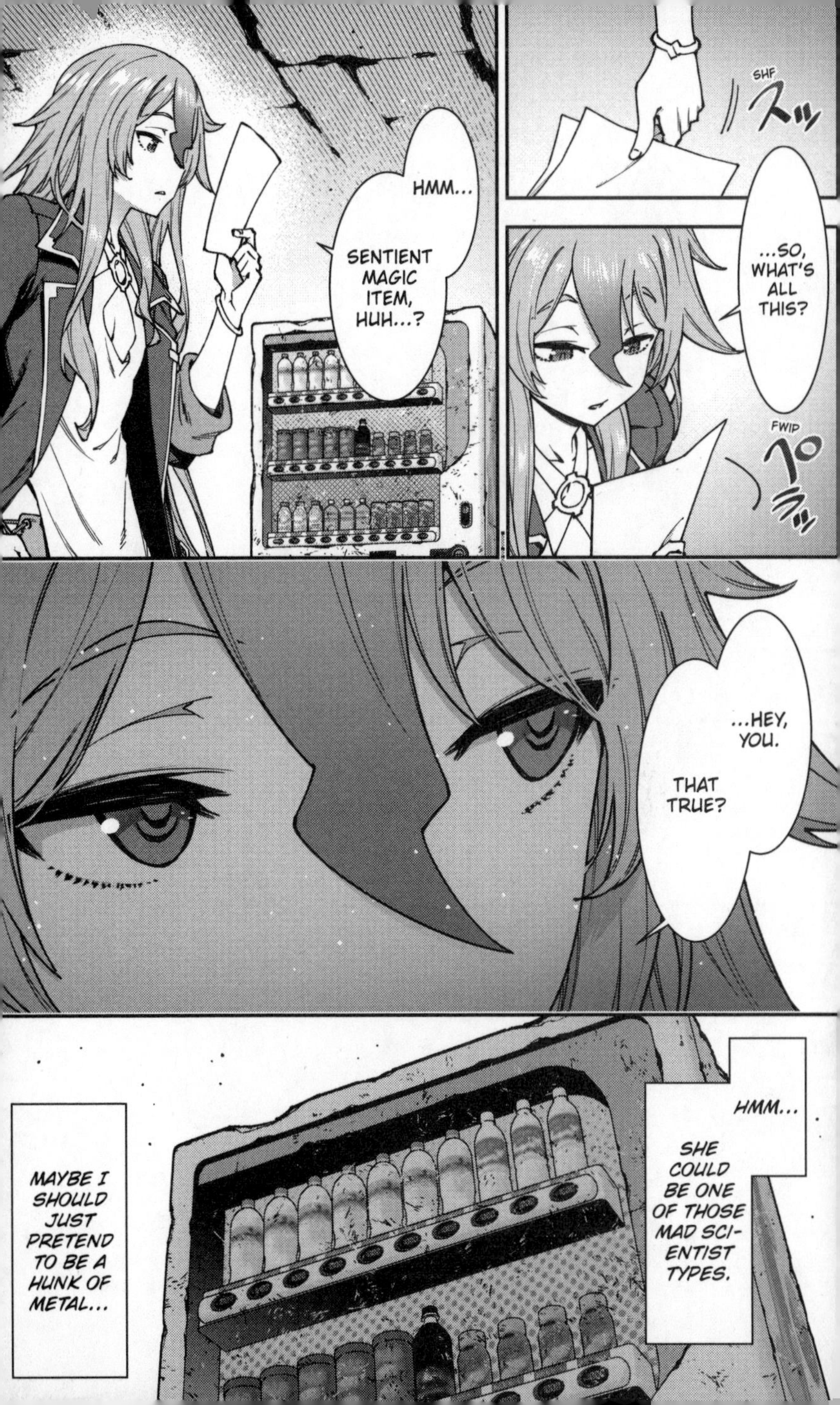
SHF
スッ
...SO, WHAT'S ALL THIS?
FWIP
ペラッ
HMM...
SENTIENT MAGIC ITEM, HUH...?
...HEY, YOU.
THAT TRUE?
HMM...
SHE COULD BE ONE OF THOSE MAD SCI-ENTIST TYPES.
MAYBE I SHOULD JUST PRETEND TO BE A HUNK OF METAL...

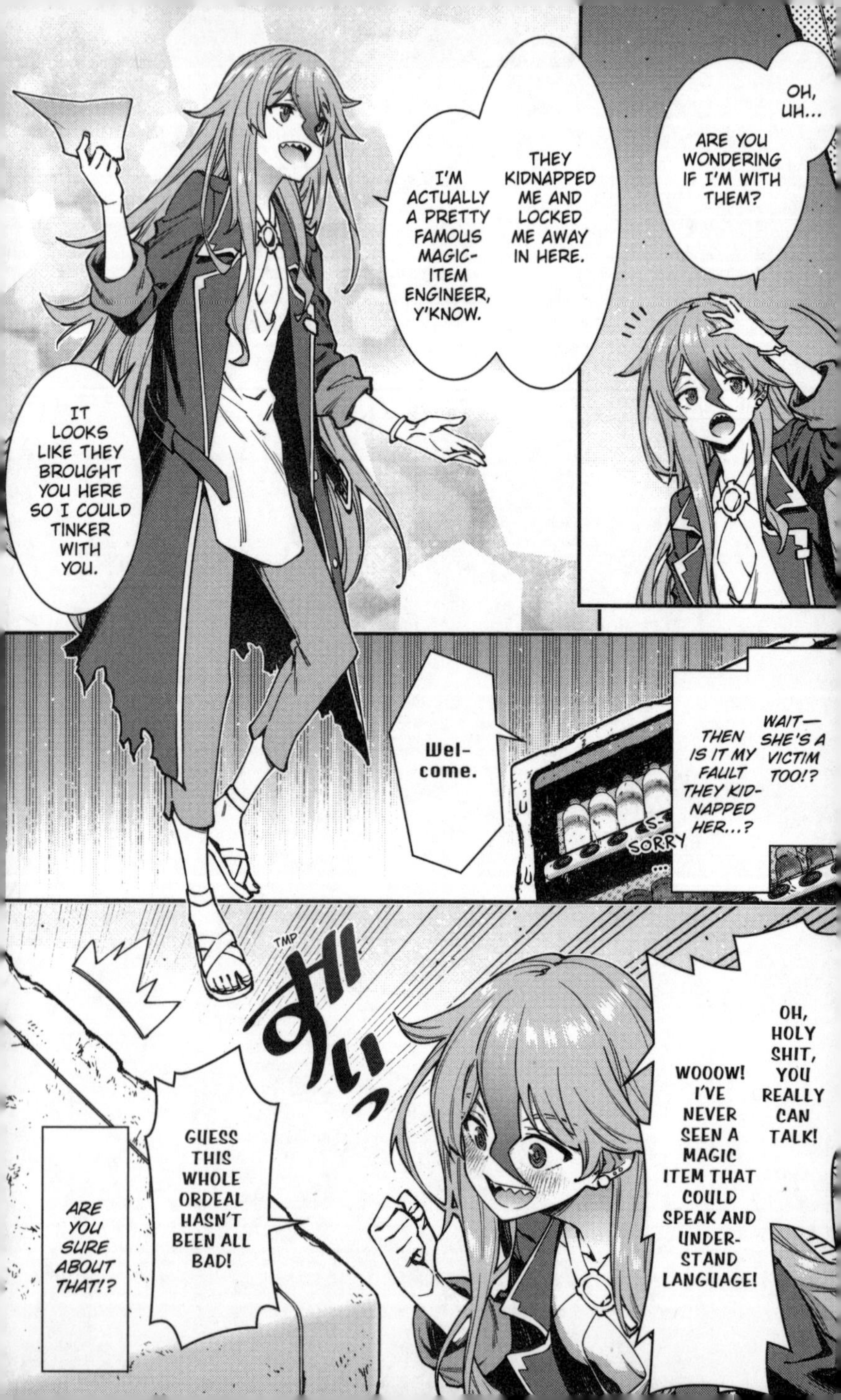

OH, UH...
ARE YOU WONDERING IF I'M WITH THEM?
WAIT— SHE'S A VICTIM TOO!?
THEN IS IT MY FAULT THEY KIDNAPPED HER...?
S-SORRY...
Wel-come.
THEY KIDNAPPED ME AND LOCKED ME AWAY IN HERE.
I'M ACTUALLY A PRETTY FAMOUS MAGIC-ITEM ENGINEER, Y'KNOW.
IT LOOKS LIKE THEY BROUGHT YOU HERE SO I COULD TINKER WITH YOU.
TMP
OH, HOLY SHIT, YOU REALLY CAN TALK!
WOOOW! I'VE NEVER SEEN A MAGIC ITEM THAT COULD SPEAK AND UNDER-STAND LANGUAGE!
GUESS THIS WHOLE ORDEAL HASN'T BEEN ALL BAD!
ARE YOU SURE ABOUT THAT!?

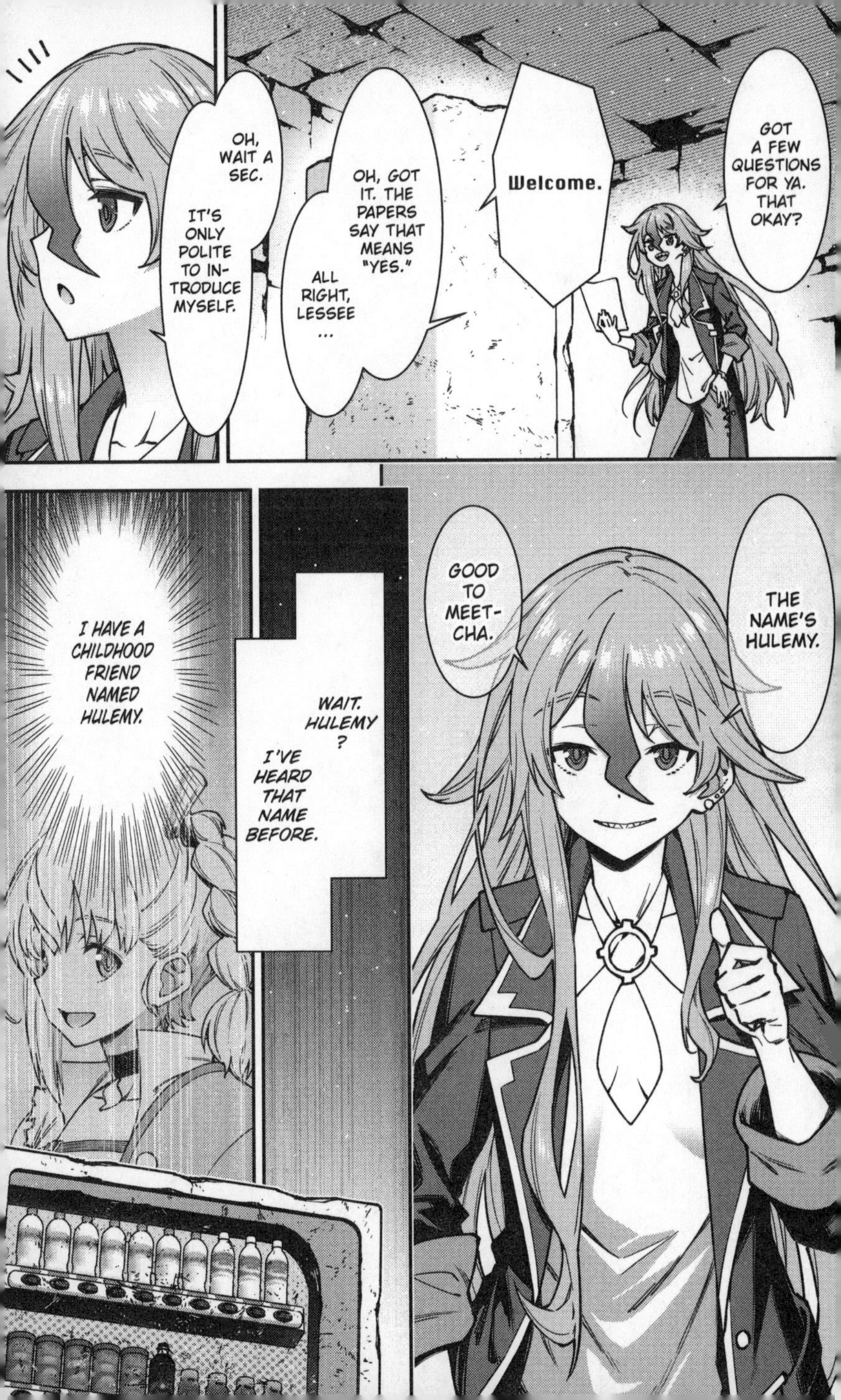
GOT A FEW QUESTIONS FOR YA. THAT OKAY?
Welcome.
OH, GOT IT. THE PAPERS SAY THAT MEANS "YES."
ALL RIGHT, LESSEE ...
OH, WAIT A SEC.
IT'S ONLY POLITE TO INTRODUCE MYSELF.
THE NAME'S HULEMY.
GOOD TO MEET-CHA.
WAIT. HULEMY?
I'VE HEARD THAT NAME BEFORE.
I HAVE A CHILDHOOD FRIEND NAMED HULEMY.

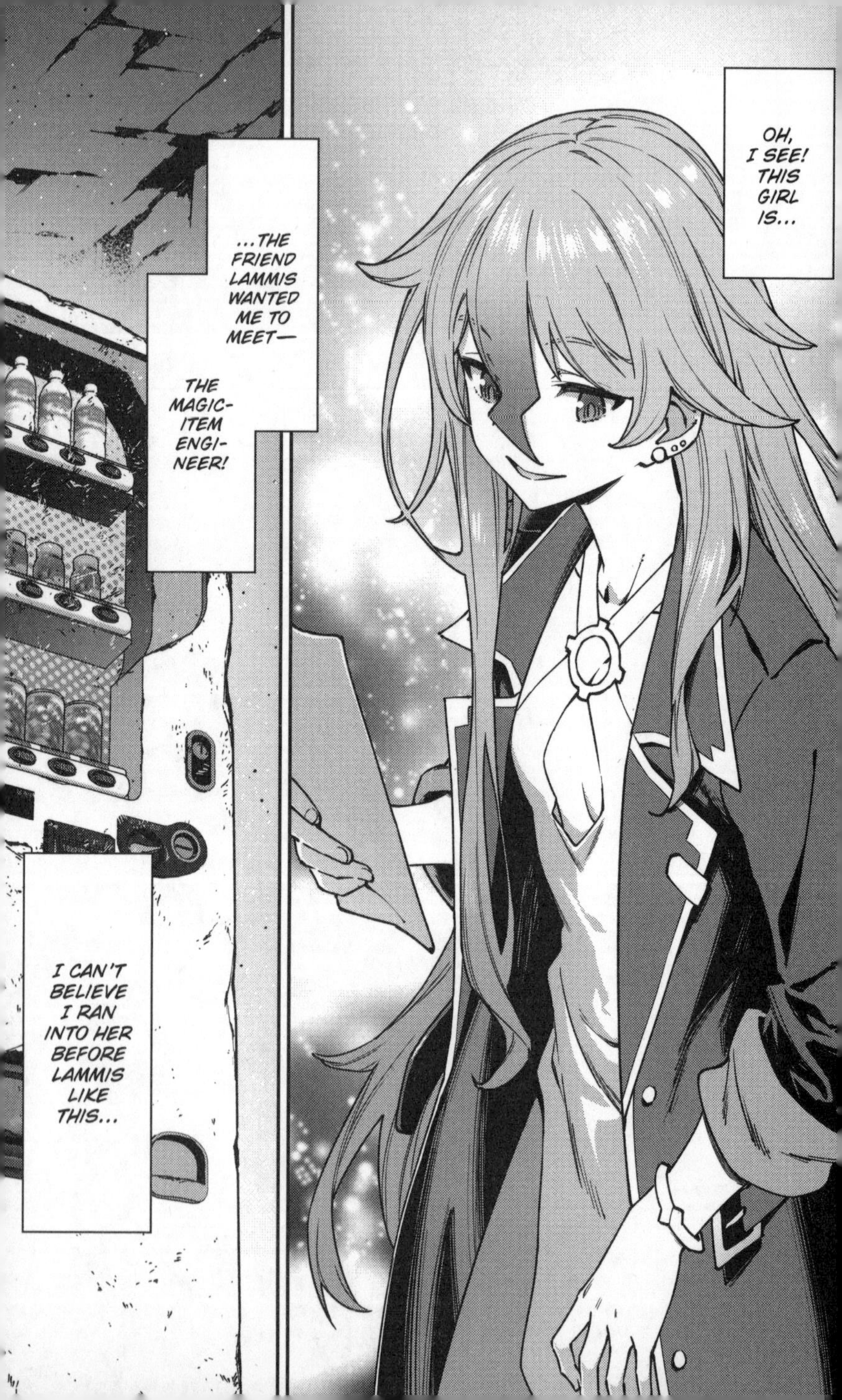
OH, I SEE! THIS GIRL IS...
...THE FRIEND LAMMIS WANTED ME TO MEET—
THE MAGIC-ITEM ENGINEER!
I CAN'T BELIEVE I RAN INTO HER BEFORE LAMMIS LIKE THIS...

Reborn as a Vending Machine, I Now Wander the Dungeon

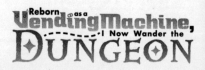

CHAPTER 12 AS A VENDING MACHINE MEGAFAN

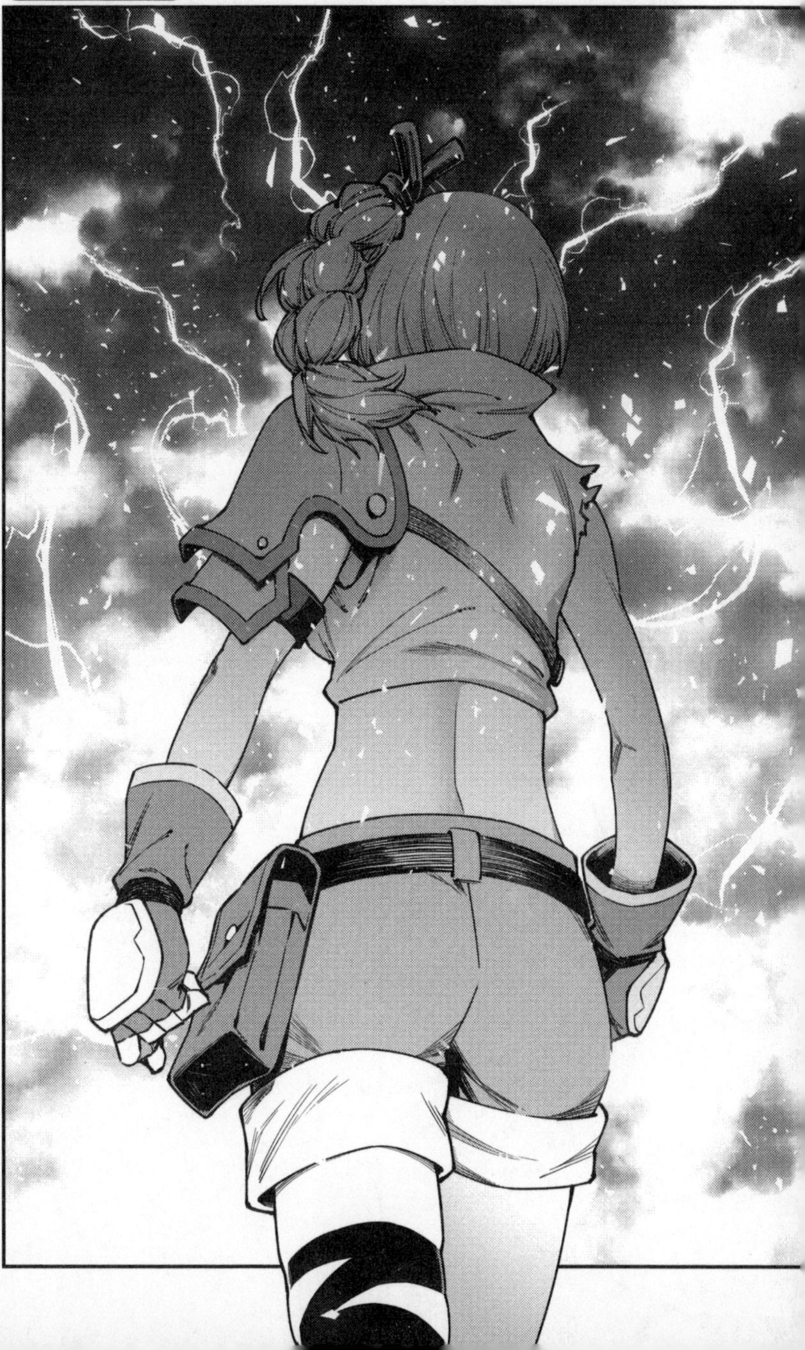

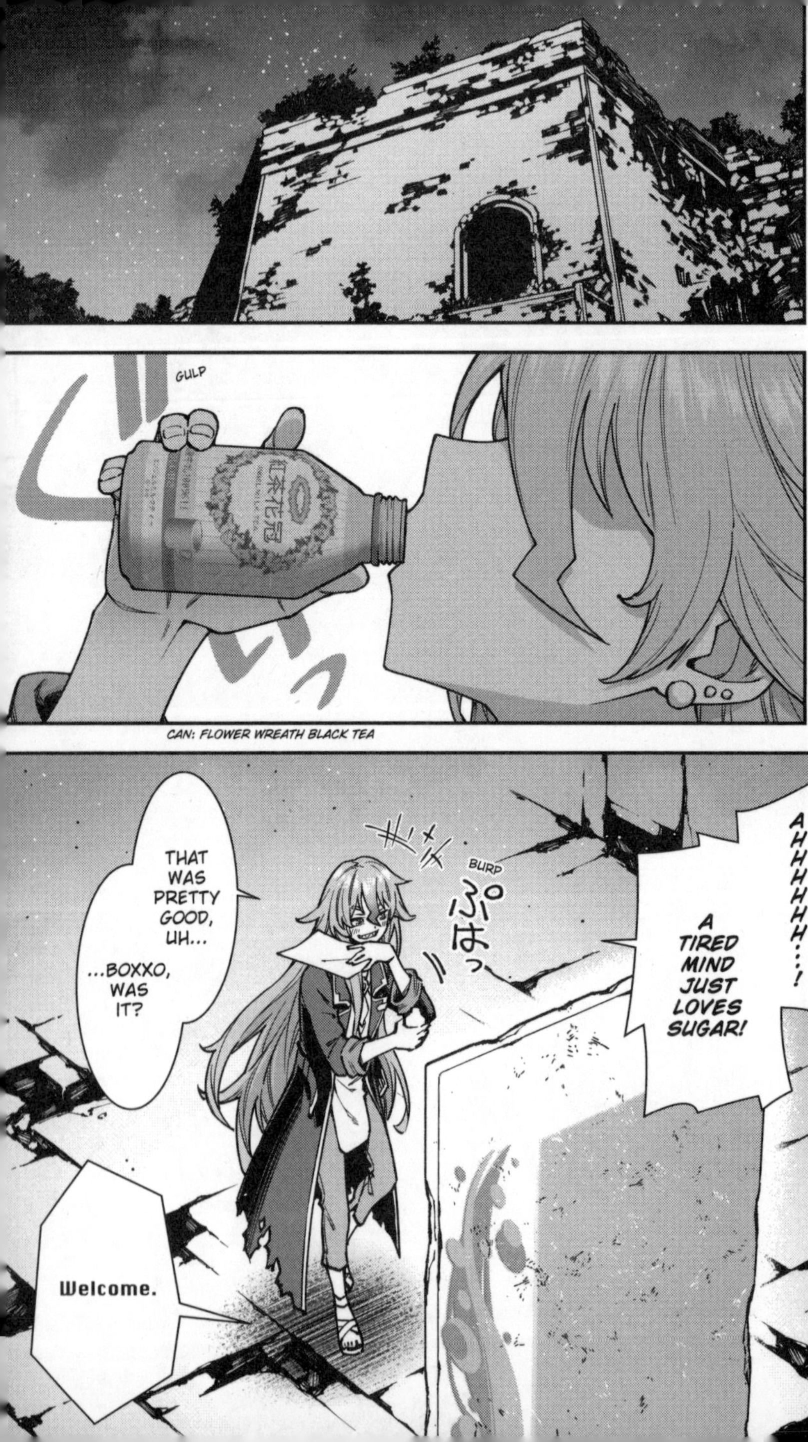
GULP
CAN: FLOWER WREATH BLACK TEA
AHHHHHH...!
A TIRED MIND JUST LOVES SUGAR!
BURP
ぷはっ
THAT WAS PRETTY GOOD, UH...
...BOXXO, WAS IT?
Welcome.

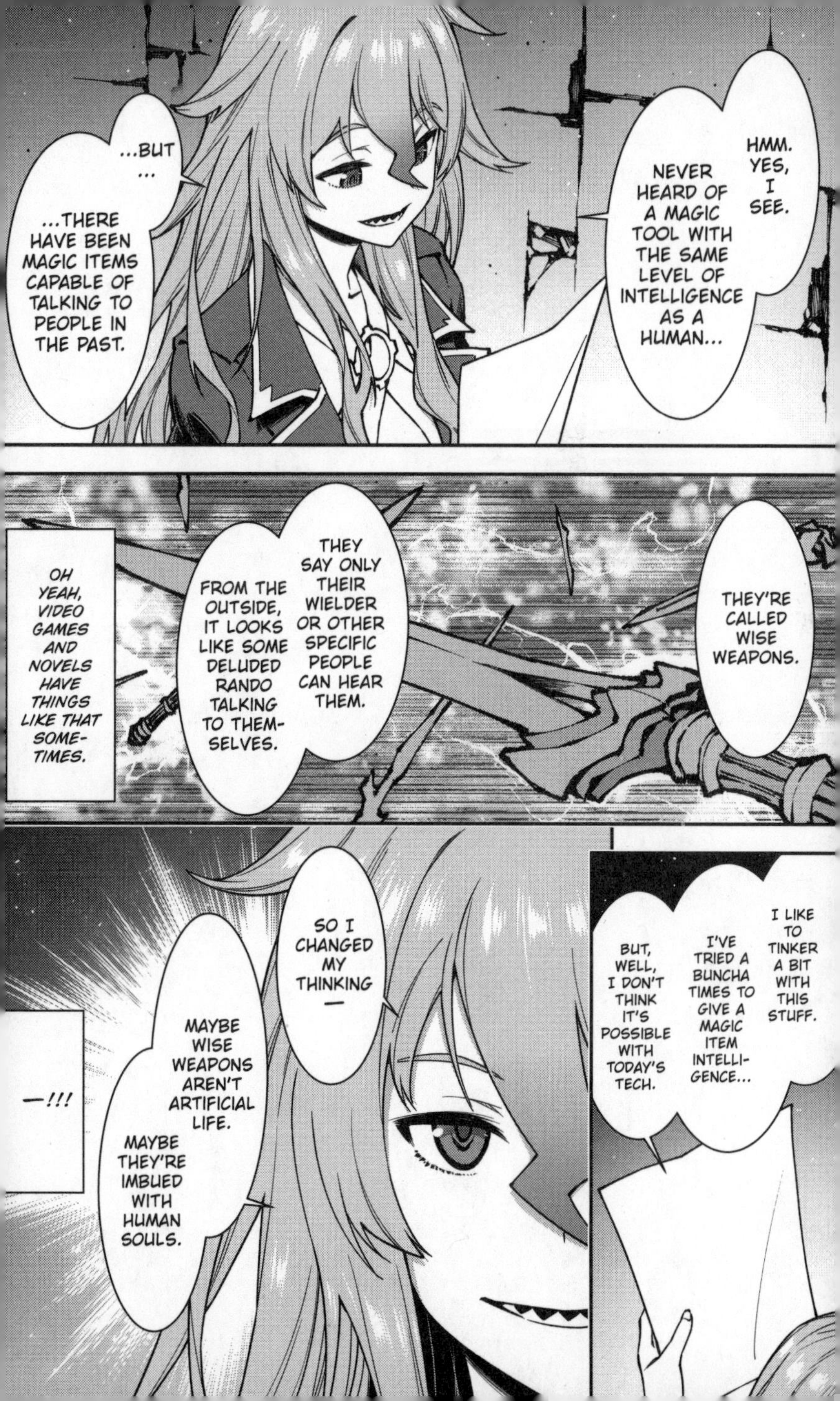
HMM. YES, I SEE.
NEVER HEARD OF A MAGIC TOOL WITH THE SAME LEVEL OF INTELLIGENCE AS A HUMAN...
...BUT ...
...THERE HAVE BEEN MAGIC ITEMS CAPABLE OF TALKING TO PEOPLE IN THE PAST.
THEY'RE CALLED WISE WEAPONS.
THEY SAY ONLY THEIR WIELDER OR OTHER SPECIFIC PEOPLE CAN HEAR THEM.
FROM THE OUTSIDE, IT LOOKS LIKE SOME DELUDED RANDO TALKING TO THEM-SELVES.
OH YEAH, VIDEO GAMES AND NOVELS HAVE THINGS LIKE THAT SOME-TIMES.
I LIKE TO TINKER A BIT WITH THIS STUFF.
I'VE TRIED A BUNCHA TIMES TO GIVE A MAGIC ITEM INTELLI-GENCE...
BUT, WELL, I DON'T THINK IT'S POSSIBLE WITH TODAY'S TECH.
SO I CHANGED MY THINKING —
MAYBE WISE WEAPONS AREN'T ARTIFICIAL LIFE.
MAYBE THEY'RE IMBUED WITH HUMAN SOULS.
—!!!

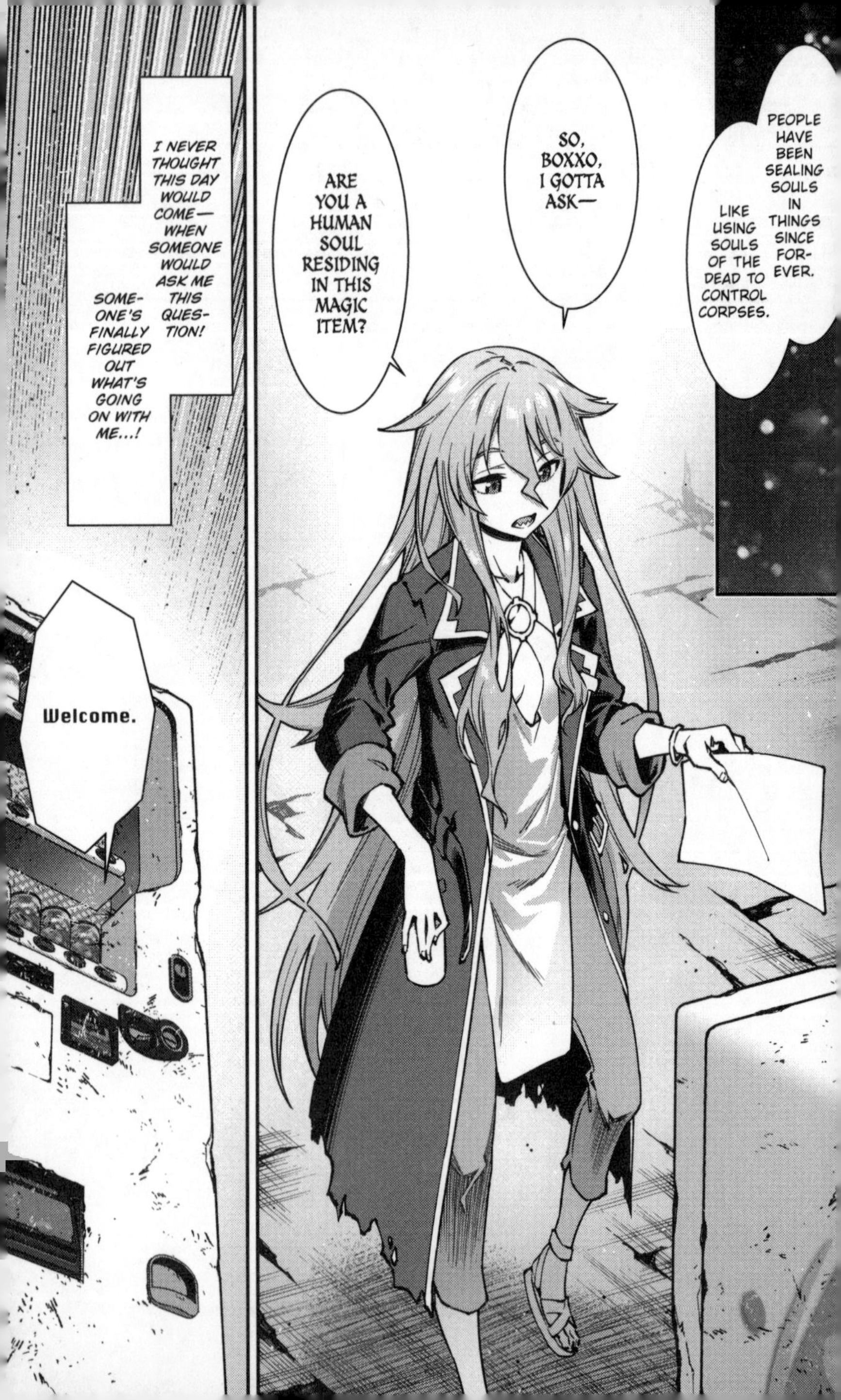
PEOPLE HAVE BEEN SEALING SOULS IN THINGS SINCE FOREVER.
LIKE USING SOULS OF THE DEAD TO CONTROL CORPSES.
SO, BOXXO, I GOTTA ASK—
ARE YOU A HUMAN SOUL RESIDING IN THIS MAGIC ITEM?
I NEVER THOUGHT THIS DAY WOULD COME—WHEN SOMEONE WOULD ASK ME THIS QUESTION!
SOMEONE'S FINALLY FIGURED OUT WHAT'S GOING ON WITH ME...!
Welcome.

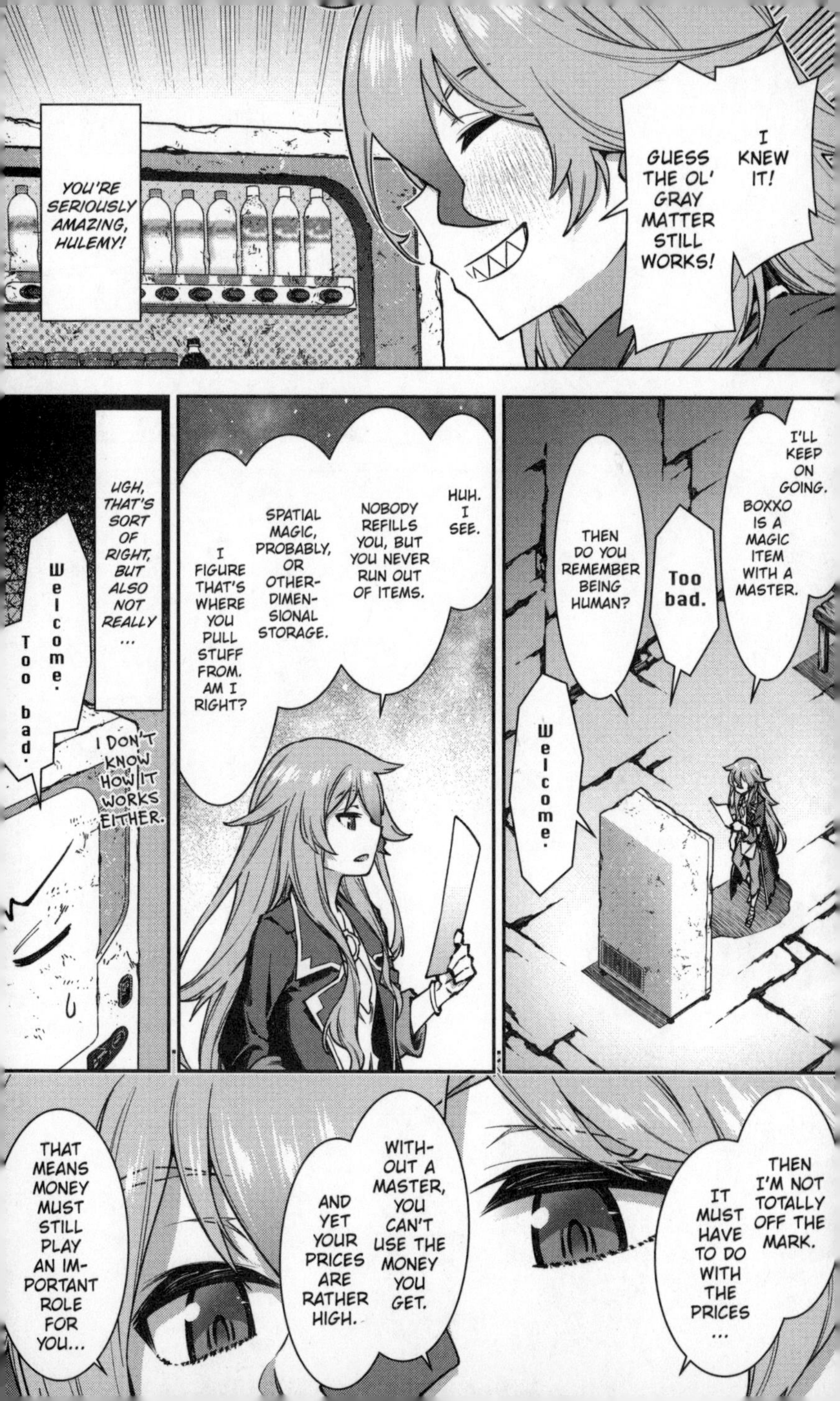
I KNEW IT!
GUESS THE OL' GRAY MATTER STILL WORKS!
YOU'RE SERIOUSLY AMAZING, HULEMY!
I'LL KEEP ON GOING. BOXXO IS A MAGIC ITEM WITH A MASTER.
Too bad.
THEN DO YOU REMEMBER BEING HUMAN?
Welcome.
HUH. I SEE.
NOBODY REFILLS YOU, BUT YOU NEVER RUN OUT OF ITEMS.
SPATIAL MAGIC, PROBABLY, OR OTHER-DIMENSIONAL STORAGE.
I FIGURE THAT'S WHERE YOU PULL STUFF FROM. AM I RIGHT?
UGH, THAT'S SORT OF RIGHT, BUT ALSO NOT REALLY ...
Welcome. Too bad.
I DON'T KNOW HOW IT WORKS EITHER.
THEN I'M NOT TOTALLY OFF THE MARK.
IT MUST HAVE TO DO WITH THE PRICES ...
WITHOUT A MASTER, YOU CAN'T USE THE MONEY YOU GET.
AND YET YOUR PRICES ARE RATHER HIGH.
THAT MEANS MONEY MUST STILL PLAY AN IMPORTANT ROLE FOR YOU...

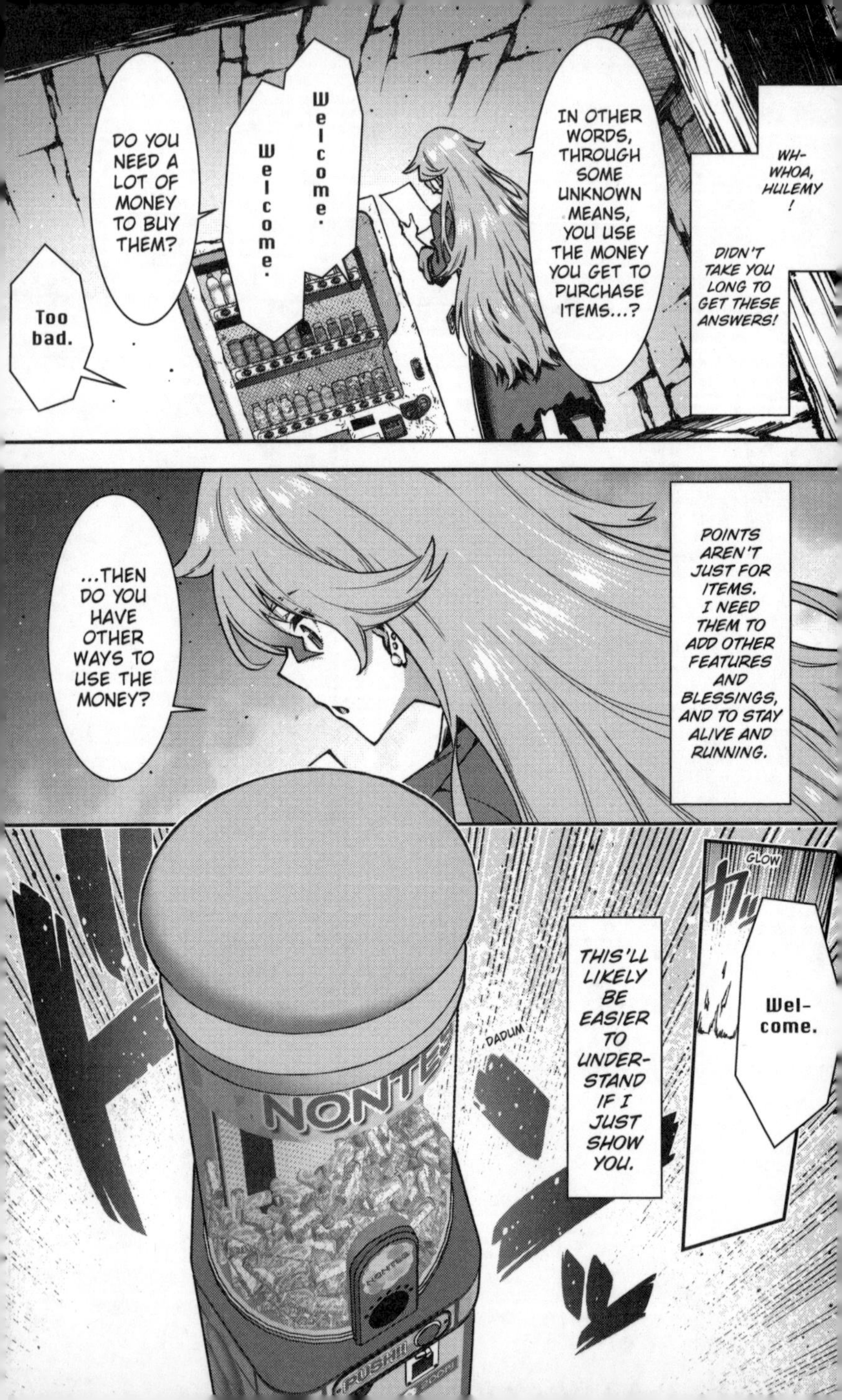
WH-WHOA, HULEMY!
DIDN'T TAKE YOU LONG TO GET THESE ANSWERS!
IN OTHER WORDS, THROUGH SOME UNKNOWN MEANS, YOU USE THE MONEY YOU GET TO PURCHASE ITEMS...?
Welcome. Welcome.
DO YOU NEED A LOT OF MONEY TO BUY THEM?
Too bad.
POINTS AREN'T JUST FOR ITEMS. I NEED THEM TO ADD OTHER FEATURES AND BLESSINGS, AND TO STAY ALIVE AND RUNNING.
...THEN DO YOU HAVE OTHER WAYS TO USE THE MONEY?
GLOW
Wel-come.
THIS'LL LIKELY BE EASIER TO UNDER-STAND IF I JUST SHOW YOU.
DADUM
PUSH!!

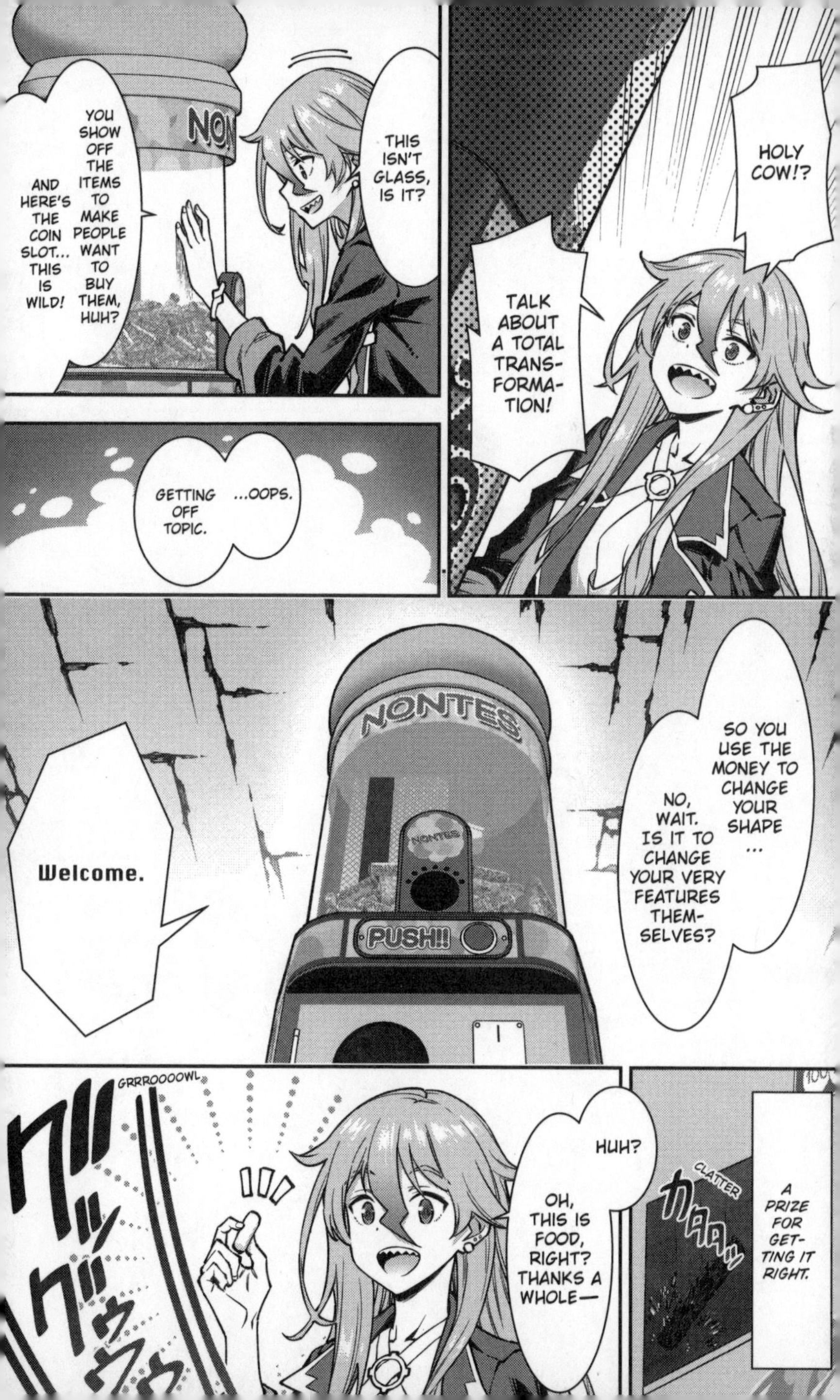
HOLY COW!?
TALK ABOUT A TOTAL TRANSFORMATION!
THIS ISN'T GLASS, IS IT?
YOU SHOW OFF THE ITEMS TO MAKE PEOPLE WANT TO BUY THEM, HUH?
AND HERE'S THE COIN SLOT... THIS IS WILD!
NON
...OOPS.
GETTING OFF TOPIC.
SO YOU USE THE MONEY TO CHANGE YOUR SHAPE ...
NO, WAIT. IS IT TO CHANGE YOUR VERY FEATURES THEMSELVES?
NONTES
NONTES
PUSH!!
Welcome.
CLATTER
A PRIZE FOR GET-TING IT RIGHT.
HUH?
OH, THIS IS FOOD, RIGHT? THANKS A WHOLE—
GRRROOOOWL

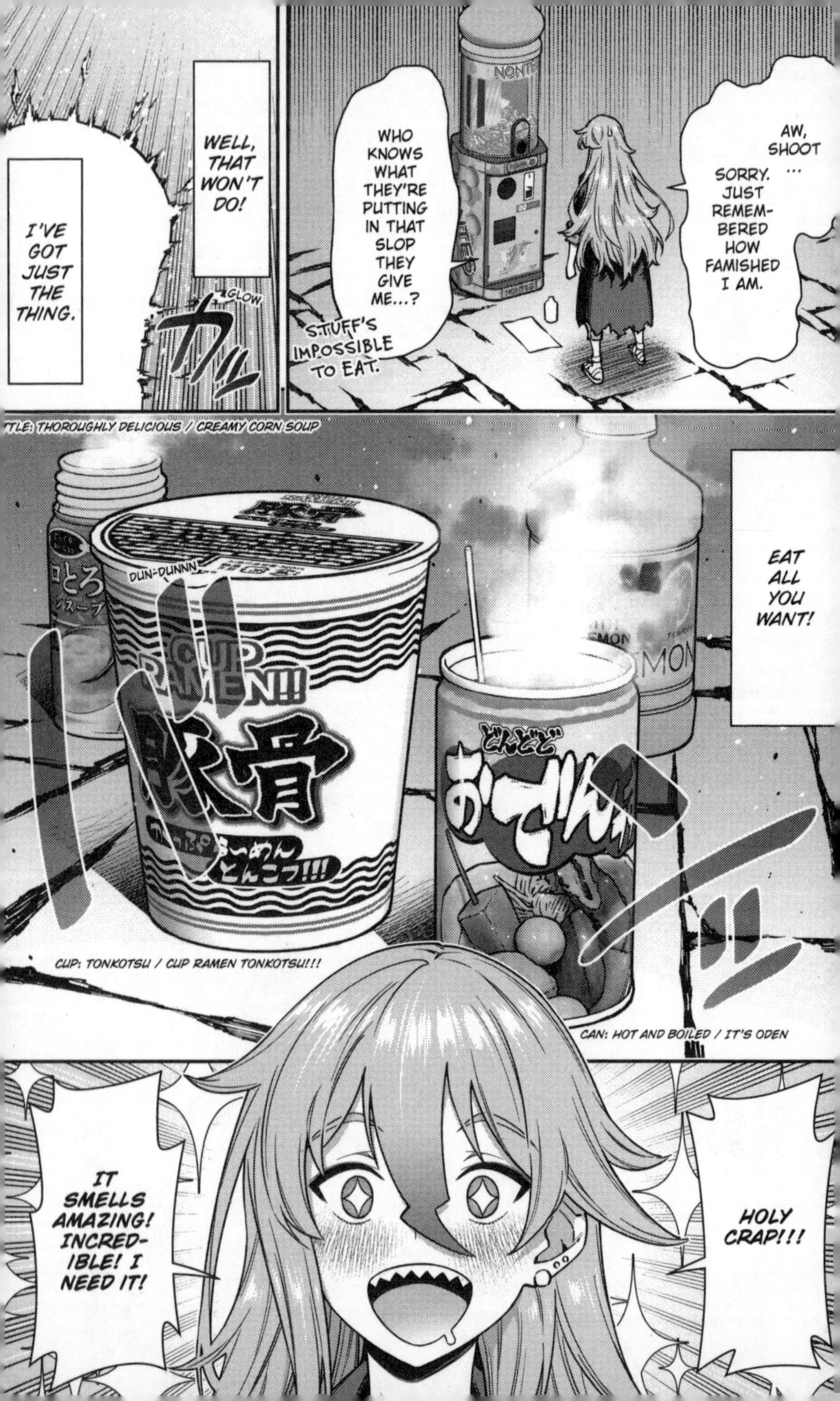
AW, SHOOT ...
SORRY. JUST REMEM-BERED HOW FAMISHED I AM.
WHO KNOWS WHAT THEY'RE PUTTING IN THAT SLOP THEY GIVE ME...?
STUFF'S IMPOSSIBLE TO EAT.
WELL, THAT WON'T DO!
GLOW
I'VE GOT JUST THE THING.
TLE: THOROUGHLY DELICIOUS / CREAMY CORN SOUP
EAT ALL YOU WANT!
DUN-DUNNN
CUP RAMEN!!
CUP: TONKOTSU / CUP RAMEN TONKOTSU!!!
CAN: HOT AND BOILED / IT'S ODEN
HOLY CRAP!!!
IT SMELLS AMAZING! INCRED-IBLE! I NEED IT!

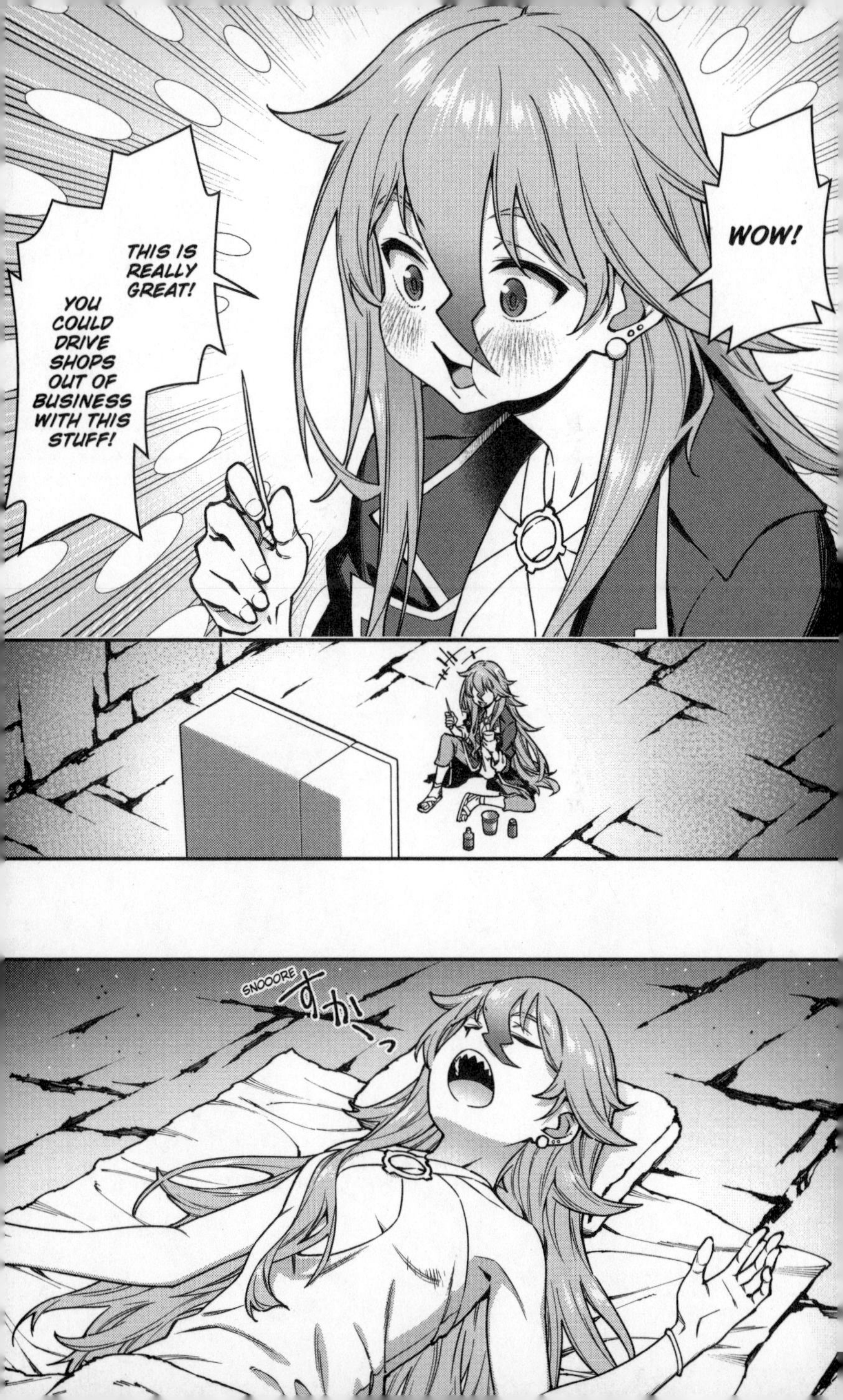
WOW!
THIS IS REALLY GREAT!
YOU COULD DRIVE SHOPS OUT OF BUSINESS WITH THIS STUFF!
SNOOORE
すかーっ

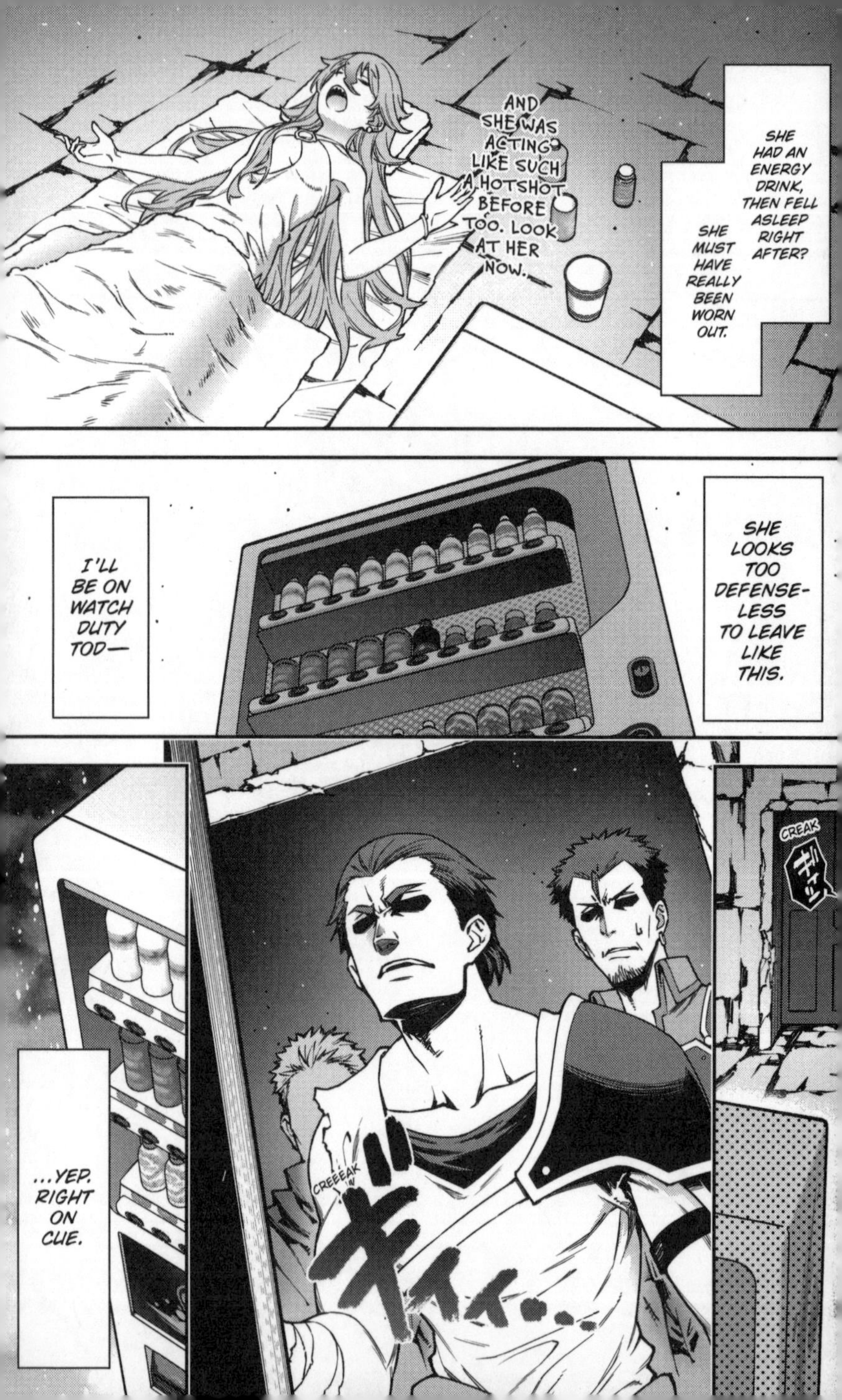
SHE HAD AN ENERGY DRINK, THEN FELL ASLEEP RIGHT AFTER?
SHE MUST HAVE REALLY BEEN WORN OUT.
AND SHE WAS ACTING LIKE SUCH A HOTSHOT BEFORE TOO. LOOK AT HER NOW.
SHE LOOKS TOO DEFENSELESS TO LEAVE LIKE THIS.
I'LL BE ON WATCH DUTY TOD—
CREAK
CREEEAK
...YEP. RIGHT ON CUE.

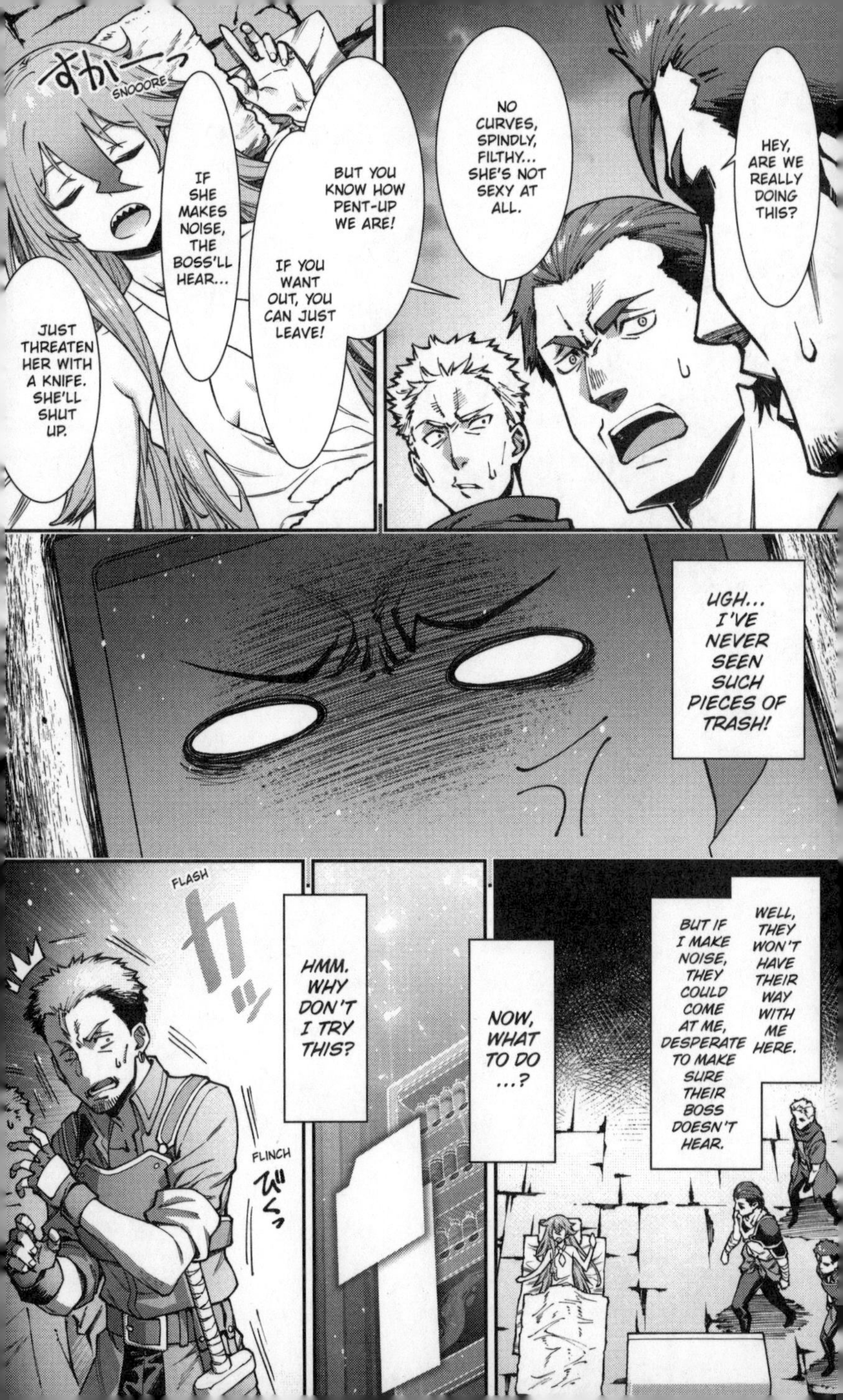
HEY, ARE WE REALLY DOING THIS?
NO CURVES, SPINDLY, FILTHY... SHE'S NOT SEXY AT ALL.
BUT YOU KNOW HOW PENT-UP WE ARE!
IF YOU WANT OUT, YOU CAN JUST LEAVE!
すかーっ
SNOOORE
IF SHE MAKES NOISE, THE BOSS'LL HEAR...
JUST THREATEN HER WITH A KNIFE. SHE'LL SHUT UP.
UGH... I'VE NEVER SEEN SUCH PIECES OF TRASH!
WELL, THEY WON'T HAVE THEIR WAY WITH ME HERE.
BUT IF I MAKE NOISE, THEY COULD COME AT ME, DESPERATE TO MAKE SURE THEIR BOSS DOESN'T HEAR.
NOW, WHAT TO DO ...?
HMM. WHY DON'T I TRY THIS?
FLASH
カッ
FLINCH
びくっ

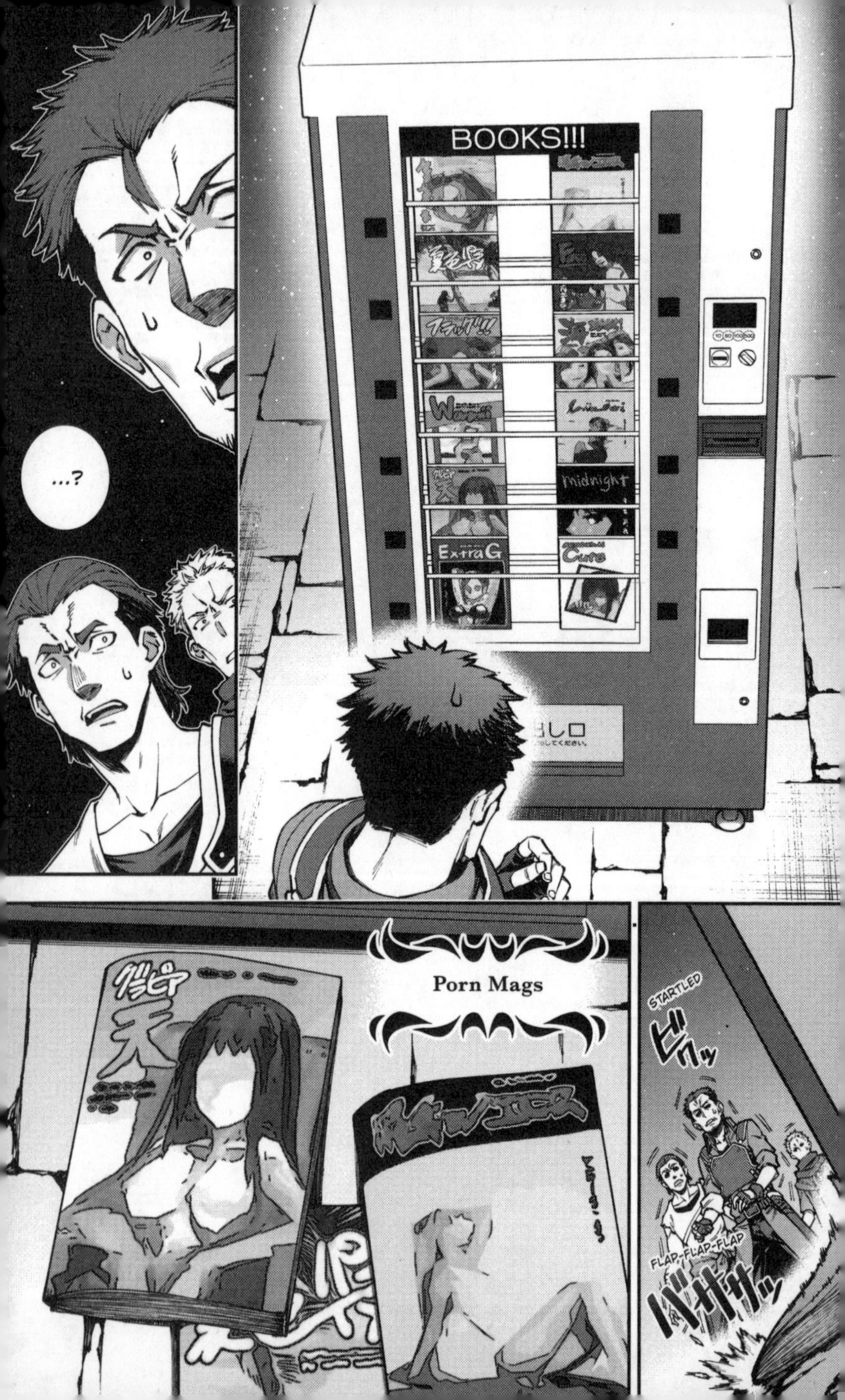
BOOKS!!!
midnight
Extra G
...?
STARTLED
FLAP-FLAP-FLAP
Porn Mags

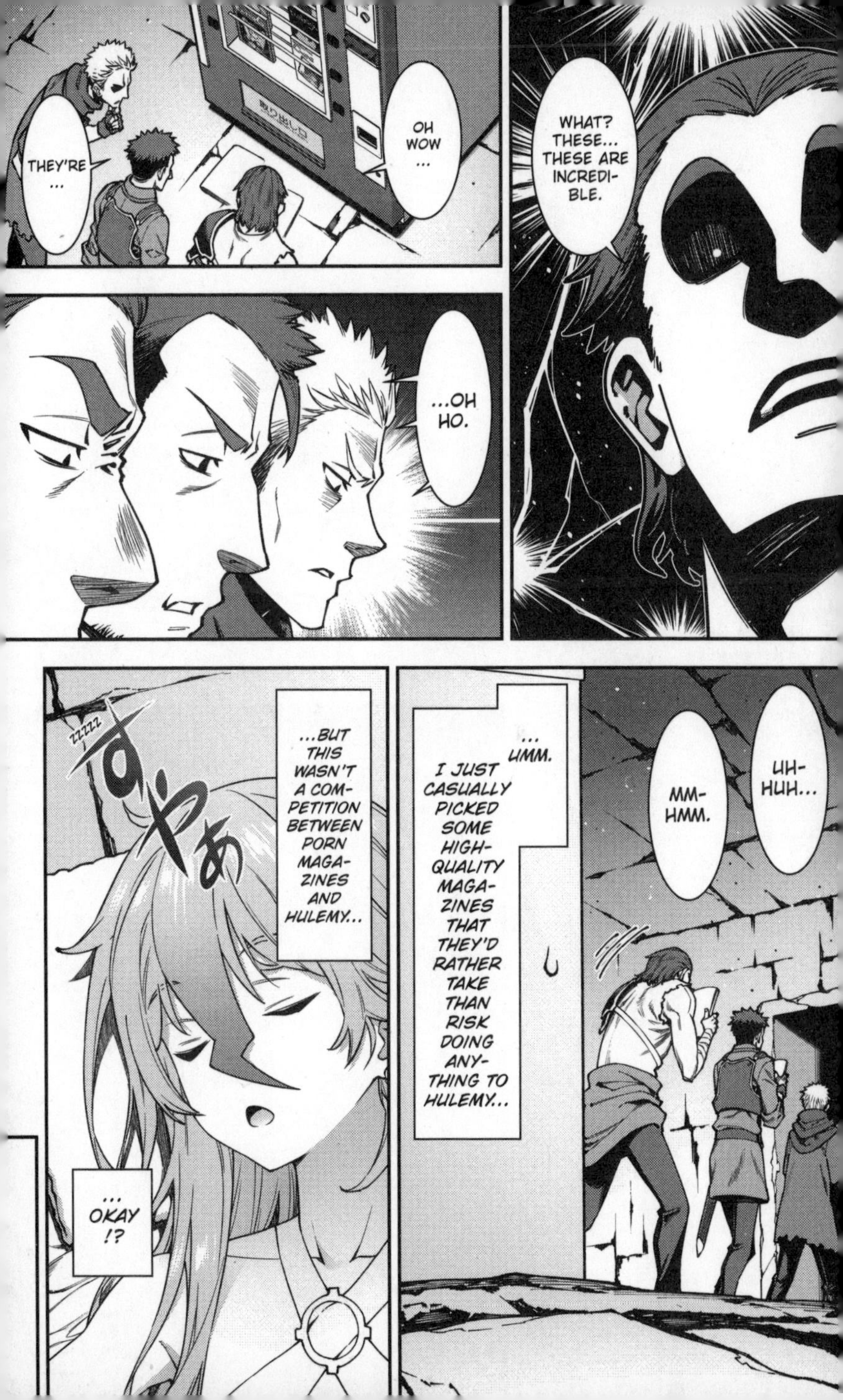
WHAT? THESE... THESE ARE INCREDI-BLE.
OH WOW ...
THEY'RE ...
...OH HO.
UH-HUH...
MM-HMM.
... UMM. I JUST CASUALLY PICKED SOME HIGH-QUALITY MAGA-ZINES THAT THEY'D RATHER TAKE THAN RISK DOING ANY-THING TO HULEMY...
...BUT THIS WASN'T A COM-PETITION BETWEEN PORN MAGA-ZINES AND HULEMY...
zzzzz
すやぁ
... OKAY !?

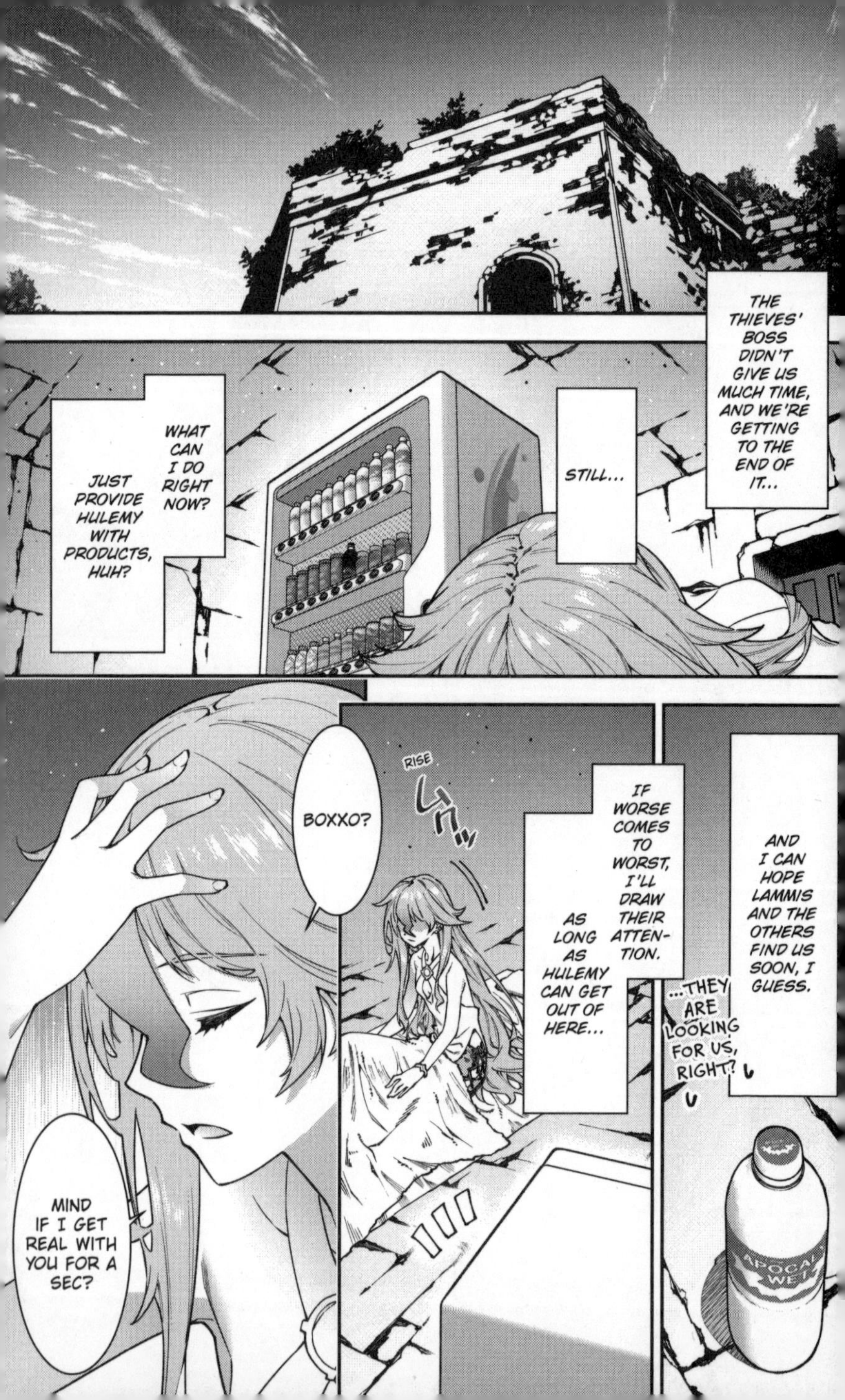
THE THIEVES' BOSS DIDN'T GIVE US MUCH TIME, AND WE'RE GETTING TO THE END OF IT...
STILL...
WHAT CAN I DO RIGHT NOW?
JUST PROVIDE HULEMY WITH PRODUCTS, HUH?
AND I CAN HOPE LAMMIS AND THE OTHERS FIND US SOON, I GUESS.
...THEY ARE LOOKING FOR US, RIGHT?
IF WORSE COMES TO WORST, I'LL DRAW THEIR ATTENTION.
AS LONG AS HULEMY CAN GET OUT OF HERE...
RISE
BOXXO?
MIND IF I GET REAL WITH YOU FOR A SEC?

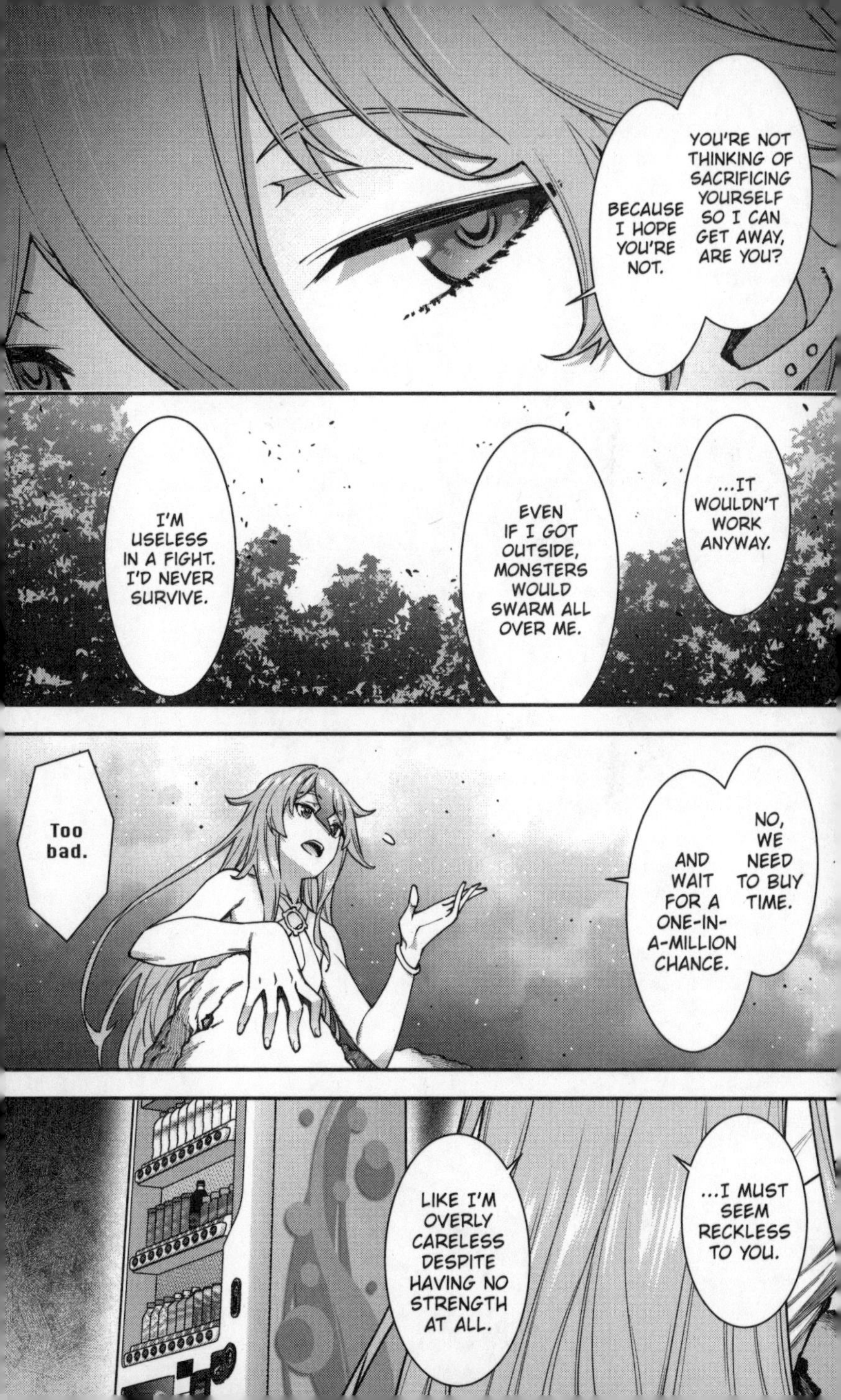
YOU'RE NOT THINKING OF SACRIFICING YOURSELF SO I CAN GET AWAY, ARE YOU?
BECAUSE I HOPE YOU'RE NOT.
...IT WOULDN'T WORK ANYWAY.
EVEN IF I GOT OUTSIDE, MONSTERS WOULD SWARM ALL OVER ME.
I'M USELESS IN A FIGHT. I'D NEVER SURVIVE.
NO, WE NEED TO BUY TIME.
AND WAIT FOR A ONE-IN-A-MILLION CHANCE.
Too bad.
...I MUST SEEM RECKLESS TO YOU.
LIKE I'M OVERLY CARELESS DESPITE HAVING NO STRENGTH AT ALL.

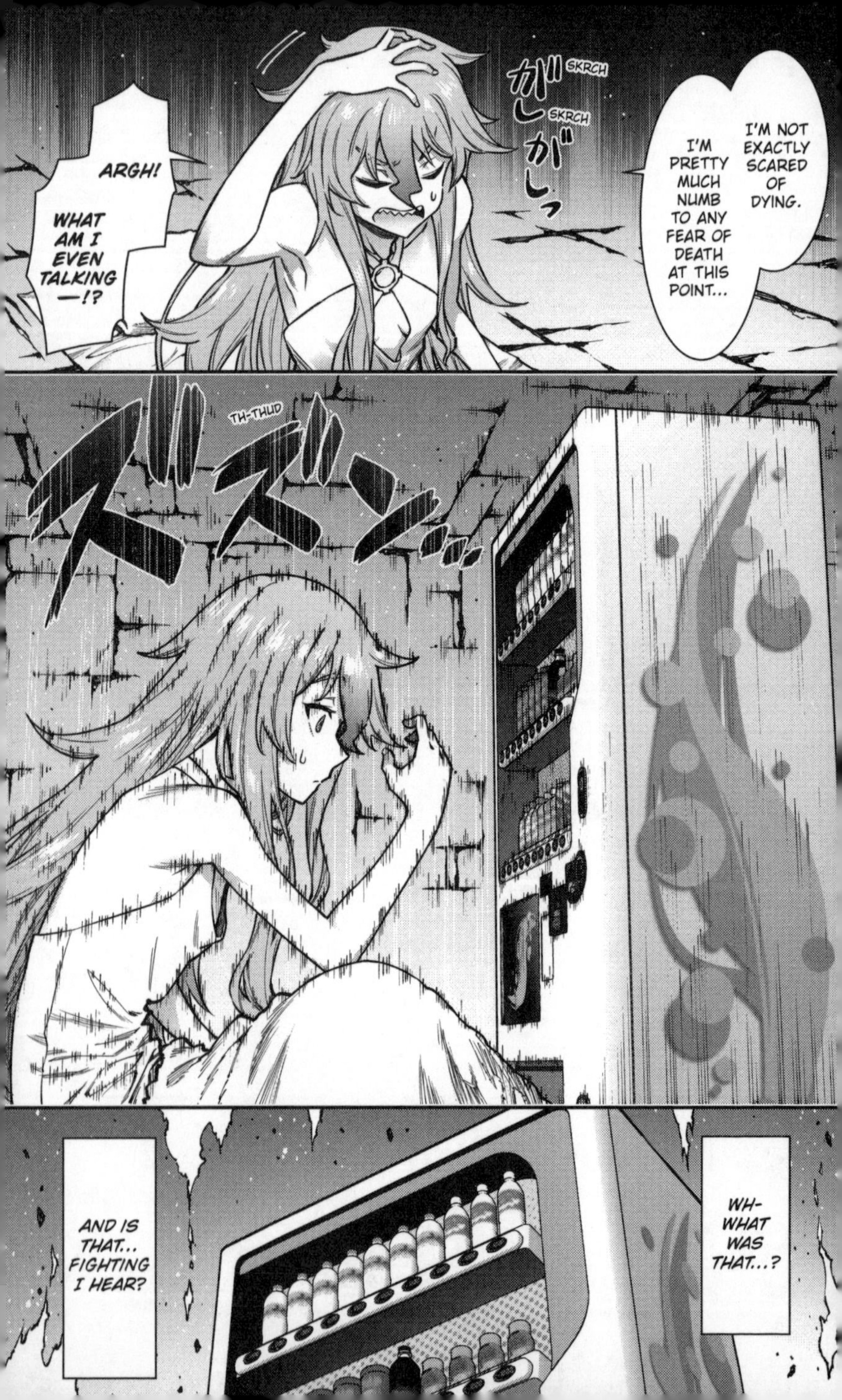
I'M NOT EXACTLY SCARED OF DYING.
I'M PRETTY MUCH NUMB TO ANY FEAR OF DEATH AT THIS POINT...
がしがしっ
SKRCH
SKRCH
ARGH!
WHAT AM I EVEN TALKING—!?
ズズン…
TH-THUD
WH-WHAT WAS THAT...?
AND IS THAT... FIGHTING I HEAR?

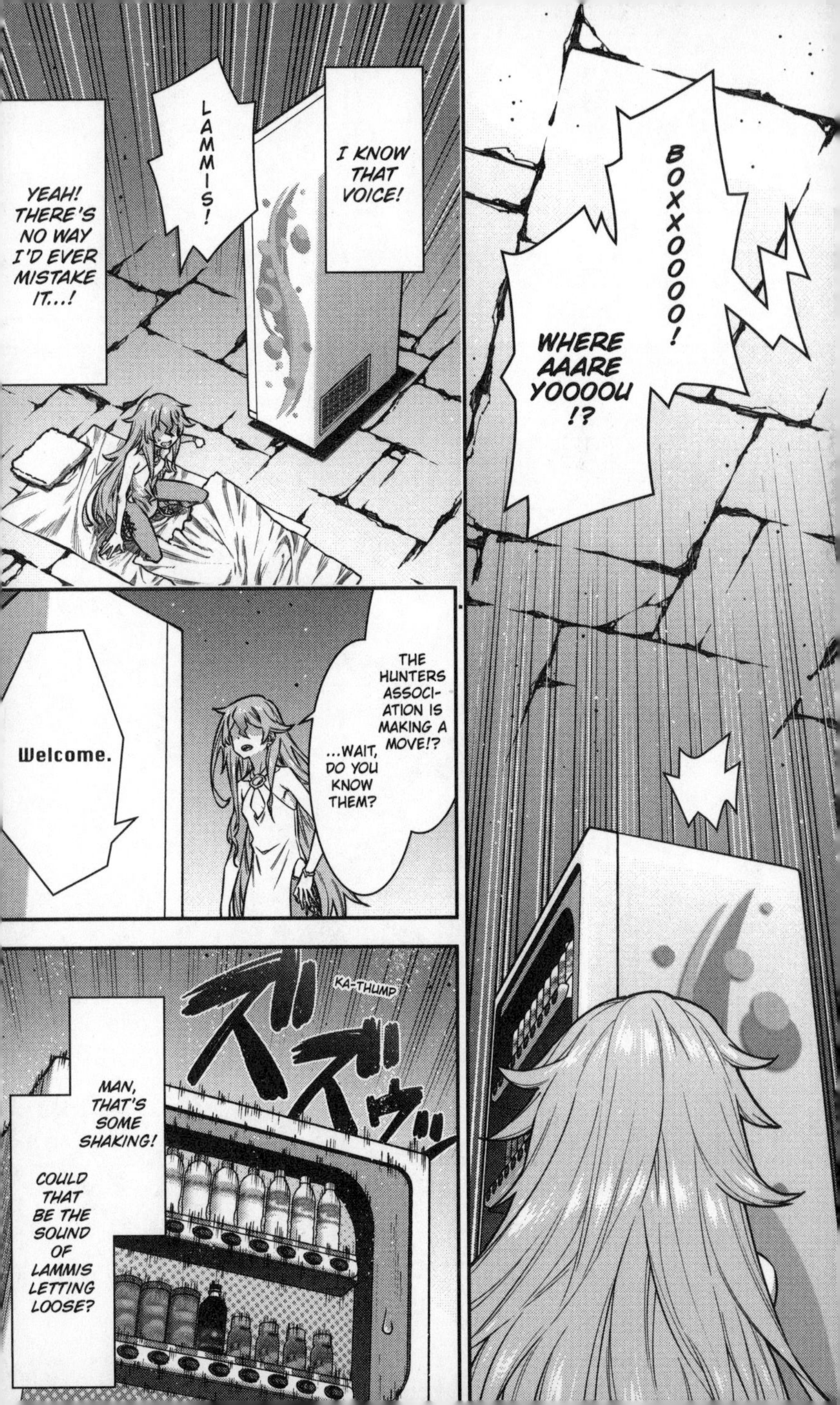
BOXXOOOO!
WHERE AAARE YOOOOU!?
I KNOW THAT VOICE!
LAMMIS!
YEAH! THERE'S NO WAY I'D EVER MISTAKE IT...!
THE HUNTERS ASSOCIATION IS MAKING A MOVE!?
...WAIT, DO YOU KNOW THEM?
Welcome.
KA-THUMP
MAN, THAT'S SOME SHAKING!
COULD THAT BE THE SOUND OF LAMMIS LETTING LOOSE?

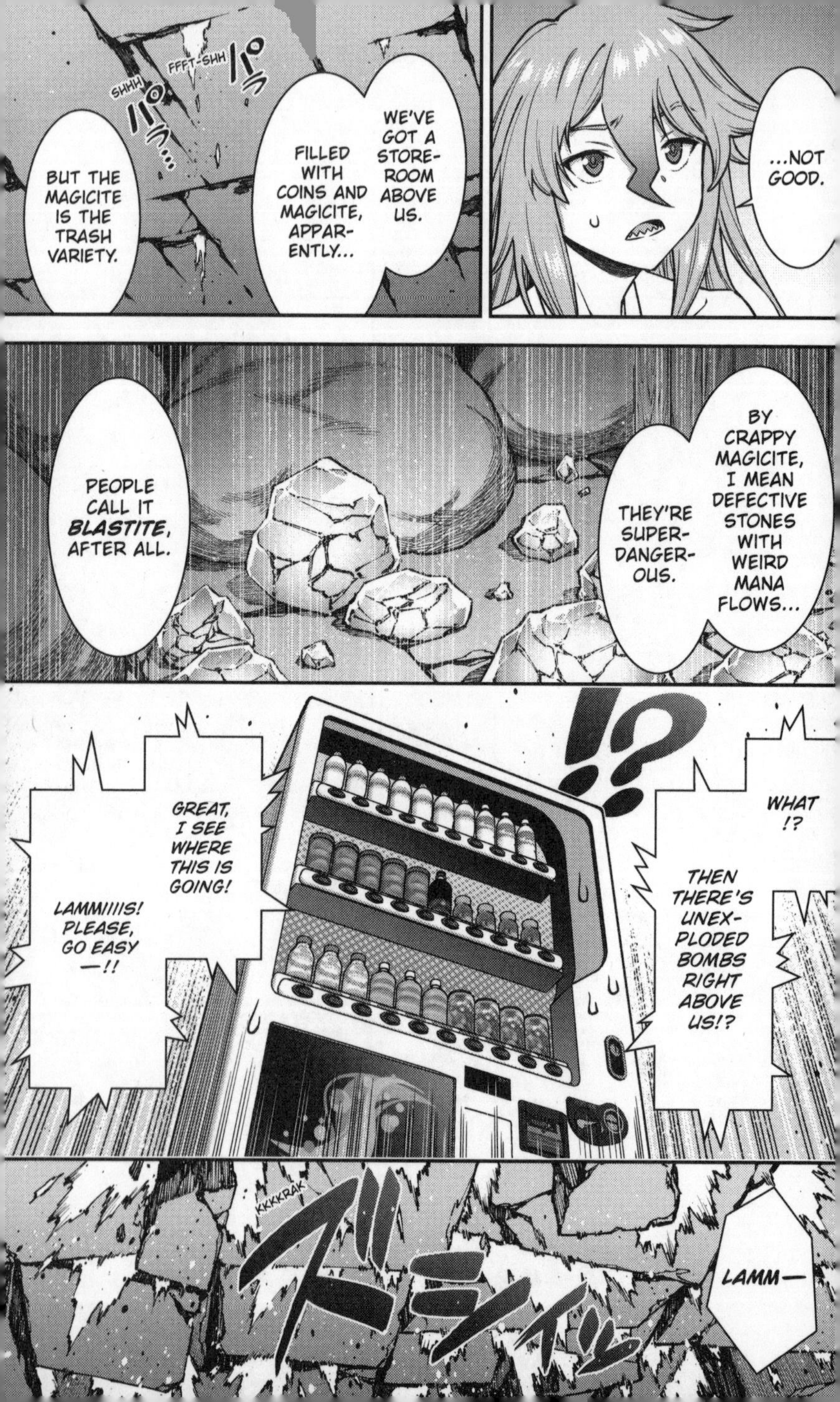
...NOT GOOD.
WE'VE GOT A STORE-ROOM ABOVE US.
FILLED WITH COINS AND MAGICITE, APPAR-ENTLY...
FFFT-SHH
SHHH
BUT THE MAGICITE IS THE TRASH VARIETY.
BY CRAPPY MAGICITE, I MEAN DEFECTIVE STONES WITH WEIRD MANA FLOWS...
THEY'RE SUPER-DANGER-OUS.
PEOPLE CALL IT *BLASTITE*, AFTER ALL.
!?
WHAT!?
THEN THERE'S UNEX-PLODED BOMBS RIGHT ABOVE US!?
GREAT, I SEE WHERE THIS IS GOING!
LAMMIIIIS! PLEASE, GO EASY—!!
LAMM—
KKKKRAK

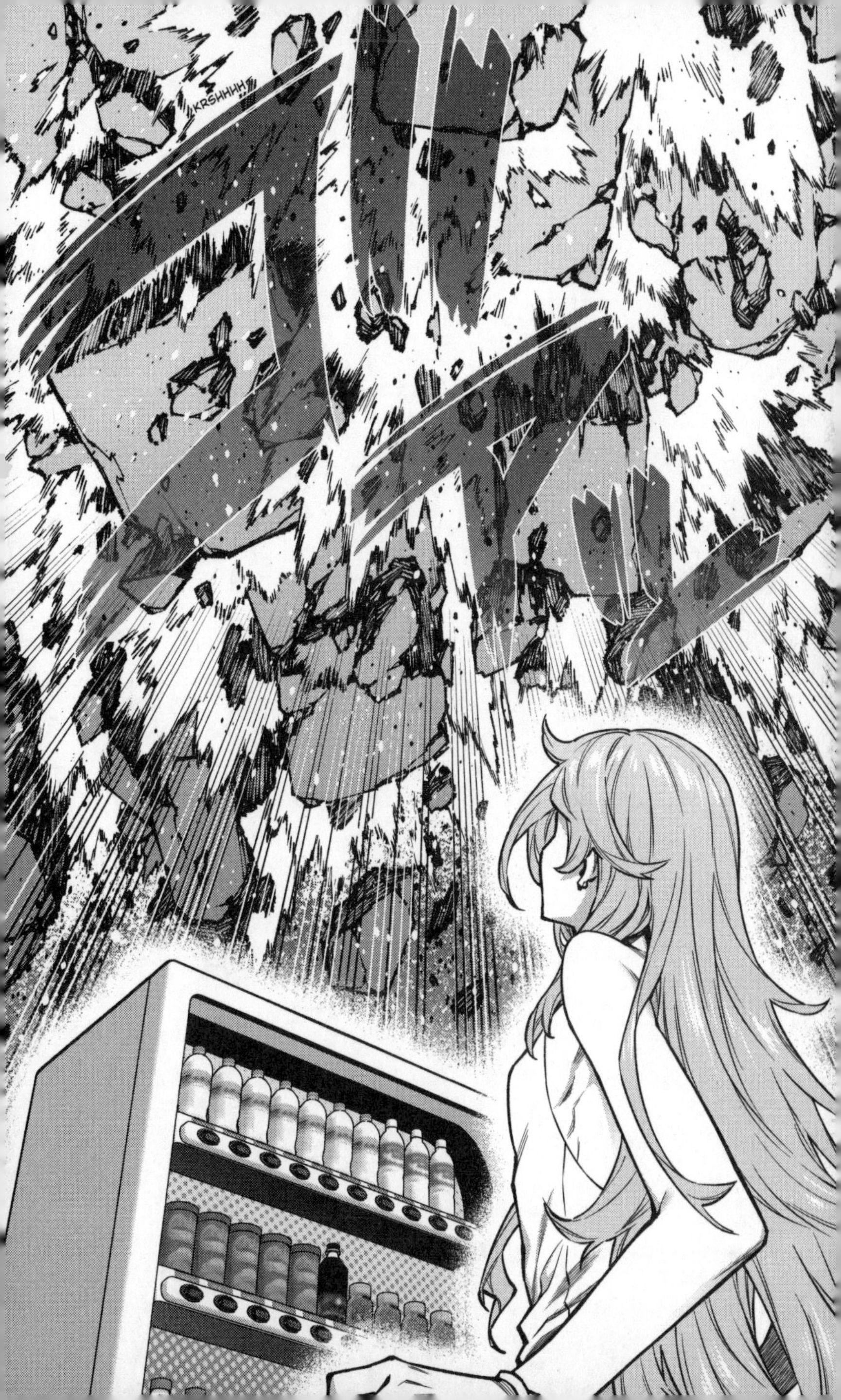
KRSHHHH

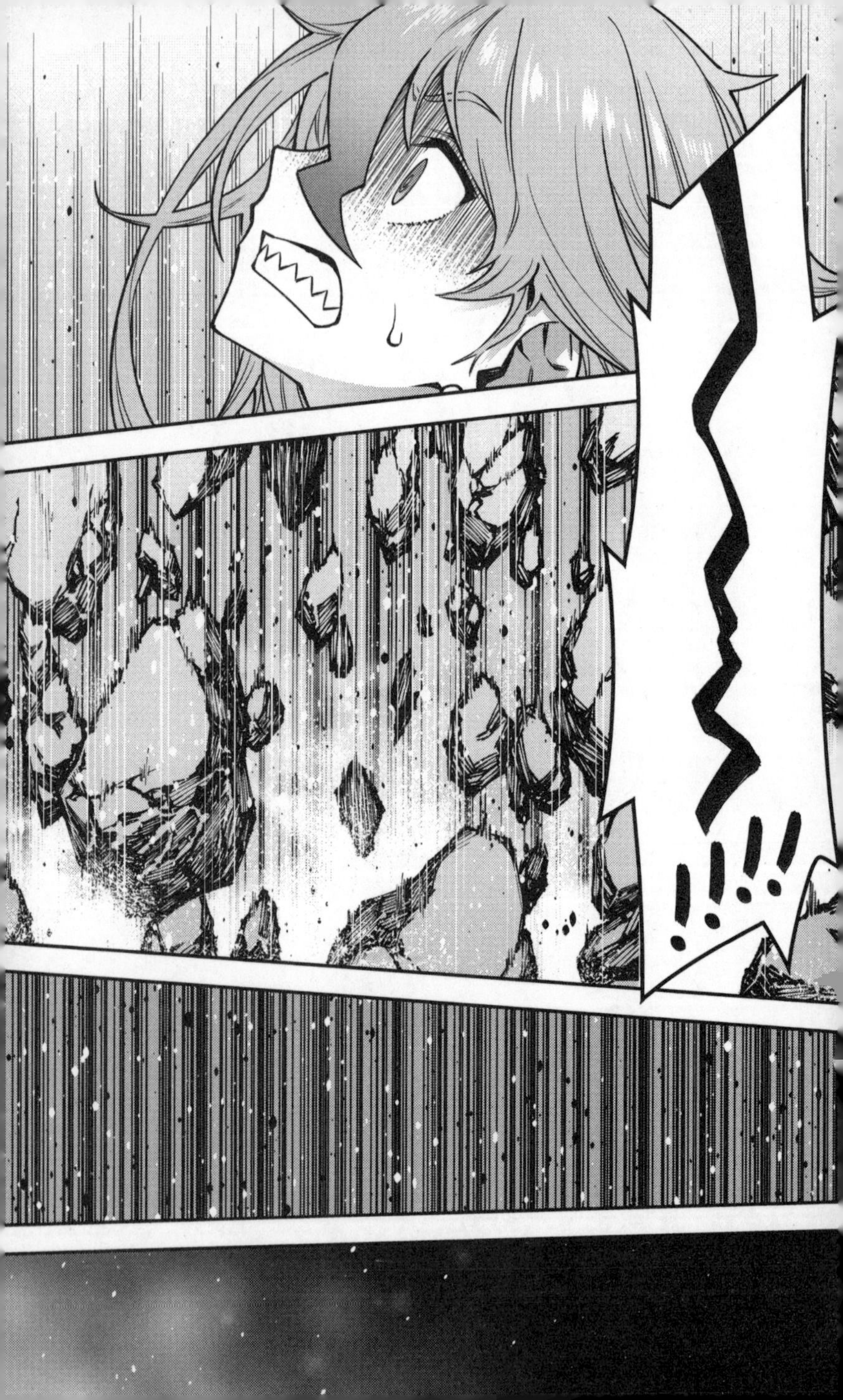
!!!!

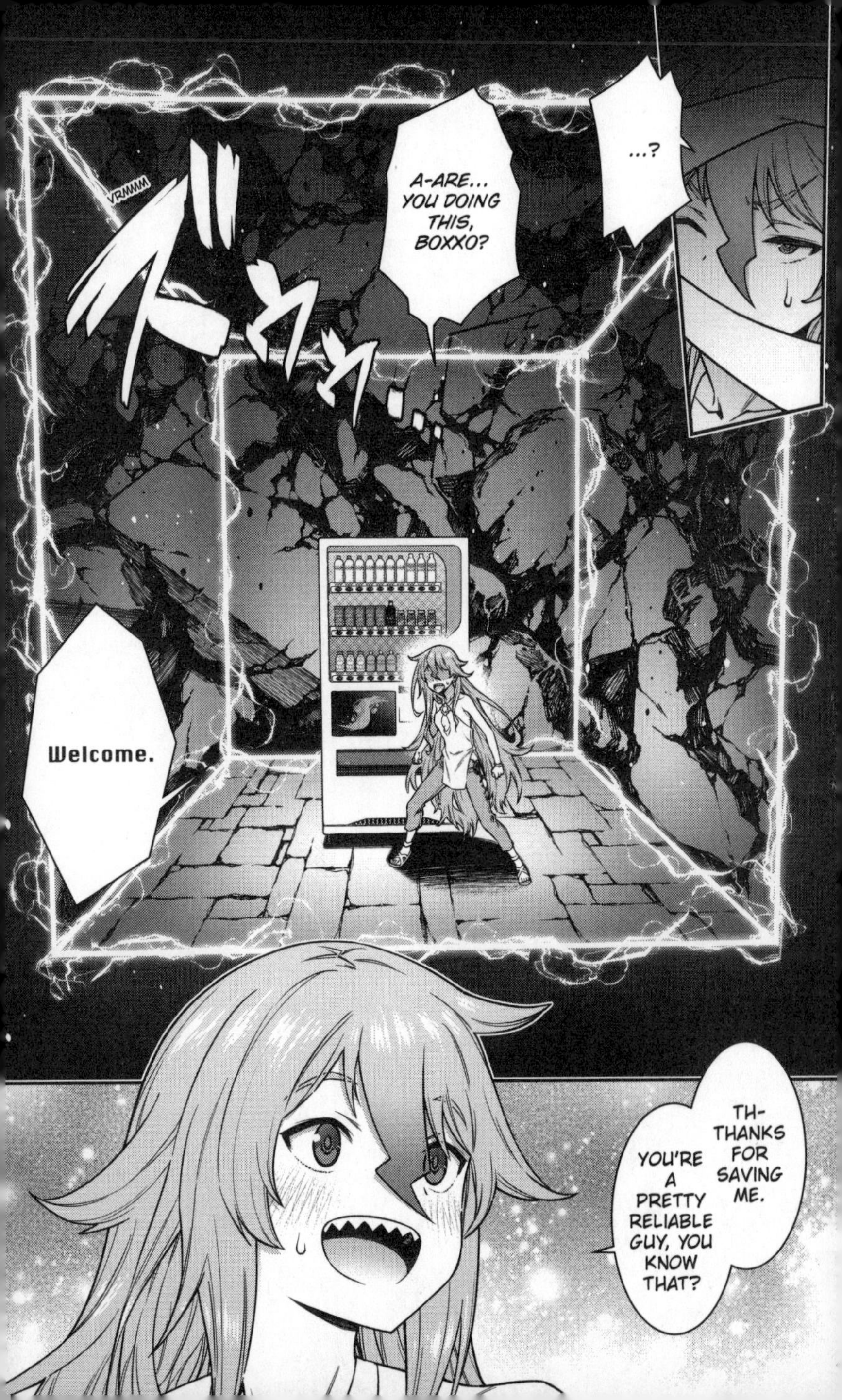
...?
A-ARE... YOU DOING THIS, BOXXO?
VRMMMM
Welcome.
TH-THANKS FOR SAVING ME.
YOU'RE A PRETTY RELIABLE GUY, YOU KNOW THAT?

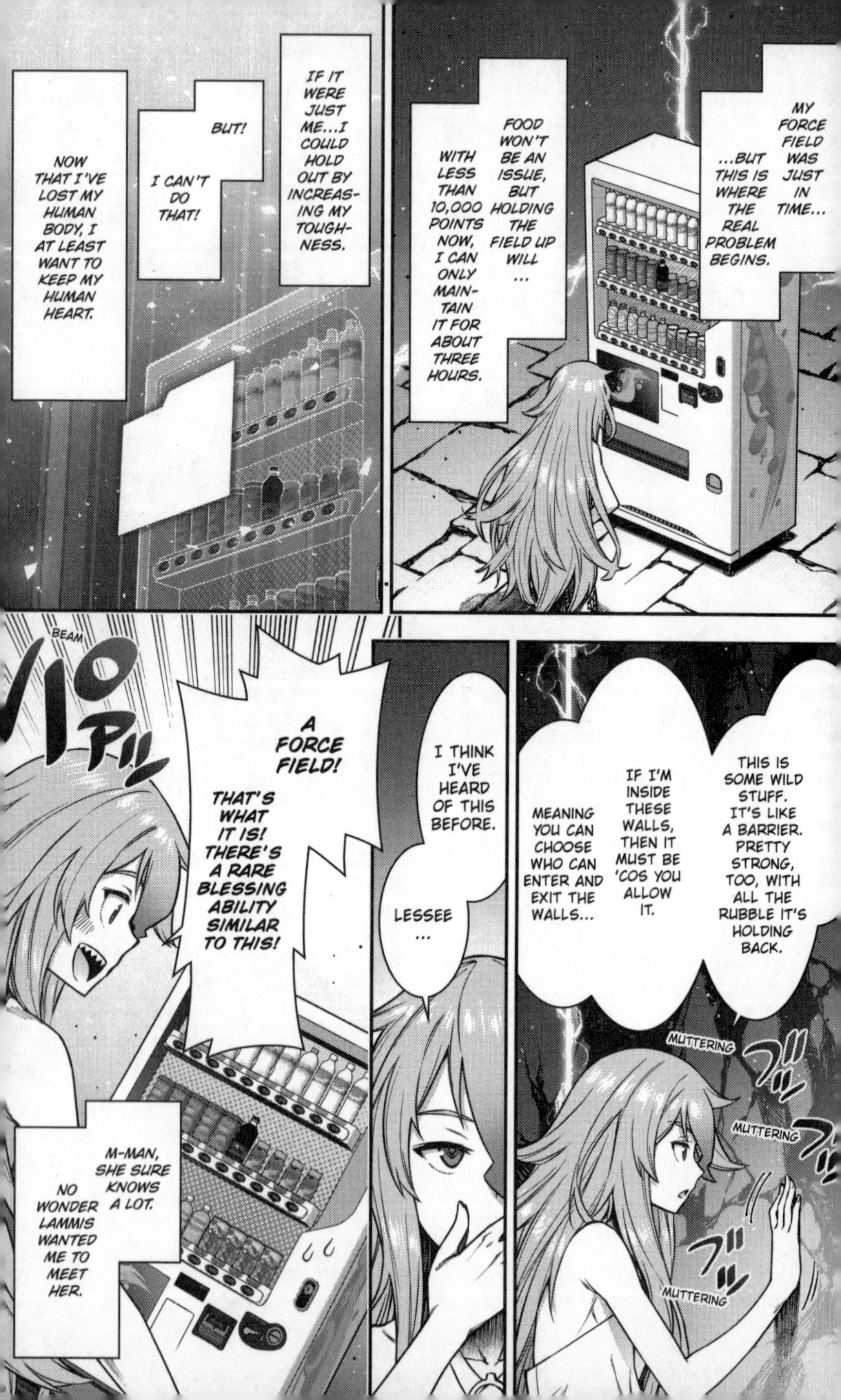
MY FORCE FIELD WAS JUST IN TIME...
...BUT THIS IS WHERE THE REAL PROBLEM BEGINS.
FOOD WON'T BE AN ISSUE, BUT HOLDING THE FIELD UP WILL ...
WITH LESS THAN 10,000 POINTS NOW, I CAN ONLY MAINTAIN IT FOR ABOUT THREE HOURS.
IF IT WERE JUST ME...I COULD HOLD OUT BY INCREASING MY TOUGHNESS.
BUT!
I CAN'T DO THAT!
NOW THAT I'VE LOST MY HUMAN BODY, I AT LEAST WANT TO KEEP MY HUMAN HEART.
THIS IS SOME WILD STUFF. IT'S LIKE A BARRIER. PRETTY STRONG, TOO, WITH ALL THE RUBBLE IT'S HOLDING BACK.
IF I'M INSIDE THESE WALLS, THEN IT MUST BE 'COS YOU ALLOW IT.
MEANING YOU CAN CHOOSE WHO CAN ENTER AND EXIT THE WALLS...
MUTTERING
MUTTERING
MUTTERING
I THINK I'VE HEARD OF THIS BEFORE.
LESSEE ...
BEAM
A FORCE FIELD!
THAT'S WHAT IT IS! THERE'S A RARE BLESSING ABILITY SIMILAR TO THIS!
M-MAN, SHE SURE KNOWS A LOT.
NO WONDER LAMMIS WANTED ME TO MEET HER.

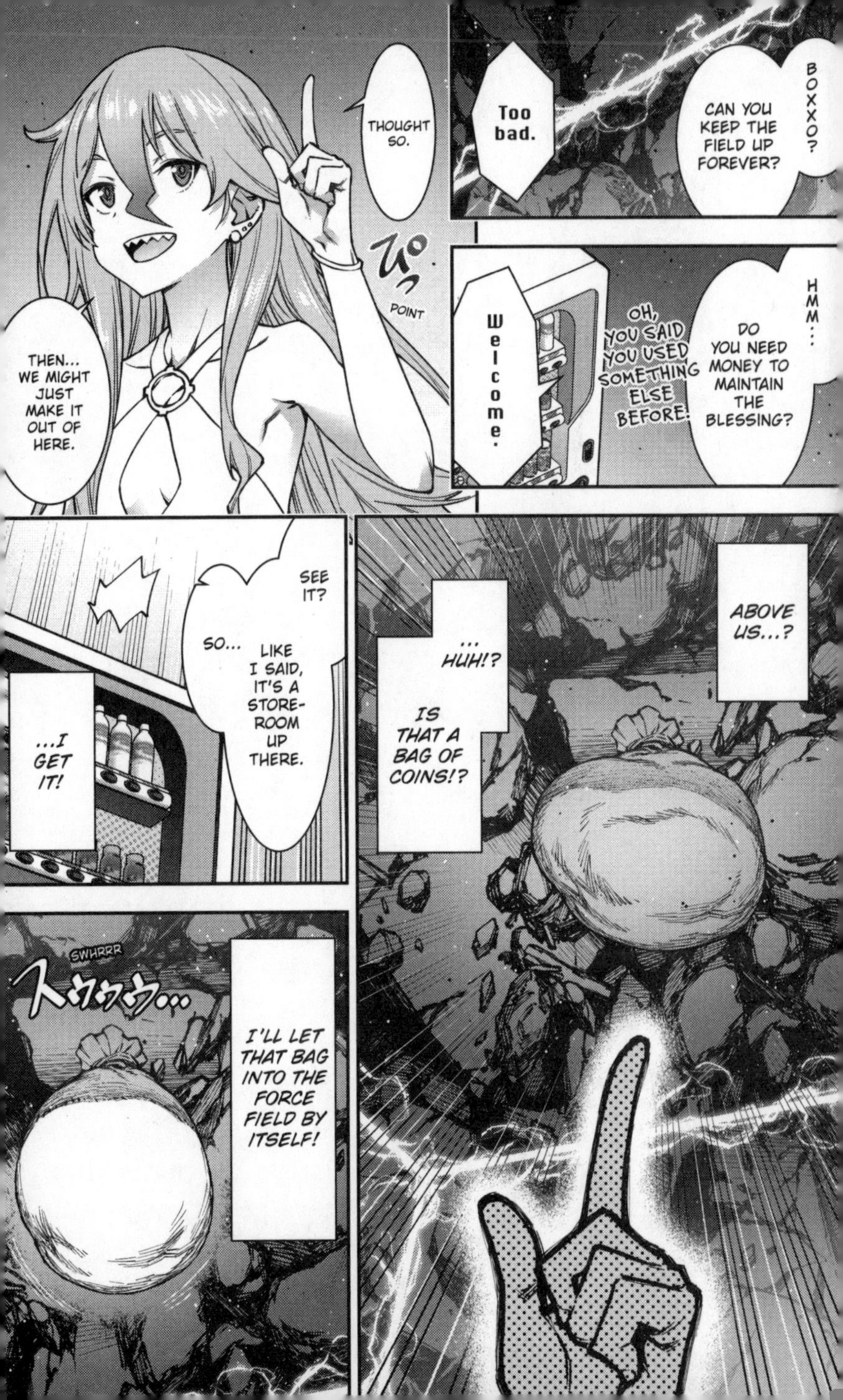
BOXXO?
CAN YOU KEEP THE FIELD UP FOREVER?
Too bad.
HMM...
DO YOU NEED MONEY TO MAINTAIN THE BLESSING?
OH, YOU SAID YOU USED SOMETHING ELSE BEFORE!
Welcome.
THOUGHT SO.
ぴっ
POINT
THEN... WE MIGHT JUST MAKE IT OUT OF HERE.
ABOVE US...?
...HUH!?
IS THAT A BAG OF COINS!?
SEE IT?
SO...
LIKE I SAID, IT'S A STOREROOM UP THERE.
...I GET IT!
SWHRRR
I'LL LET THAT BAG INTO THE FORCE FIELD BY ITSELF!

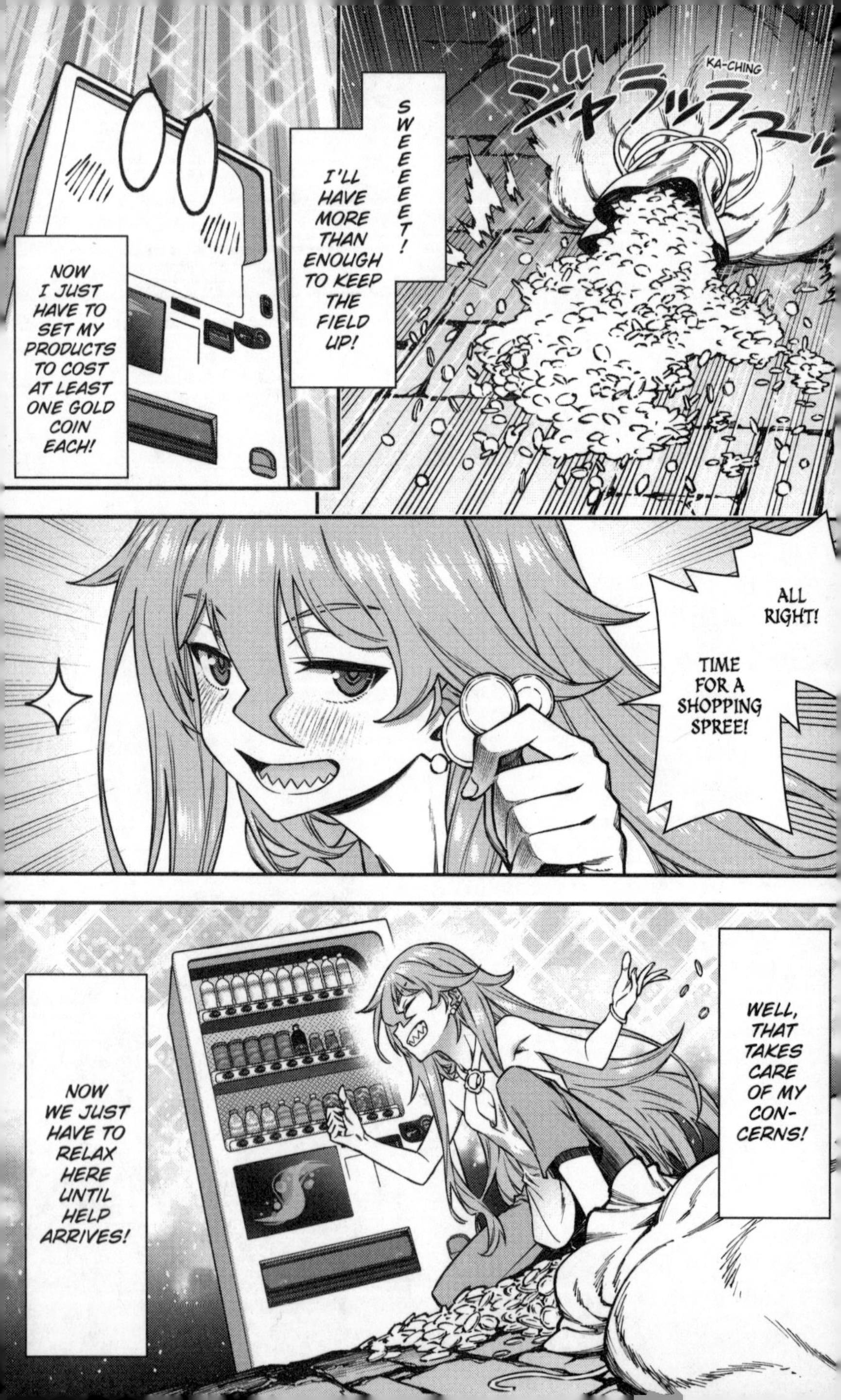

KA-CHING
SWEEEEEET!
I'LL HAVE MORE THAN ENOUGH TO KEEP THE FIELD UP!
NOW I JUST HAVE TO SET MY PRODUCTS TO COST AT LEAST ONE GOLD COIN EACH!
ALL RIGHT!
TIME FOR A SHOPPING SPREE!
WELL, THAT TAKES CARE OF MY CON-CERNS!
NOW WE JUST HAVE TO RELAX HERE UNTIL HELP ARRIVES!

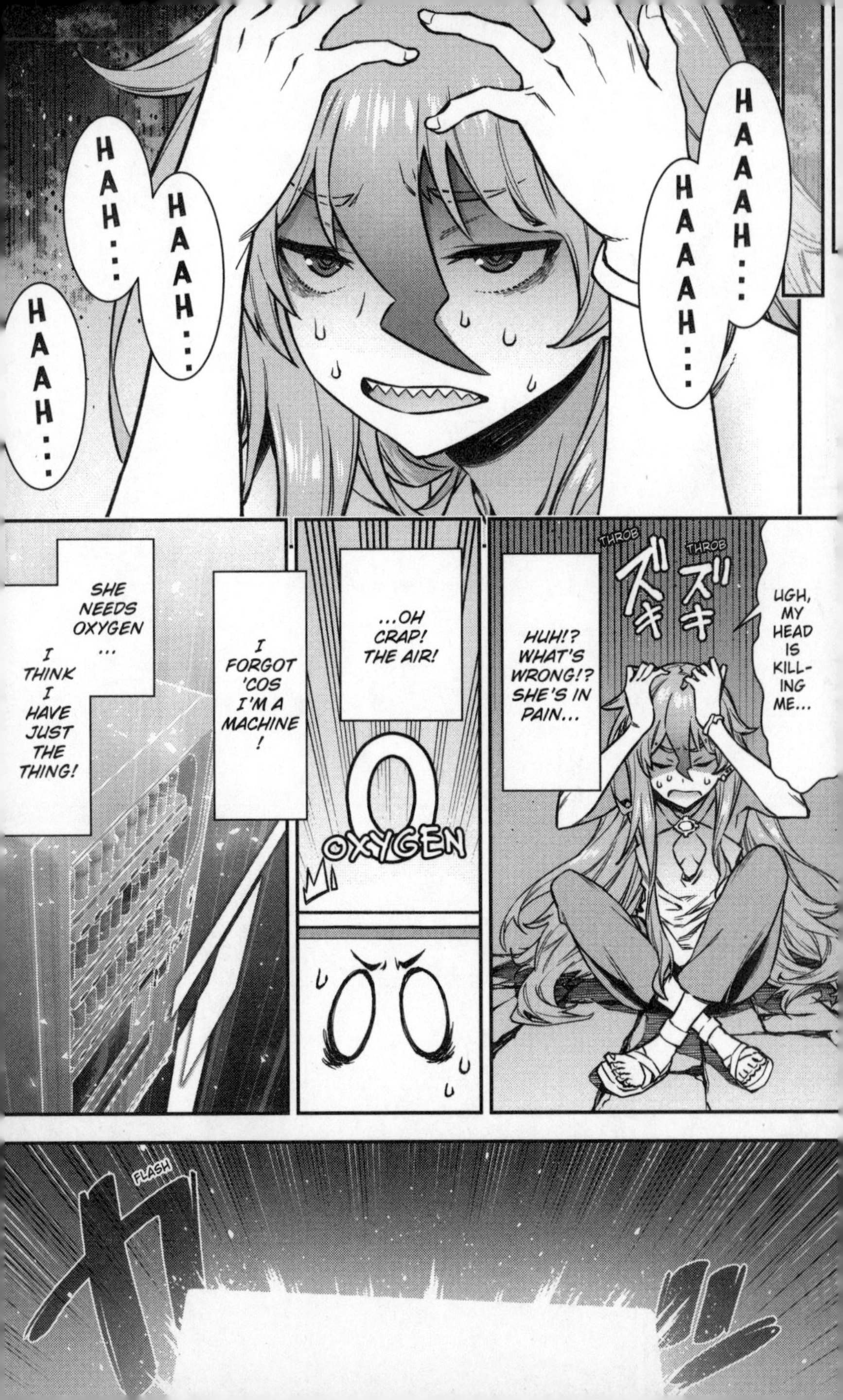
HAAAH...
HAAAH...
HAAH...
HAH...
HAAH...
THROB
THROB
UGH, MY HEAD IS KILLING ME...
HUH!? WHAT'S WRONG!? SHE'S IN PAIN...
...OH CRAP! THE AIR!
OXYGEN
I FORGOT 'COS I'M A MACHINE!
SHE NEEDS OXYGEN...
I THINK I HAVE JUST THE THING!
FLASH

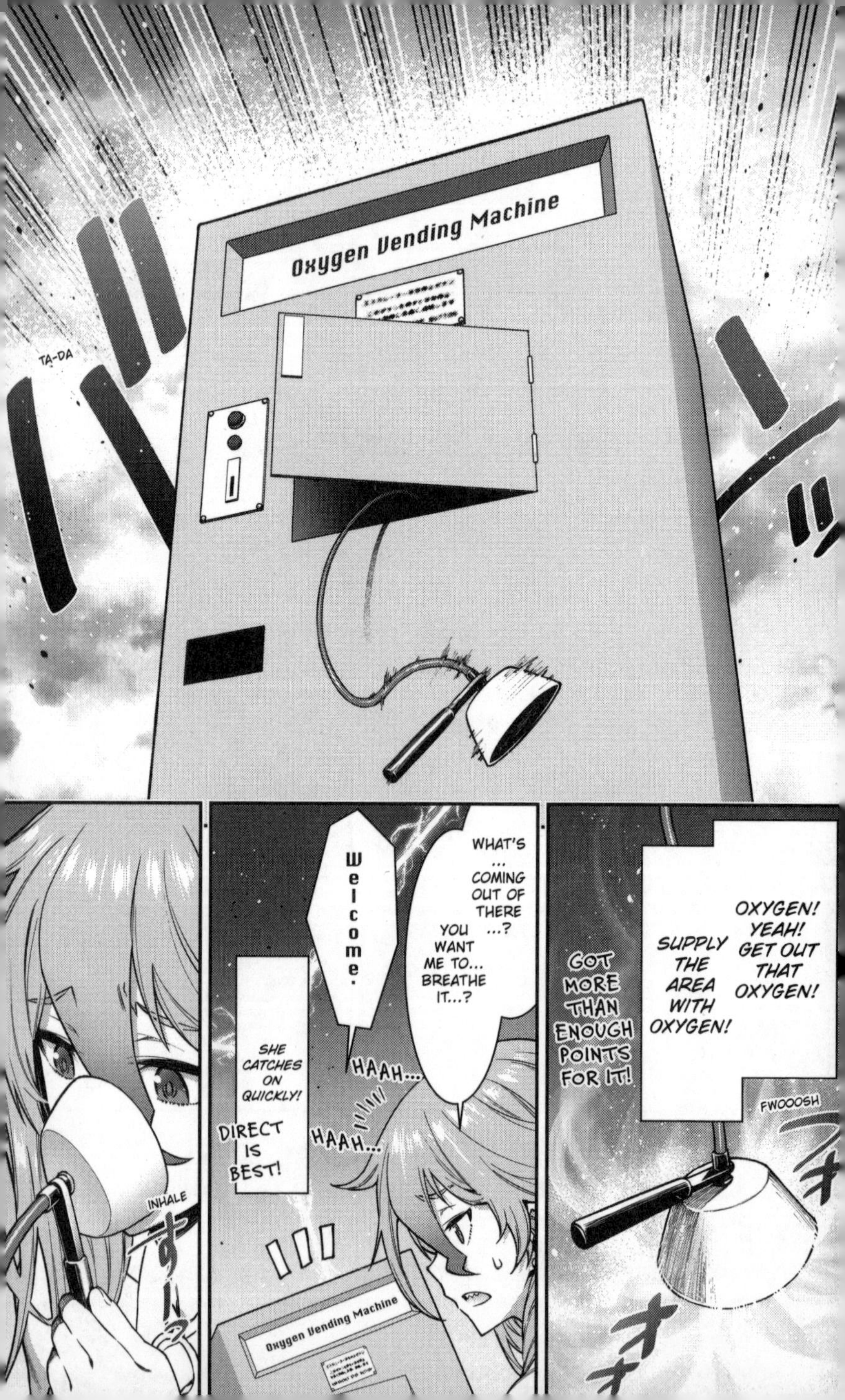
Oxygen Vending Machine
TA-DA
FWOOOSH
OXYGEN! YEAH! GET OUT THAT OXYGEN!
SUPPLY THE AREA WITH OXYGEN!
GOT MORE THAN ENOUGH POINTS FOR IT!
WHAT'S ... COMING OUT OF THERE ...?
YOU WANT ME TO... BREATHE IT...?
Welcome.
HAAH...
SHE CATCHES ON QUICKLY!
DIRECT IS BEST!
HAAH...
Oxygen Vending Machine
INHALE

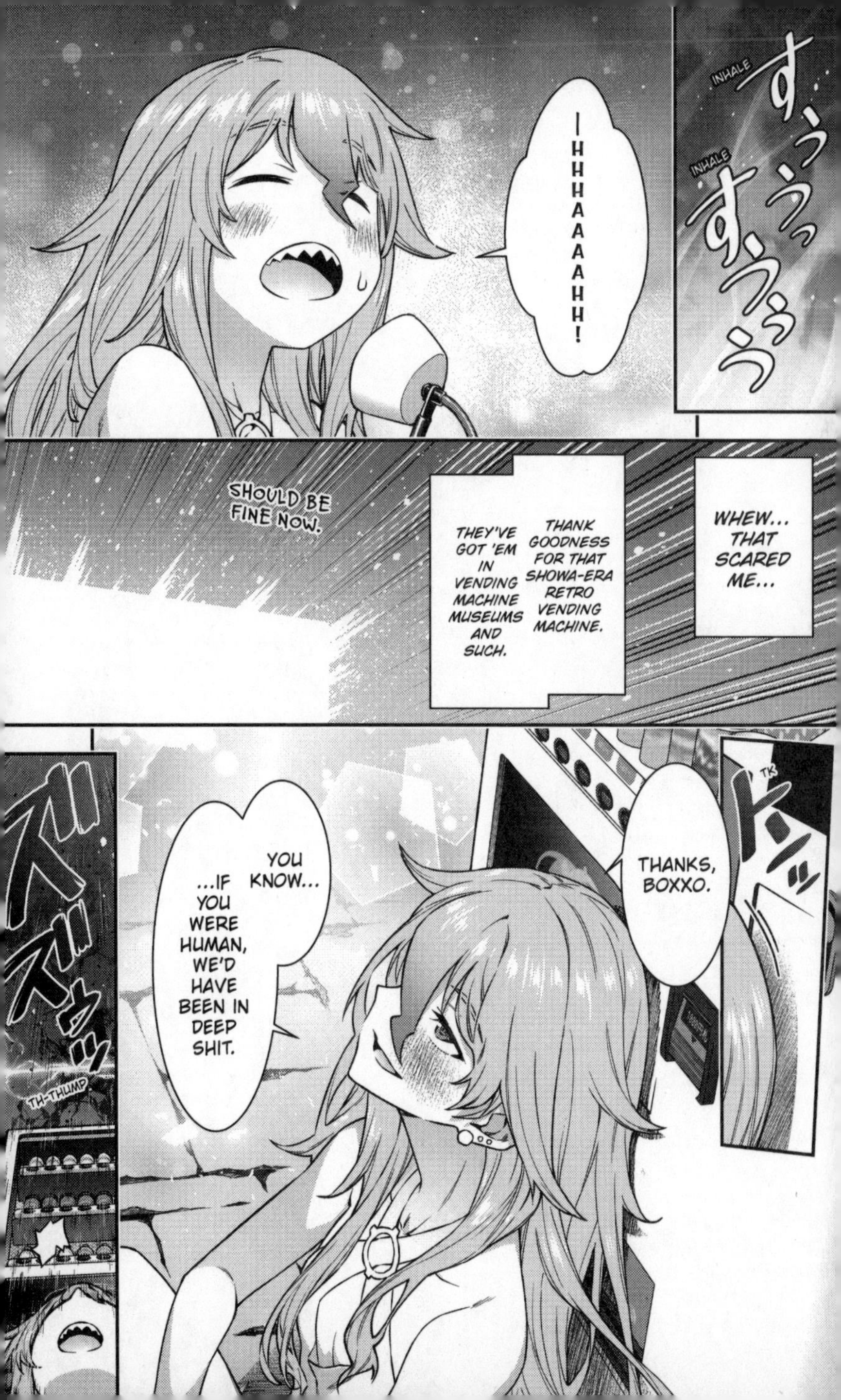
INHALE
すぅぅっ
INHALE
すぅぅぅう
IHHHAAAAAAHH!
WHEW... THAT SCARED ME...
THANK GOODNESS FOR THAT SHOWA-ERA RETRO VENDING MACHINE.
THEY'VE GOT 'EM IN VENDING MACHINE MUSEUMS AND SUCH.
SHOULD BE FINE NOW.
TK
トンッ
THANKS, BOXXO.
YOU KNOW...
...IF YOU WERE HUMAN, WE'D HAVE BEEN IN DEEP SHIT.
ズズゥッ
TH-THUMP

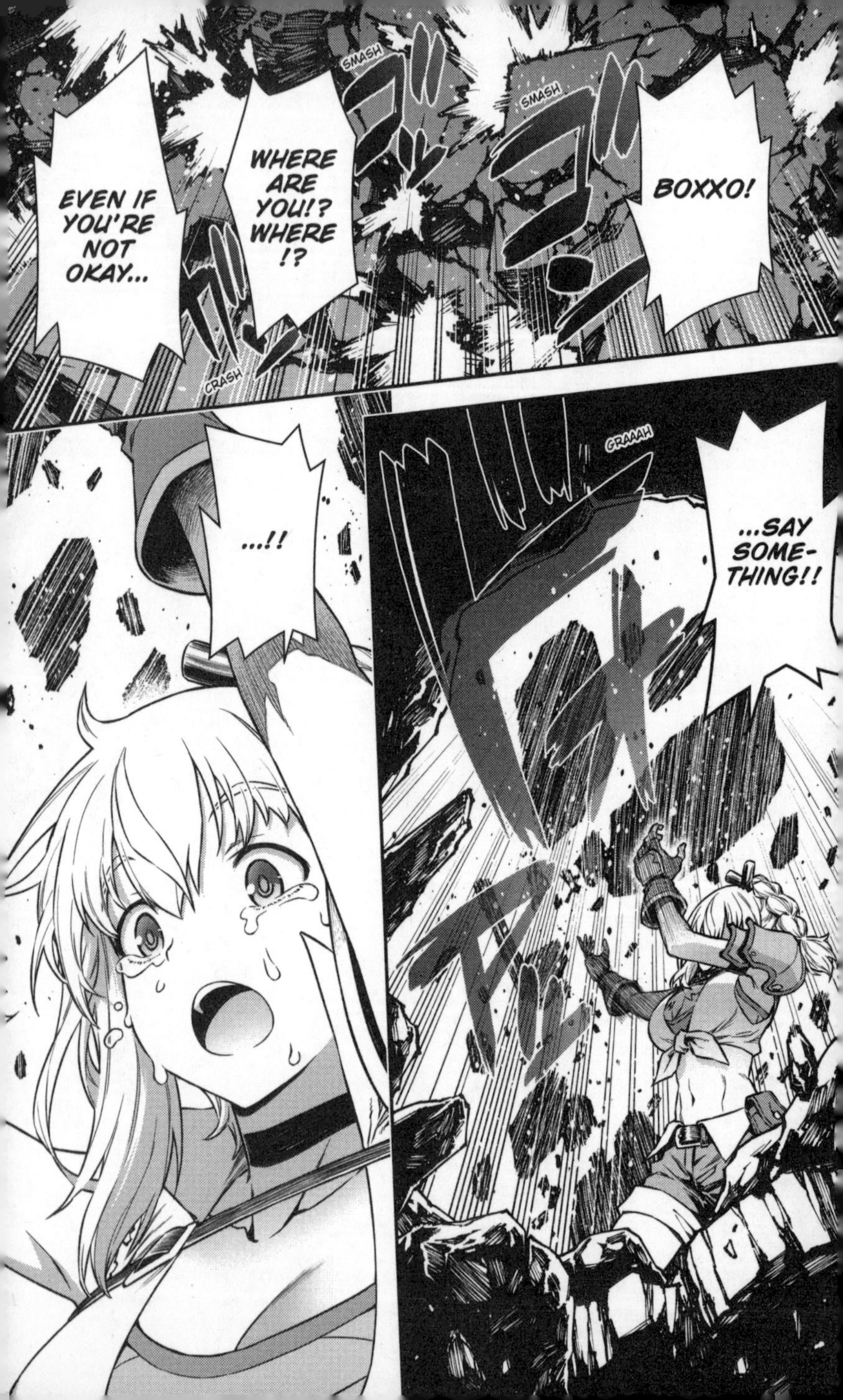
SMASH
BOXXO!
SMASH
WHERE ARE YOU!? WHERE !?
EVEN IF YOU'RE NOT OKAY...
CRASH
GRAAAH
...SAY SOMETHING!!
...!!

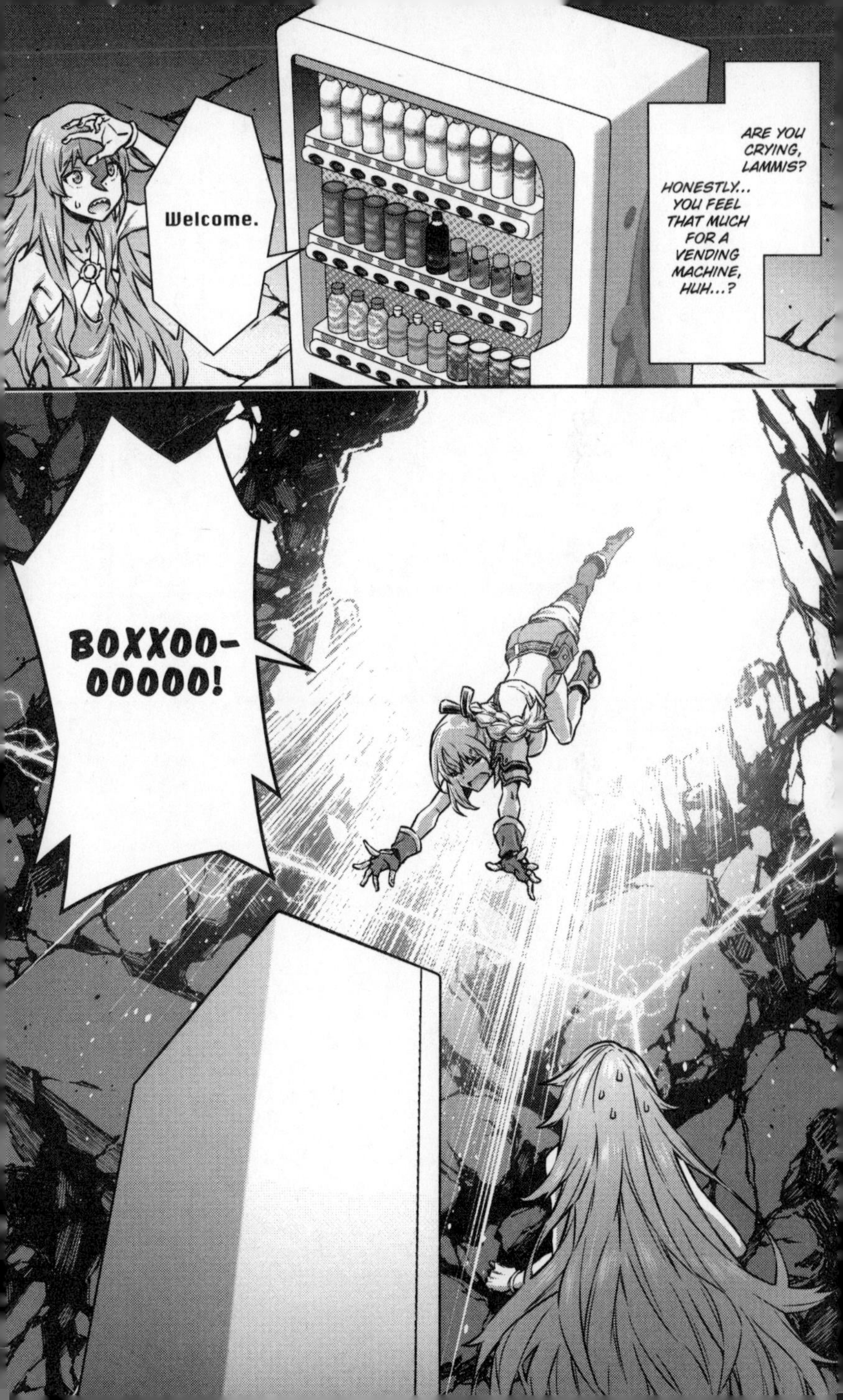

ARE YOU CRYING, LAMMIS?
HONESTLY... YOU FEEL THAT MUCH FOR A VENDING MACHINE, HUH...?
Welcome.
BOXXOO-OOOOO!

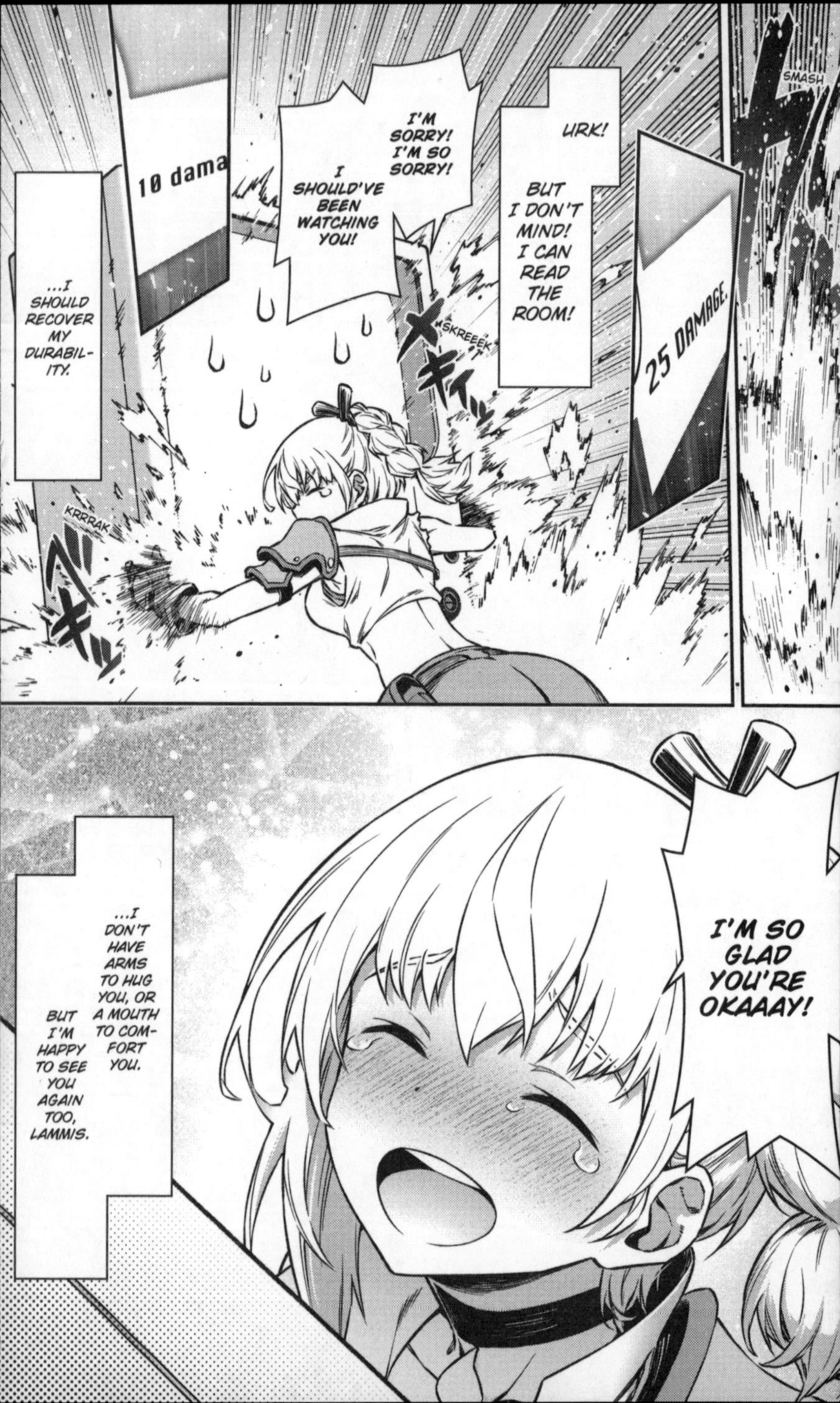
SMASH
25 DAMAGE.
URK!
BUT I DON'T MIND! I CAN READ THE ROOM!
I'M SORRY! I'M SO SORRY!
I SHOULD'VE BEEN WATCHING YOU!
SKREEEK
10 dama
...I SHOULD RECOVER MY DURABIL-ITY.
KRRRAK
I'M SO GLAD YOU'RE OKAAAY!
...I DON'T HAVE ARMS TO HUG YOU, OR A MOUTH TO COM-FORT YOU.
BUT I'M HAPPY TO SEE YOU AGAIN TOO, LAMMIS.

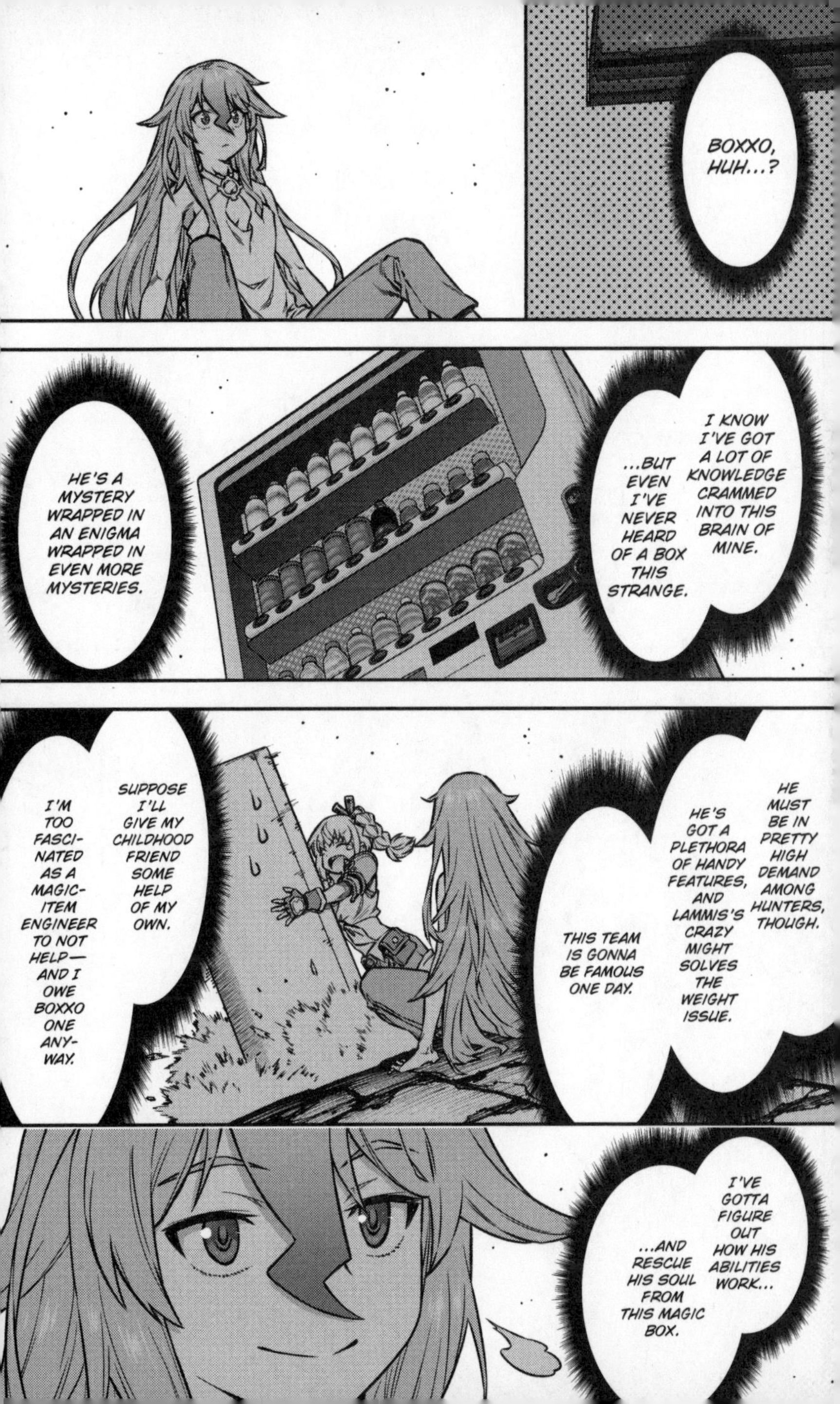
BOXXO, HUH...?
I KNOW I'VE GOT A LOT OF KNOWLEDGE CRAMMED INTO THIS BRAIN OF MINE.
...BUT EVEN I'VE NEVER HEARD OF A BOX THIS STRANGE.
HE'S A MYSTERY WRAPPED IN AN ENIGMA WRAPPED IN EVEN MORE MYSTERIES.
HE MUST BE IN PRETTY HIGH DEMAND AMONG HUNTERS, THOUGH.
HE'S GOT A PLETHORA OF HANDY FEATURES, AND LAMMIS'S CRAZY MIGHT SOLVES THE WEIGHT ISSUE.
THIS TEAM IS GONNA BE FAMOUS ONE DAY.
SUPPOSE I'LL GIVE MY CHILDHOOD FRIEND SOME HELP OF MY OWN.
I'M TOO FASCI-NATED AS A MAGIC-ITEM ENGINEER TO NOT HELP—AND I OWE BOXXO ONE ANY-WAY.
I'VE GOTTA FIGURE OUT HOW HIS ABILITIES WORK...
...AND RESCUE HIS SOUL FROM THIS MAGIC BOX.

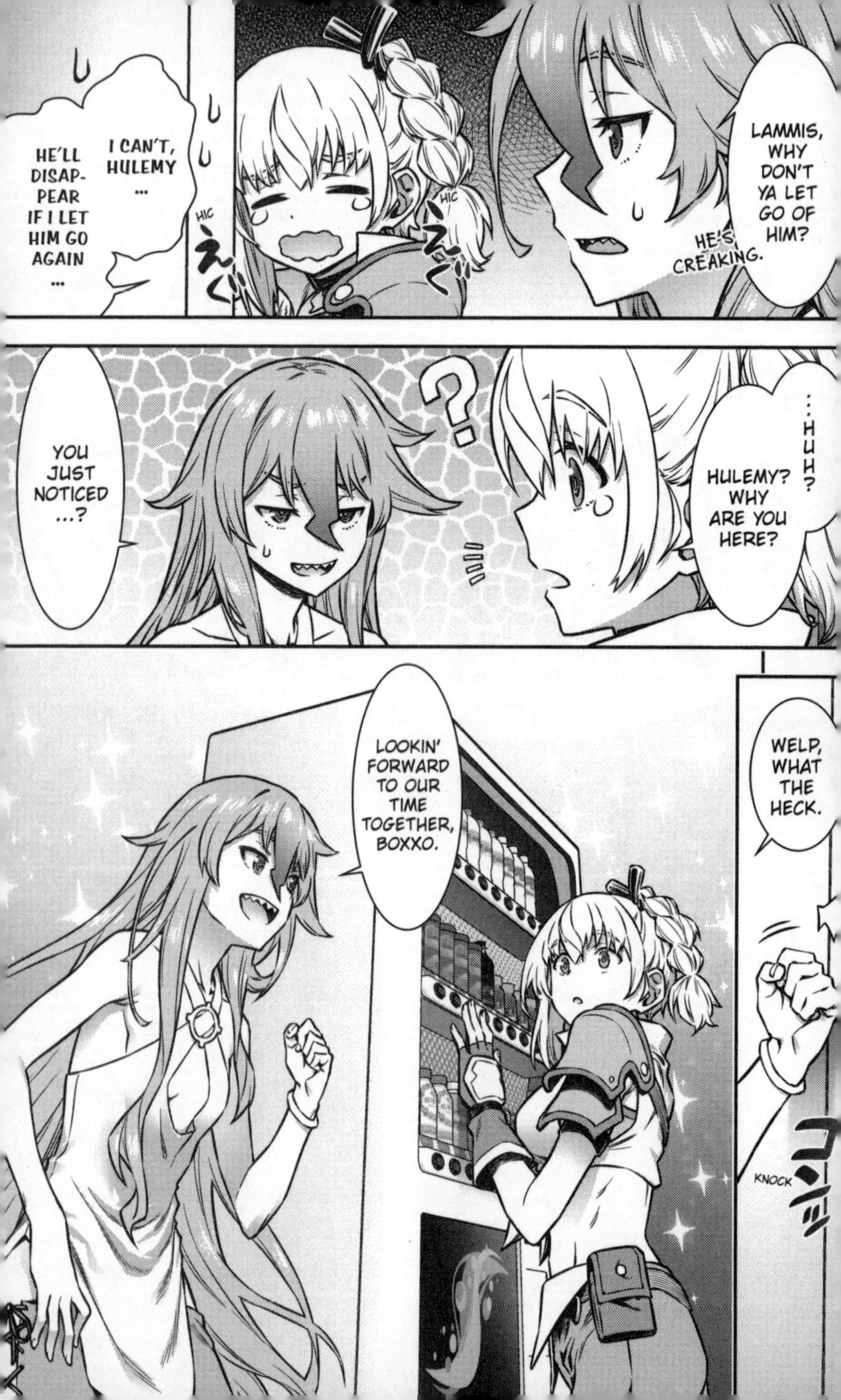
LAMMIS, WHY DON'T YA LET GO OF HIM?
HE'S CREAKING.
HIC
HIC
I CAN'T, HULEMY ...
HE'LL DISAP-PEAR IF I LET HIM GO AGAIN ...
...HUH?
HULEMY? WHY ARE YOU HERE?
YOU JUST NOTICED ...?
WELP, WHAT THE HECK.
KNOCK
LOOKIN' FORWARD TO OUR TIME TOGETHER, BOXXO.

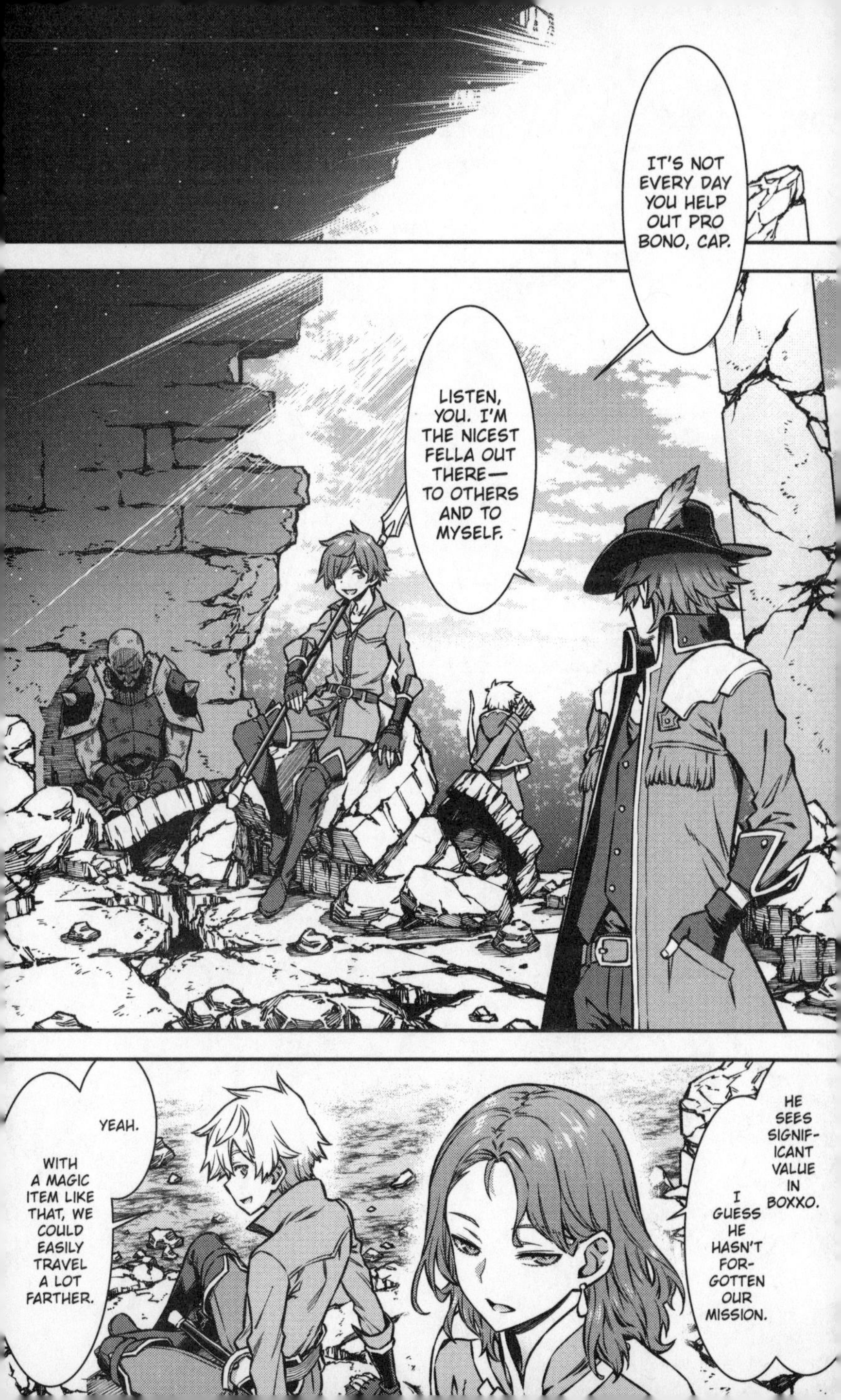
IT'S NOT EVERY DAY YOU HELP OUT PRO BONO, CAP.
LISTEN, YOU. I'M THE NICEST FELLA OUT THERE— TO OTHERS AND TO MYSELF.
HE SEES SIGNIF-ICANT VALUE IN BOXXO.
I GUESS HE HASN'T FOR-GOTTEN OUR MISSION.
YEAH.
WITH A MAGIC ITEM LIKE THAT, WE COULD EASILY TRAVEL A LOT FARTHER.

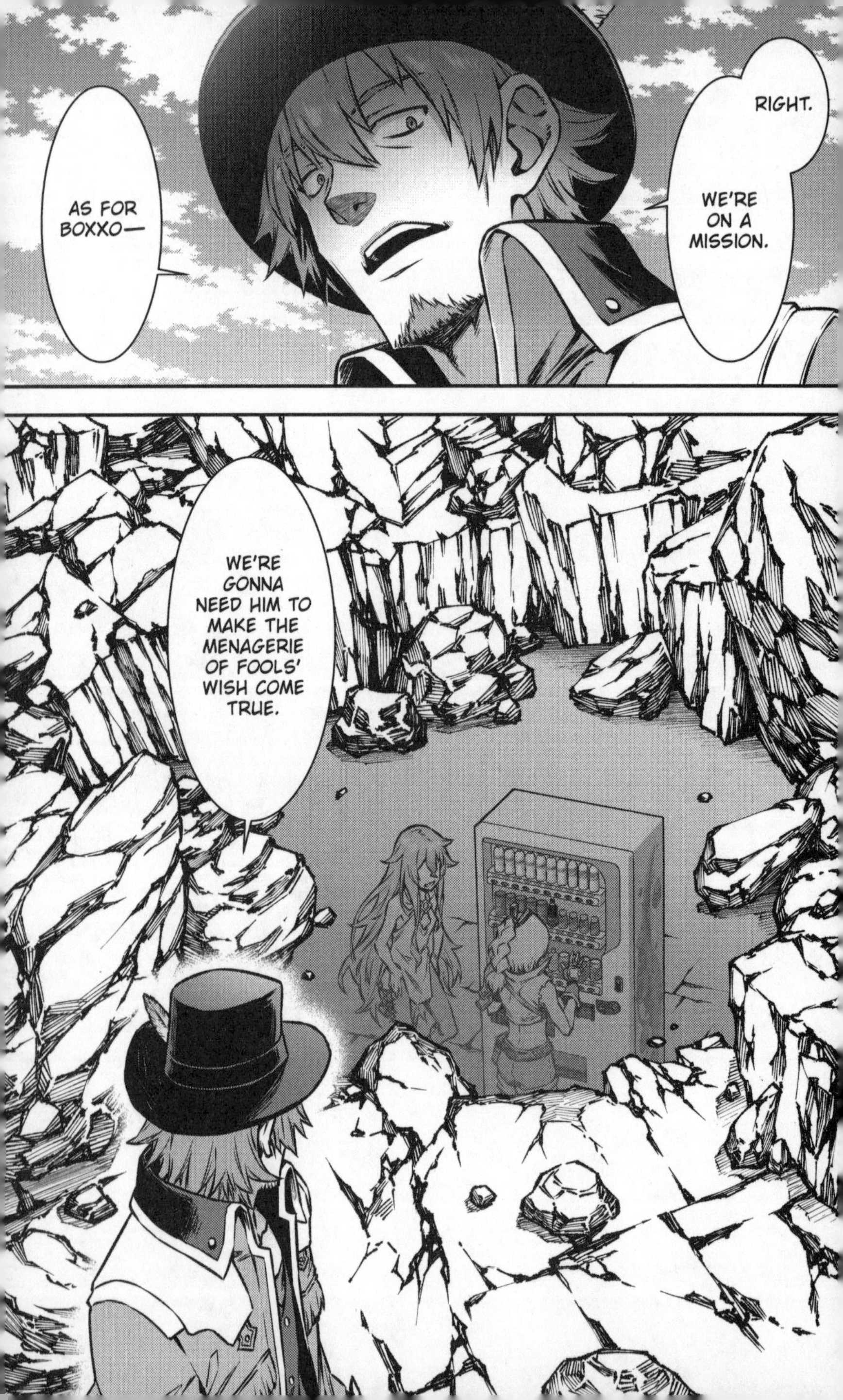
RIGHT.
WE'RE ON A MISSION.
AS FOR BOXXO—
WE'RE GONNA NEED HIM TO MAKE THE MENAGERIE OF FOOLS' WISH COME TRUE.

CHAPTER 13 TOGETHER

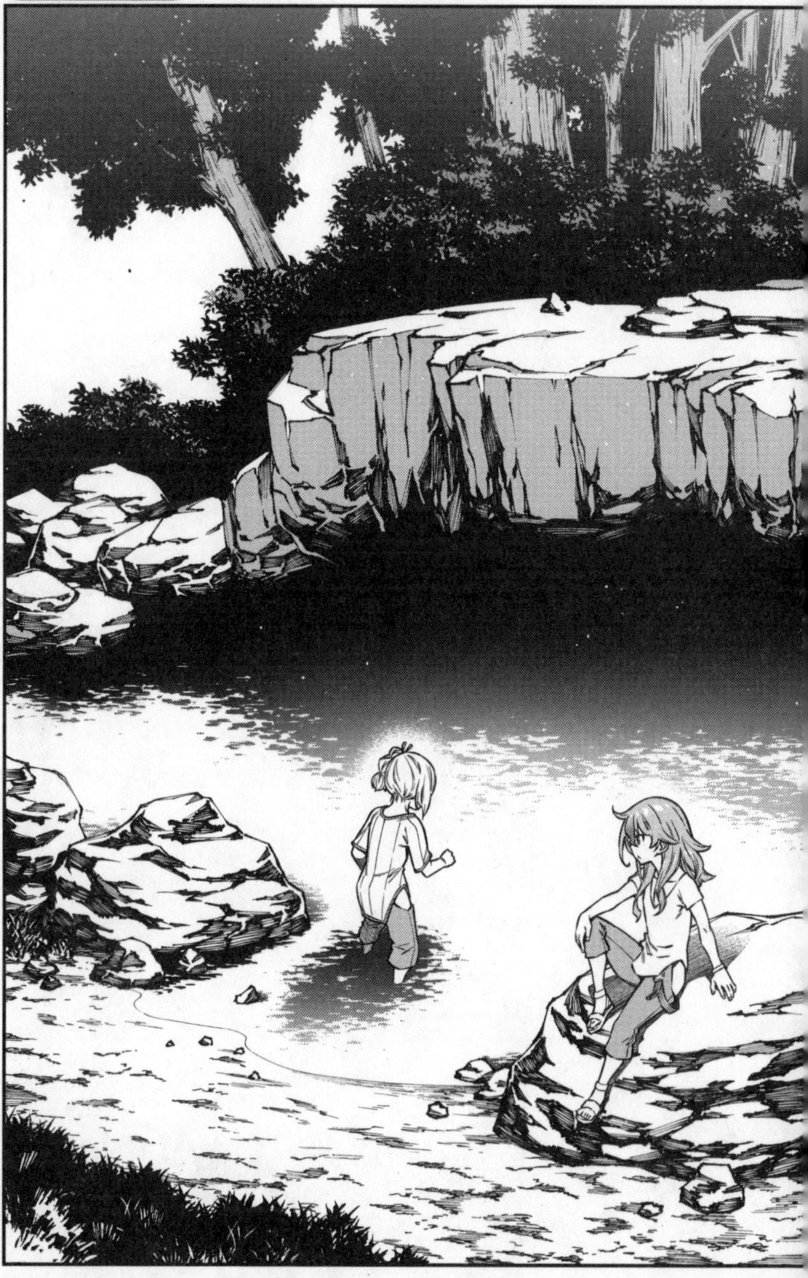

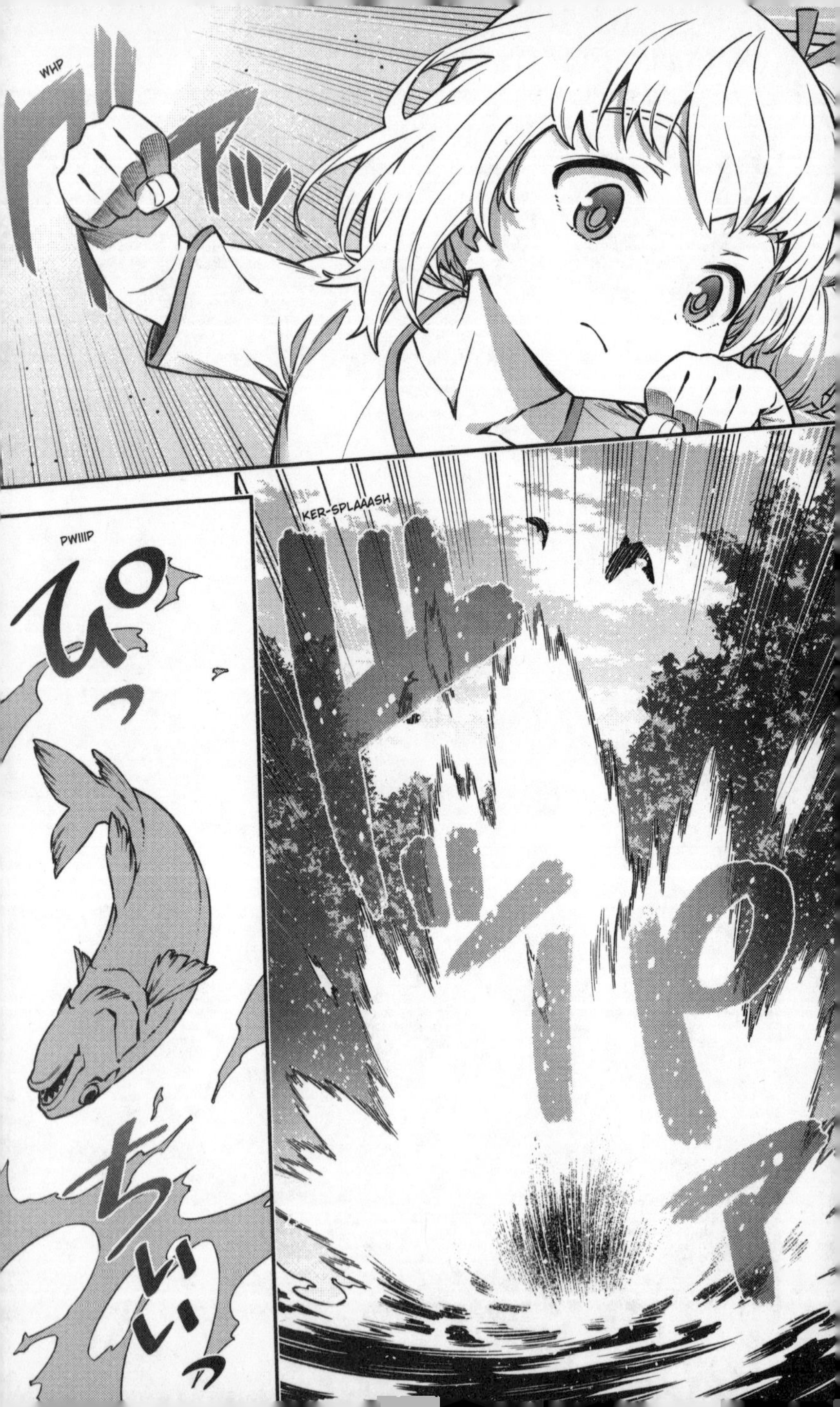
WHP
KER-SPLAAASH
PWIIIP

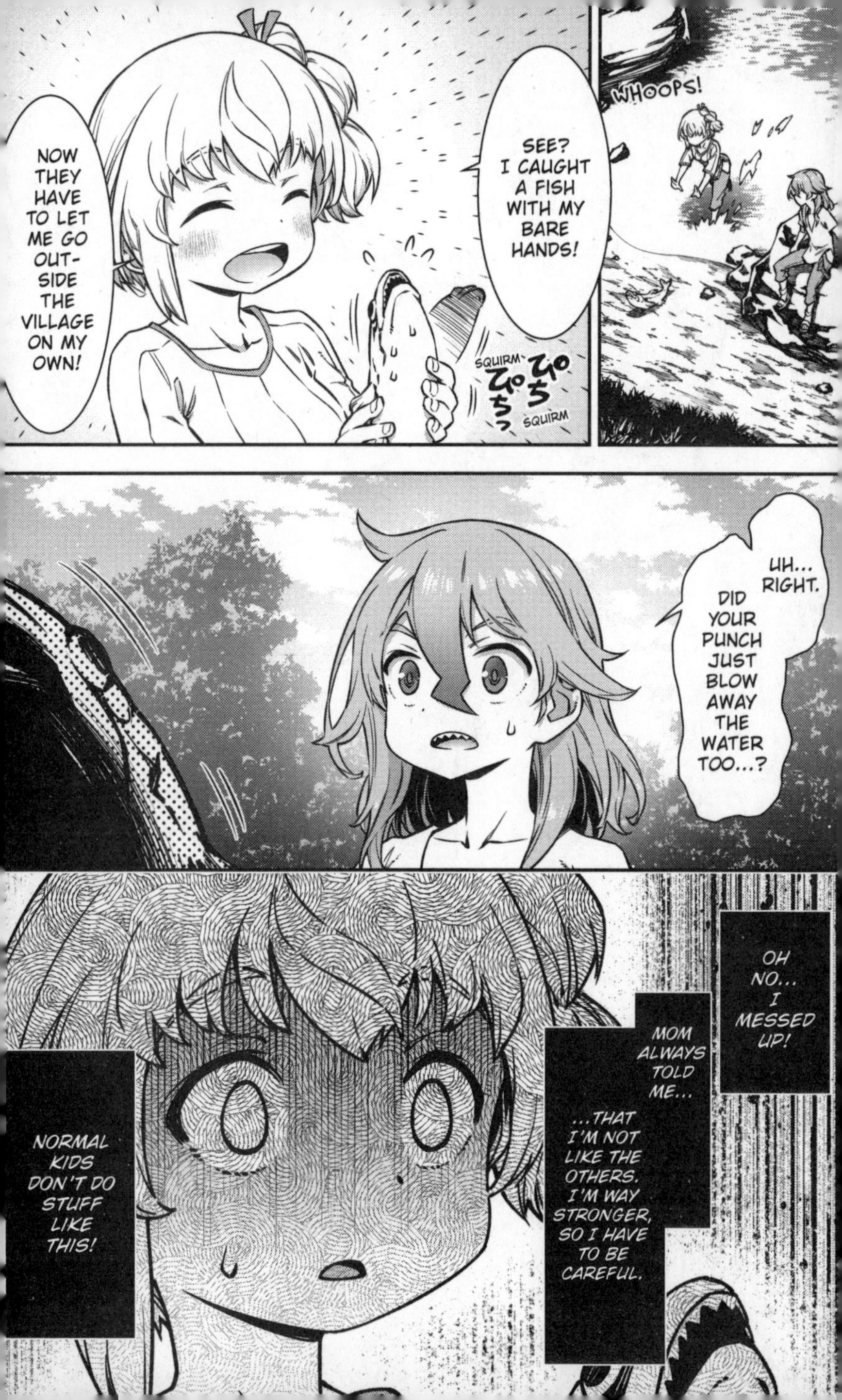
WHOOPS!
SEE? I CAUGHT A FISH WITH MY BARE HANDS!
NOW THEY HAVE TO LET ME GO OUT-SIDE THE VILLAGE ON MY OWN!
ぴち SQUIRM
ぴちっ SQUIRM
UH... RIGHT. DID YOUR PUNCH JUST BLOW AWAY THE WATER TOO...?
OH NO... I MESSED UP!
MOM ALWAYS TOLD ME...
...THAT I'M NOT LIKE THE OTHERS. I'M WAY STRONGER, SO I HAVE TO BE CAREFUL.
NORMAL KIDS DON'T DO STUFF LIKE THIS!

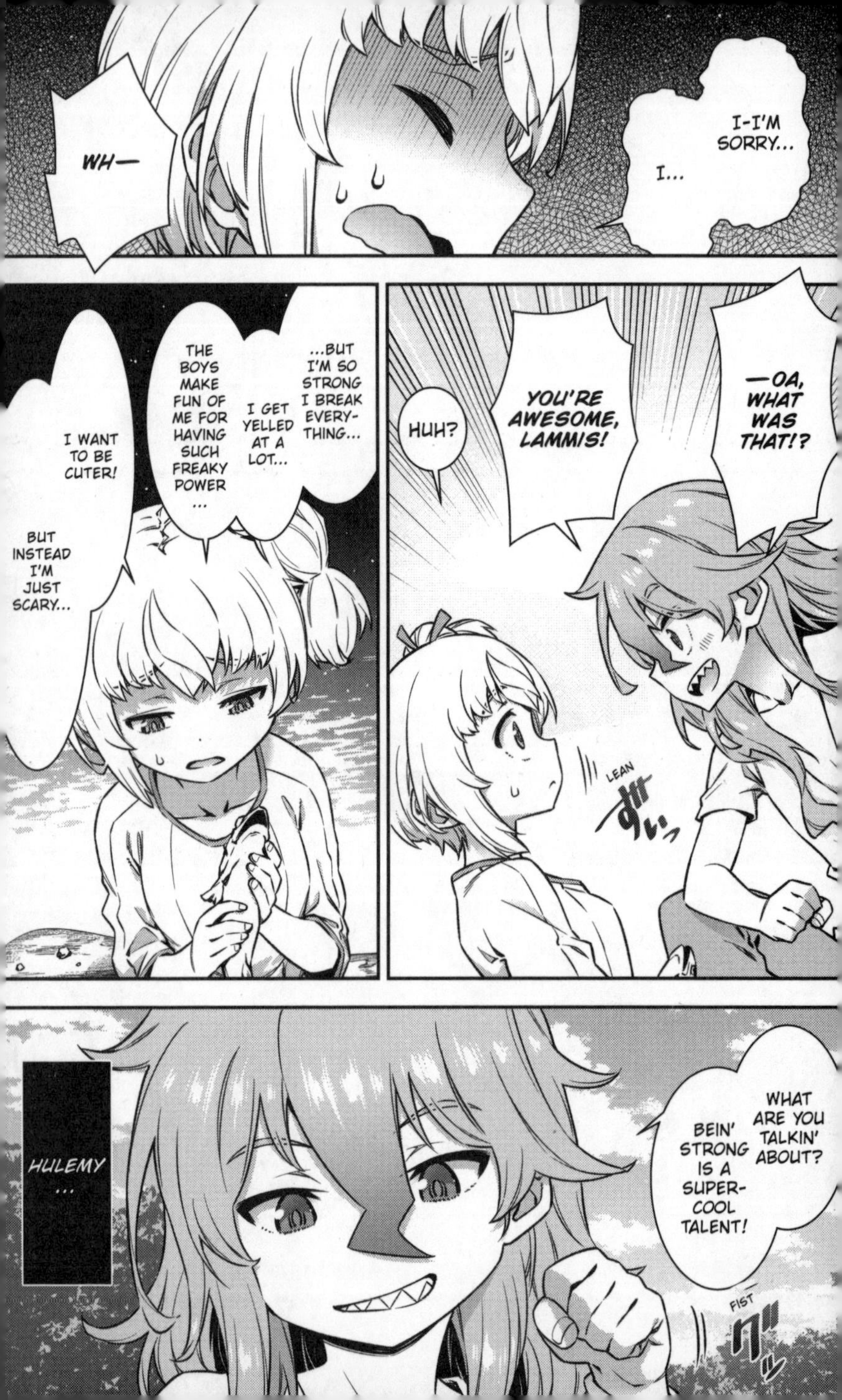
I-I'M SORRY...
I...
WH—
—OA, WHAT WAS THAT!?
YOU'RE AWESOME, LAMMIS!
HUH?
LEAN
...BUT I'M SO STRONG I BREAK EVERY-THING...
I GET YELLED AT A LOT...
THE BOYS MAKE FUN OF ME FOR HAVING SUCH FREAKY POWER...
I WANT TO BE CUTER!
BUT INSTEAD I'M JUST SCARY...
WHAT ARE YOU TALKIN' ABOUT?
BEIN' STRONG IS A SUPER-COOL TALENT!
FIST
HULEMY...

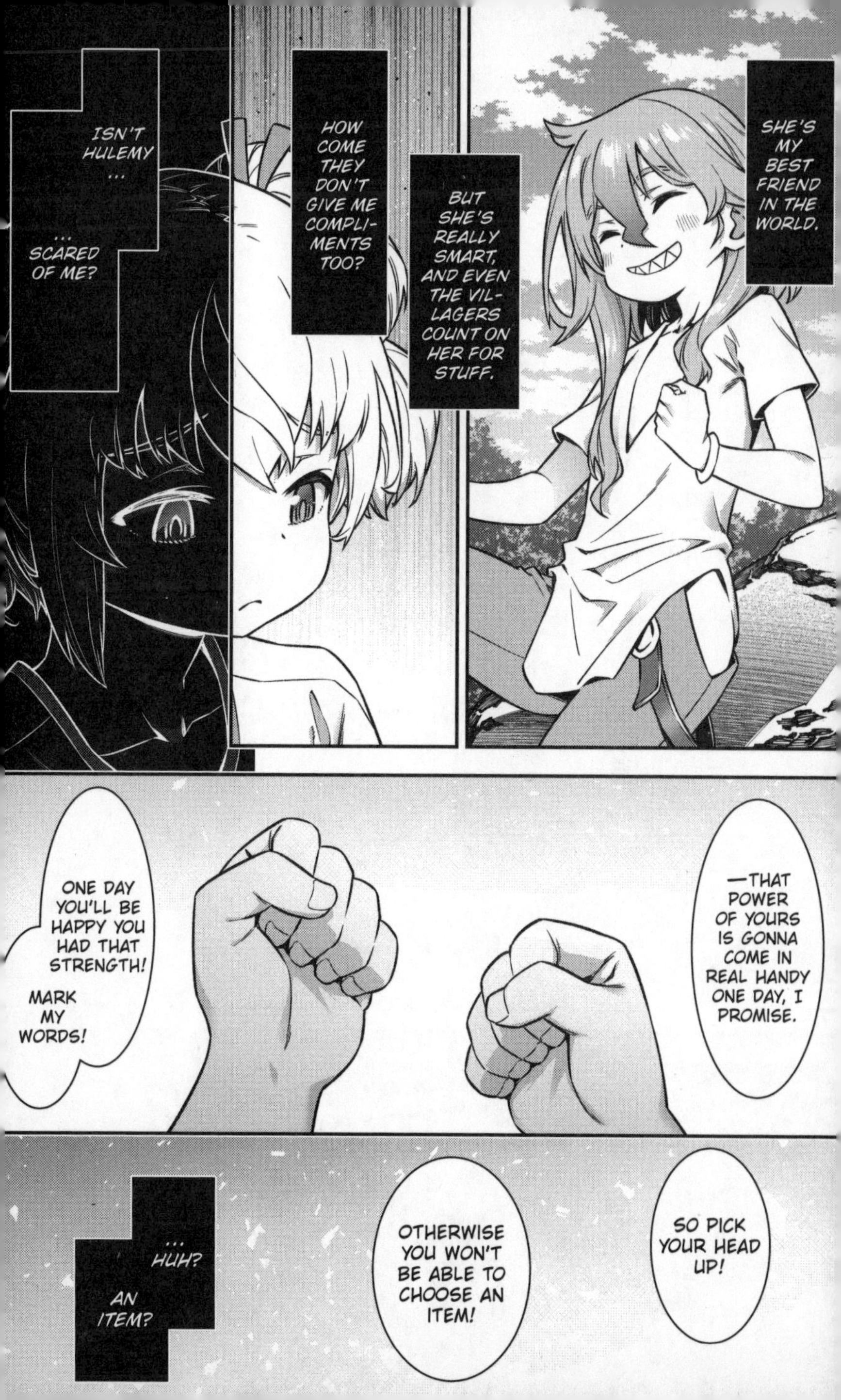
SHE'S MY BEST FRIEND IN THE WORLD.
BUT SHE'S REALLY SMART, AND EVEN THE VILLAGERS COUNT ON HER FOR STUFF.
HOW COME THEY DON'T GIVE ME COMPLIMENTS TOO?
ISN'T HULEMY...
...SCARED OF ME?
—THAT POWER OF YOURS IS GONNA COME IN REAL HANDY ONE DAY, I PROMISE.
ONE DAY YOU'LL BE HAPPY YOU HAD THAT STRENGTH!
MARK MY WORDS!
SO PICK YOUR HEAD UP!
OTHERWISE YOU WON'T BE ABLE TO CHOOSE AN ITEM!
...HUH?
AN ITEM?

OH...

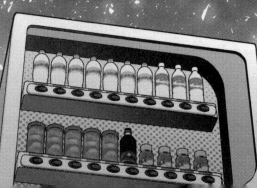

Welcome.

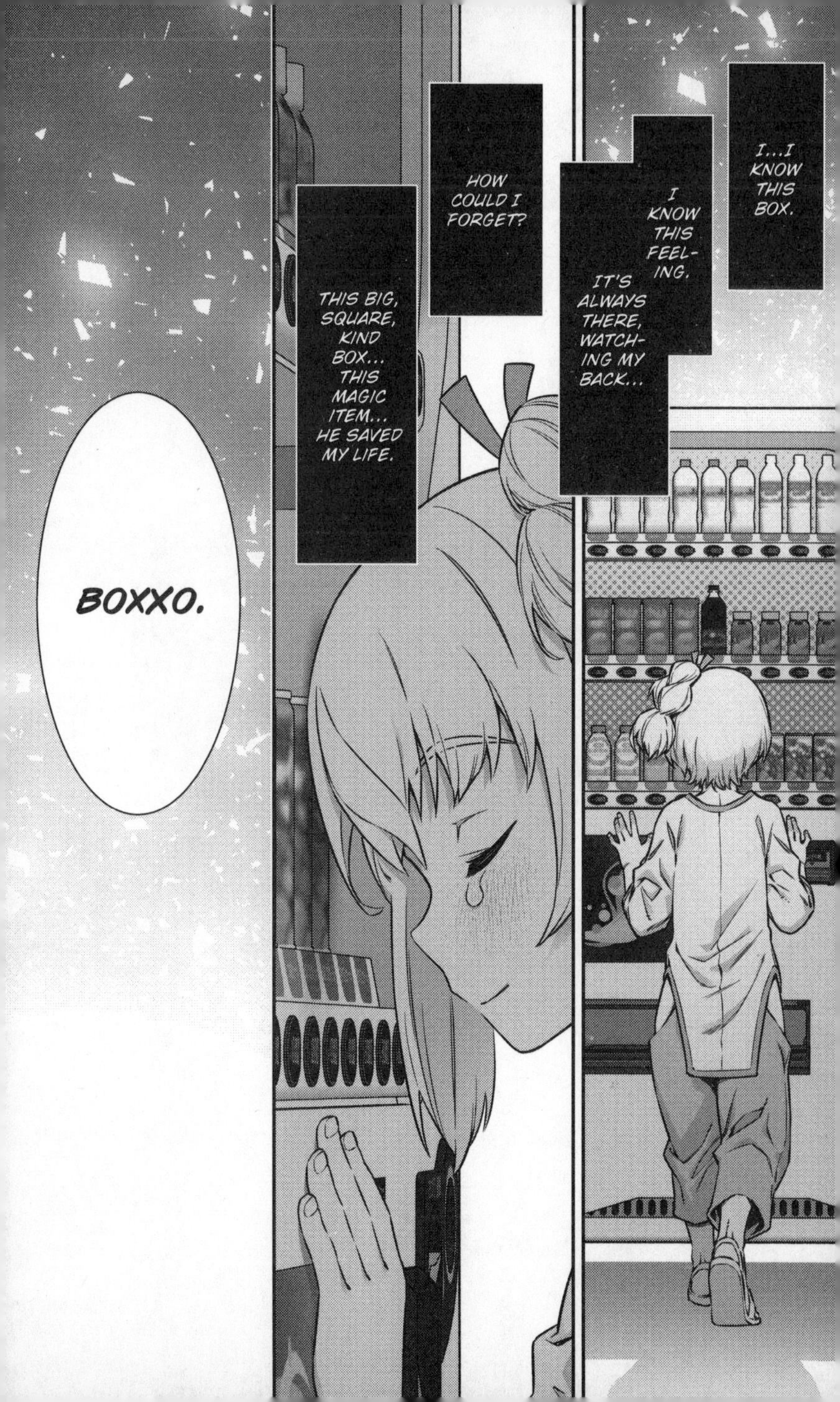
I...I KNOW THIS BOX.
I KNOW THIS FEEL-ING.
IT'S ALWAYS THERE, WATCH-ING MY BACK...
HOW COULD I FORGET?
THIS BIG, SQUARE, KIND BOX... THIS MAGIC ITEM... HE SAVED MY LIFE.
BOXXO.

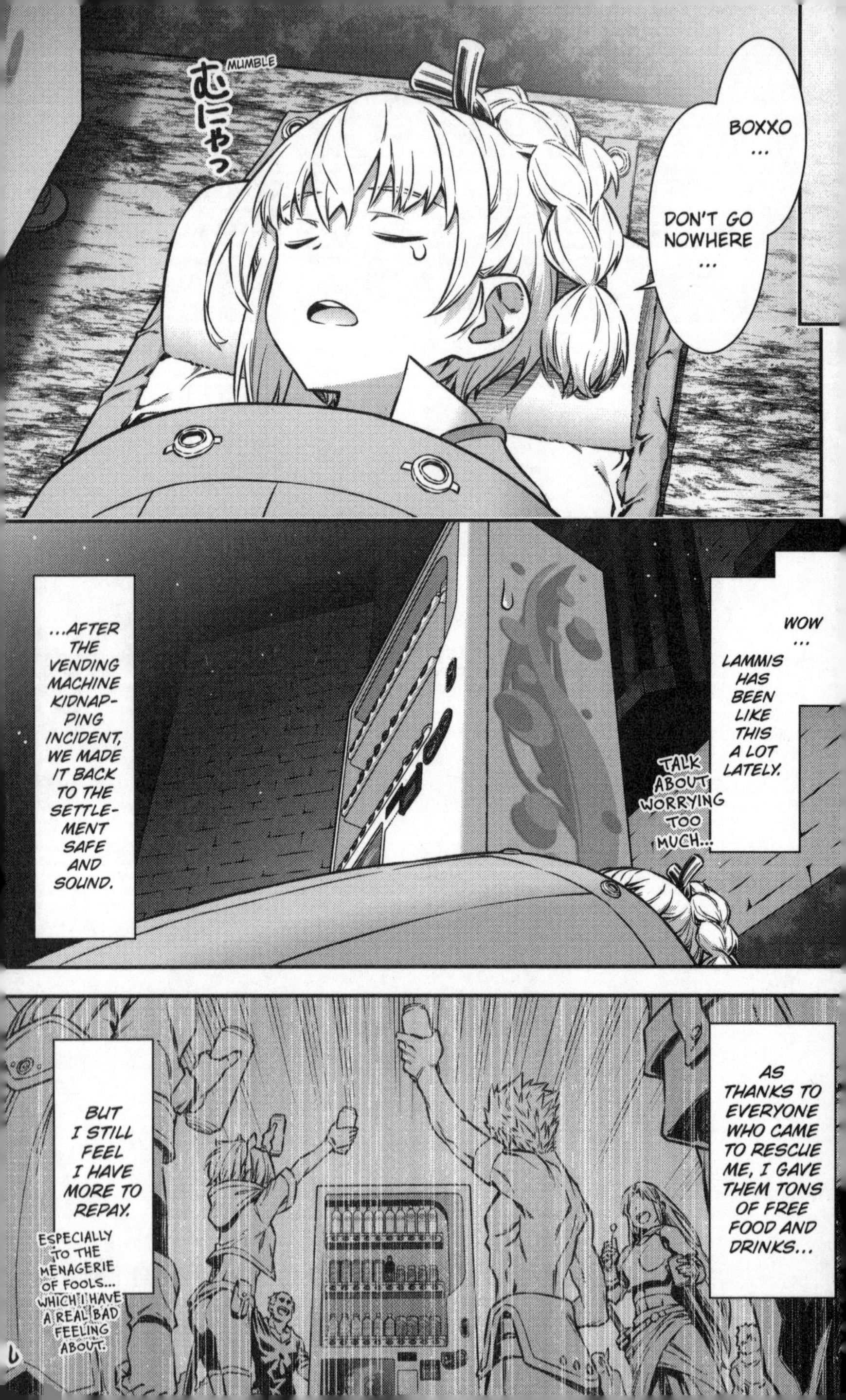
BOXXO ... DON'T GO NOWHERE ...
MUMBLE むにゃっ
WOW ... LAMMIS HAS BEEN LIKE THIS A LOT LATELY.
TALK ABOUT WORRYING TOO MUCH...
...AFTER THE VENDING MACHINE KIDNAP-PING INCIDENT, WE MADE IT BACK TO THE SETTLE-MENT SAFE AND SOUND.
AS THANKS TO EVERYONE WHO CAME TO RESCUE ME, I GAVE THEM TONS OF FREE FOOD AND DRINKS...
BUT I STILL FEEL I HAVE MORE TO REPAY.
ESPECIALLY TO THE MENAGERIE OF FOOLS... WHICH I HAVE A REAL BAD FEELING ABOUT.

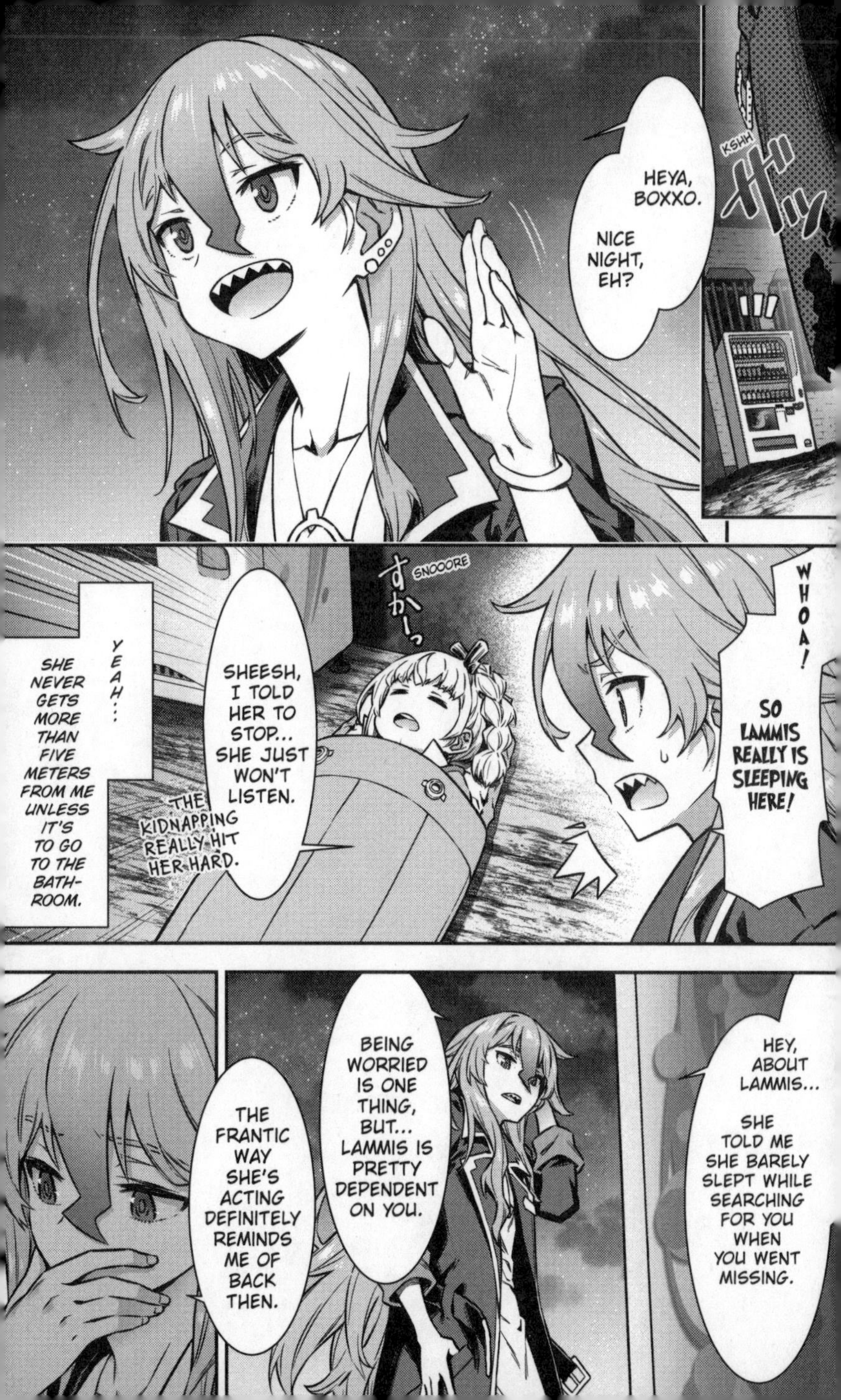

KSHH
ザッ
HEYA, BOXXO.
NICE NIGHT, EH?
WHOA!
SO LAMMIS REALLY IS SLEEPING HERE!
すかーっ
SNOOORE
SHEESH, I TOLD HER TO STOP... SHE JUST WON'T LISTEN.
THE KIDNAPPING REALLY HIT HER HARD.
YEAH...
SHE NEVER GETS MORE THAN FIVE METERS FROM ME UNLESS IT'S TO GO TO THE BATH-ROOM.
HEY, ABOUT LAMMIS...
SHE TOLD ME SHE BARELY SLEPT WHILE SEARCHING FOR YOU WHEN YOU WENT MISSING.
BEING WORRIED IS ONE THING, BUT... LAMMIS IS PRETTY DEPENDENT ON YOU.
THE FRANTIC WAY SHE'S ACTING DEFINITELY REMINDS ME OF BACK THEN.

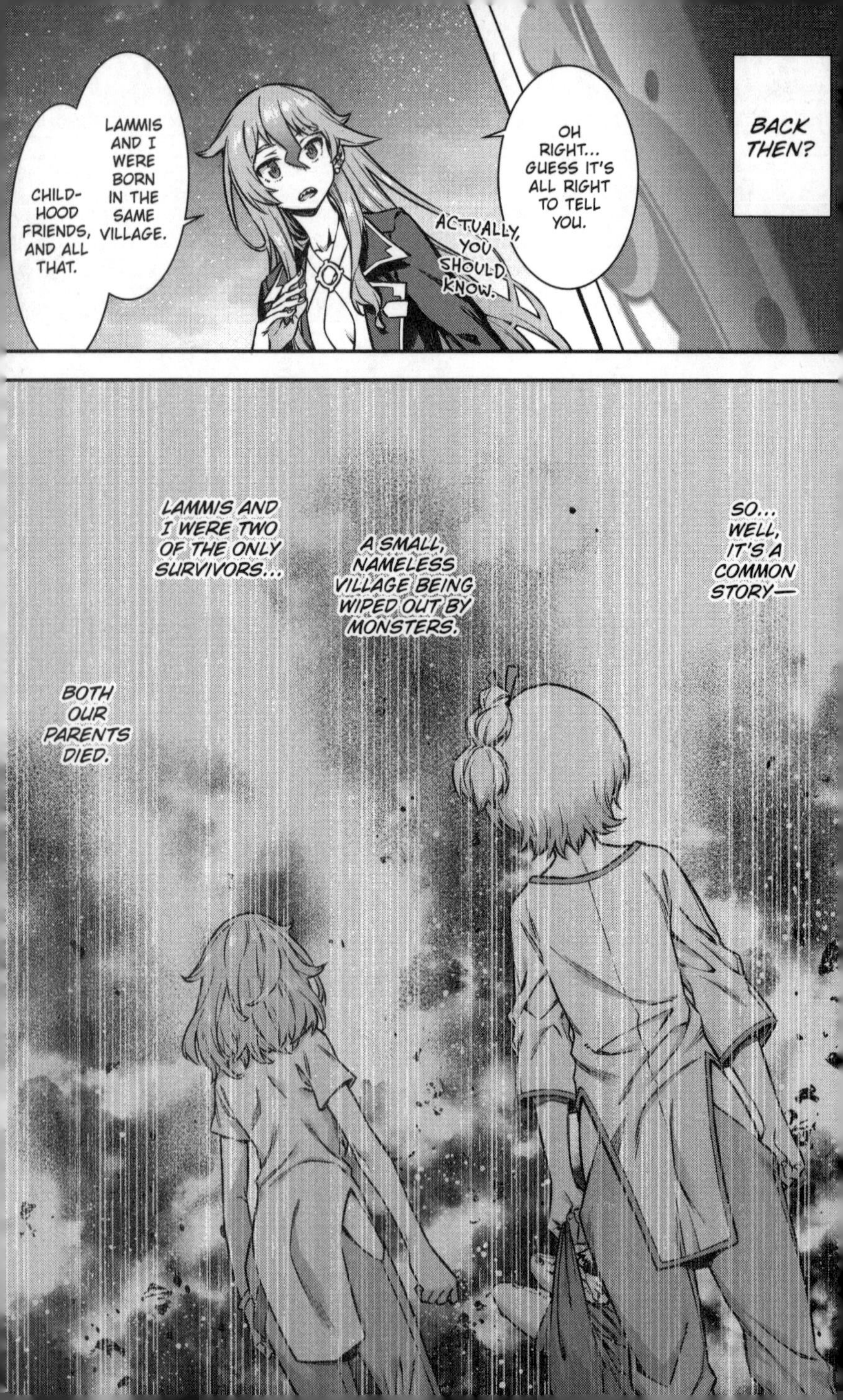
BACK THEN?
OH RIGHT... GUESS IT'S ALL RIGHT TO TELL YOU.
ACTUALLY, YOU SHOULD KNOW.
LAMMIS AND I WERE BORN IN THE SAME VILLAGE.
CHILD-HOOD FRIENDS, AND ALL THAT.
SO... WELL, IT'S A COMMON STORY—
A SMALL, NAMELESS VILLAGE BEING WIPED OUT BY MONSTERS.
LAMMIS AND I WERE TWO OF THE ONLY SURVIVORS...
BOTH OUR PARENTS DIED.

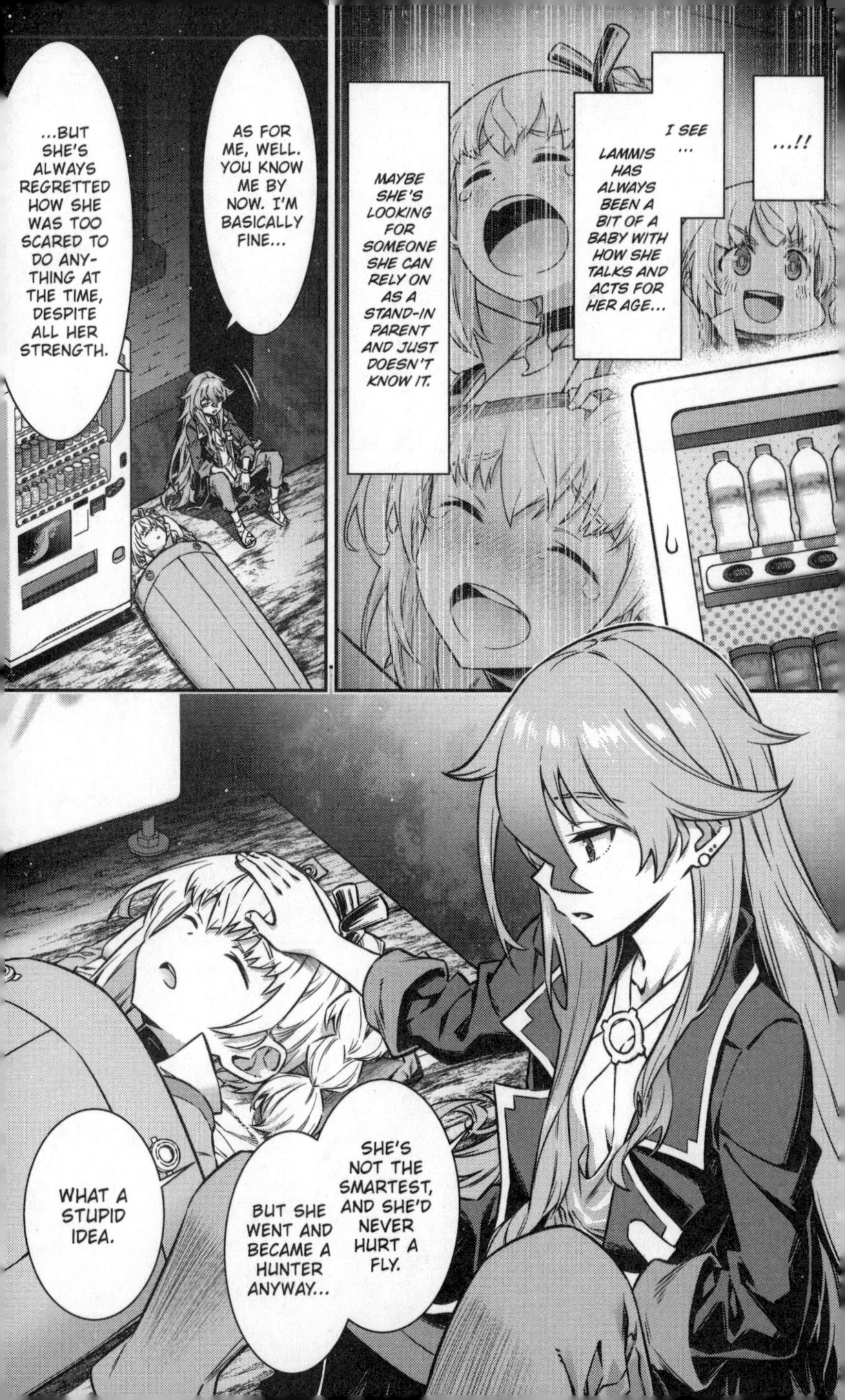
...!!
I SEE ... LAMMIS HAS ALWAYS BEEN A BIT OF A BABY WITH HOW SHE TALKS AND ACTS FOR HER AGE...
MAYBE SHE'S LOOKING FOR SOMEONE SHE CAN RELY ON AS A STAND-IN PARENT AND JUST DOESN'T KNOW IT.
AS FOR ME, WELL. YOU KNOW ME BY NOW. I'M BASICALLY FINE...
...BUT SHE'S ALWAYS REGRETTED HOW SHE WAS TOO SCARED TO DO ANY-THING AT THE TIME, DESPITE ALL HER STRENGTH.
SHE'S NOT THE SMARTEST, AND SHE'D NEVER HURT A FLY.
BUT SHE WENT AND BECAME A HUNTER ANYWAY...
WHAT A STUPID IDEA.

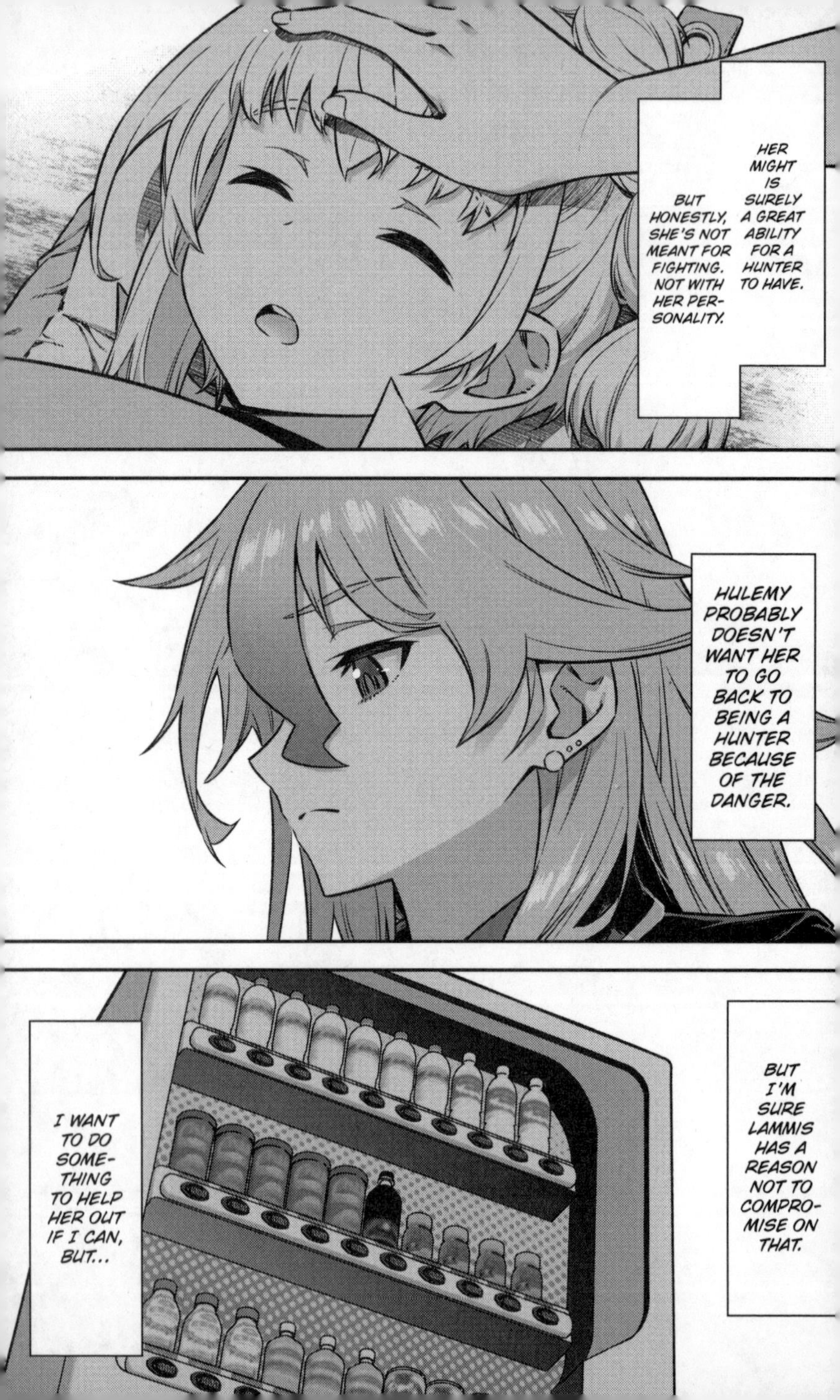
HER MIGHT IS SURELY A GREAT ABILITY FOR A HUNTER TO HAVE.
BUT HONESTLY, SHE'S NOT MEANT FOR FIGHTING. NOT WITH HER PER-SONALITY.
HULEMY PROBABLY DOESN'T WANT HER TO GO BACK TO BEING A HUNTER BECAUSE OF THE DANGER.
BUT I'M SURE LAMMIS HAS A REASON NOT TO COMPRO-MISE ON THAT.
I WANT TO DO SOME-THING TO HELP HER OUT IF I CAN, BUT...

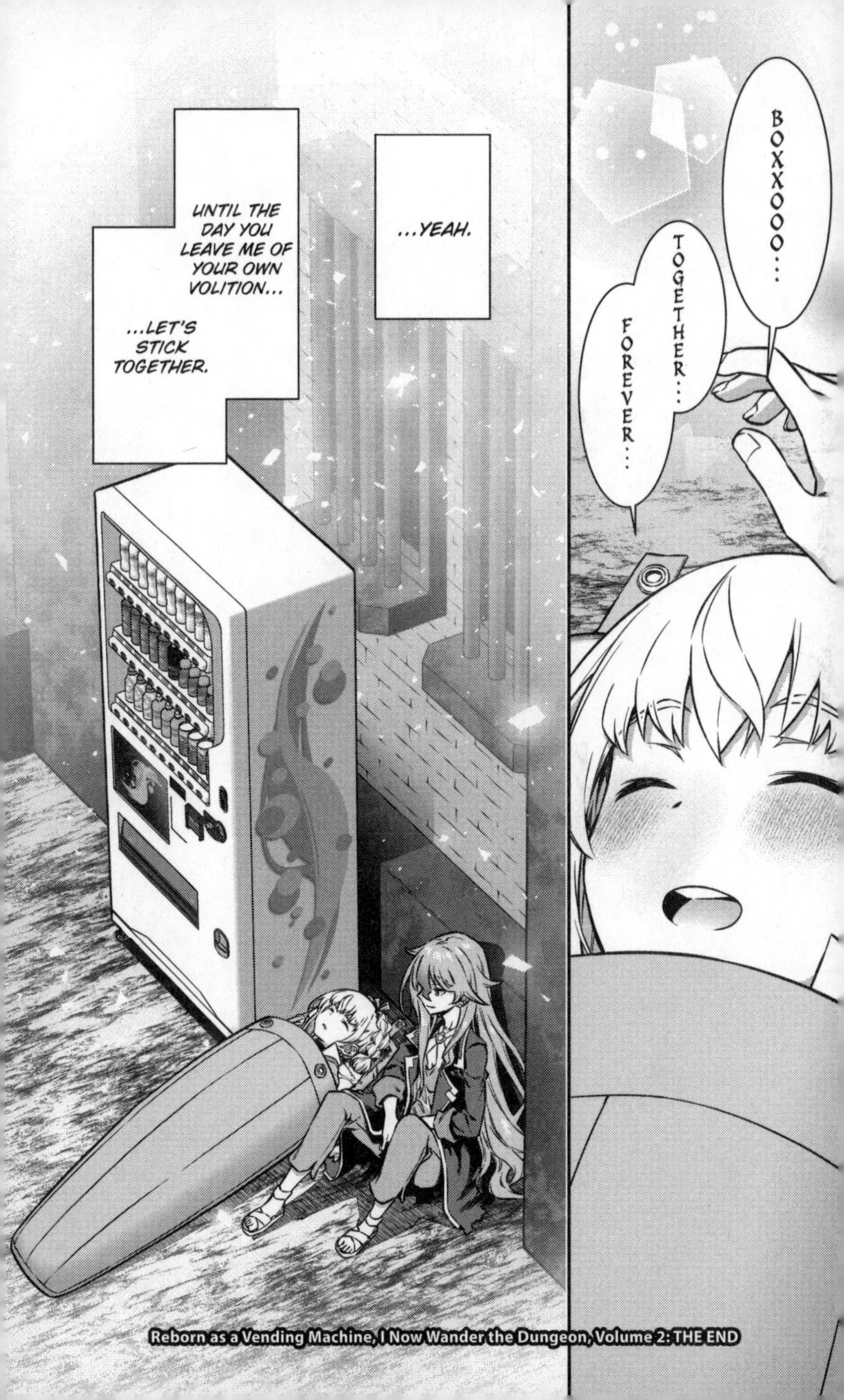
BOXOOO...
TOGETHER...
FOREVER...
UNTIL THE DAY YOU LEAVE ME OF YOUR OWN VOLITION...
...LET'S STICK TOGETHER.
...YEAH.
Reborn as a Vending Machine, I Now Wander the Dungeon, Volume 2: THE END

Reborn as a Vending Machine, I Now Wander the
DUNGEON

AFTERWORD

Thank you so much for purchasing this book. I'm Kunieda.

I've recently been buying a lot of ramen with strange soup or stew flavors. They're pretty good! Or so I say, as I eat everything I can find, occasionally feeling like I've just been punched in the gut by one...

But I tend to instantly drop the coins into any vending machine with interesting products in it. It's one of the things I look forward to when I go out.

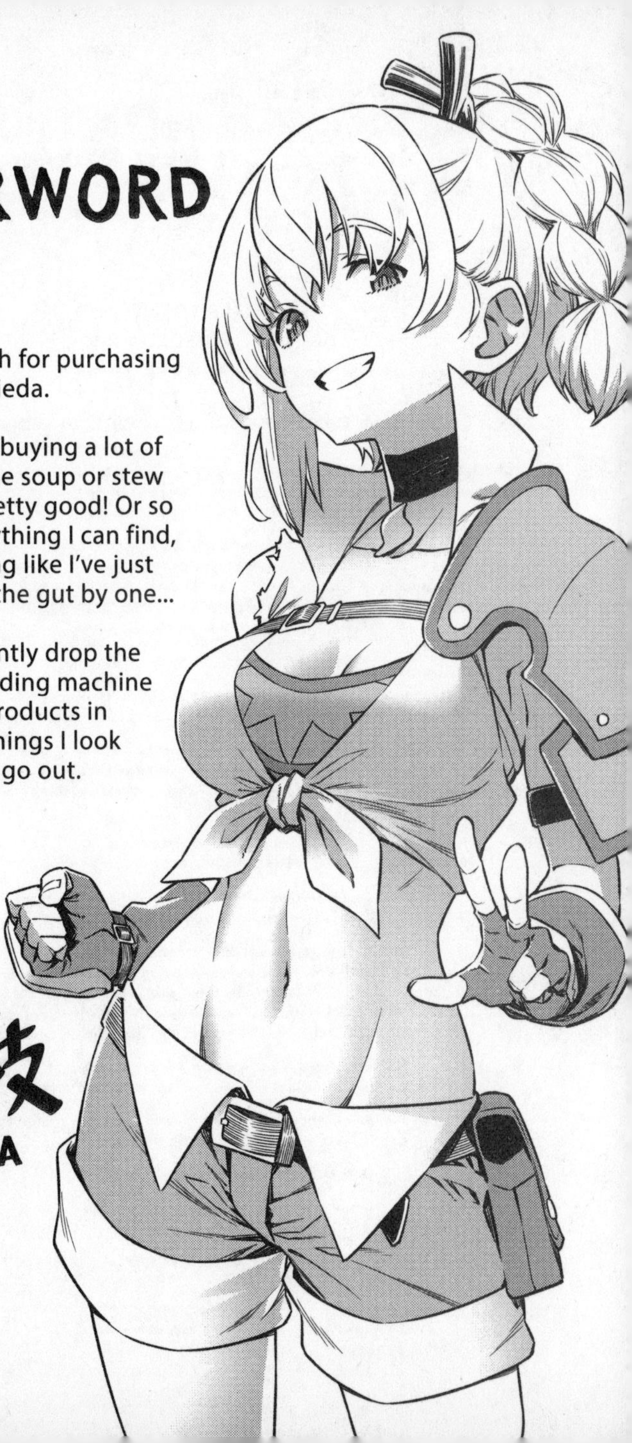

九二枝

KUNIEDA

Reborn as a Vending Machine, I Now Wander the DUNGEON

2

Art by **KUNIEDA**
Original Story by **HIRUKUMA**
Character Design by **HAGURE YUUKI**

Translation: **Alice Prowse** ★ Lettering: **Chiho Christie**

JIDO HAMBAIKI NI UMAREKAWATTA ORE WA MEIKYU O SAMAYO Vol. 2
©Kunieda/Hirukuma 2023
First published in Japan in 2023 by KADOKAWA CORPORATION, Tokyo.
English translation rights arranged with KADOKAWA CORPORATION, Tokyo
through TUTTLE-MORI AGENCY, INC., Tokyo.

English translation © 2024 by Yen Press, LLC

Yen Press
150 West 30th Street, 19th Floor
New York, NY 10001

yenpress.com • facebook.com/yenpress • twitter.com/yenpress
yenpress.tumblr.com • instagram.com/yenpress

First Yen Press Edition: March 2024
The chapters in this volume were originally published as
ebooks by Yen Press.
Edited by Yen Press Editorial: Carl Li
Designed by Yen Press Design: Lilliana Checo, Wendy Chan

Yen Press is an imprint of Yen Press, LLC.
The Yen Press name and logo are trademarks of Yen Press, LLC.

Library of Congress Control Number: 2023930044

ISBNs: 978-1-9753-9024-2 (paperback)
978-1-9753-9025-9 (ebook)

1 3 5 7 9 10 8 6 4 2

WOR

Printed in the United States of America

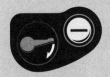

TURN TO THE BACK
OF THE BOOK TO
READ AN ORIGINAL
SHORT STORY!

Reborn as a Vending Machine, I Now Wander the DUNGEON

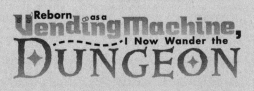

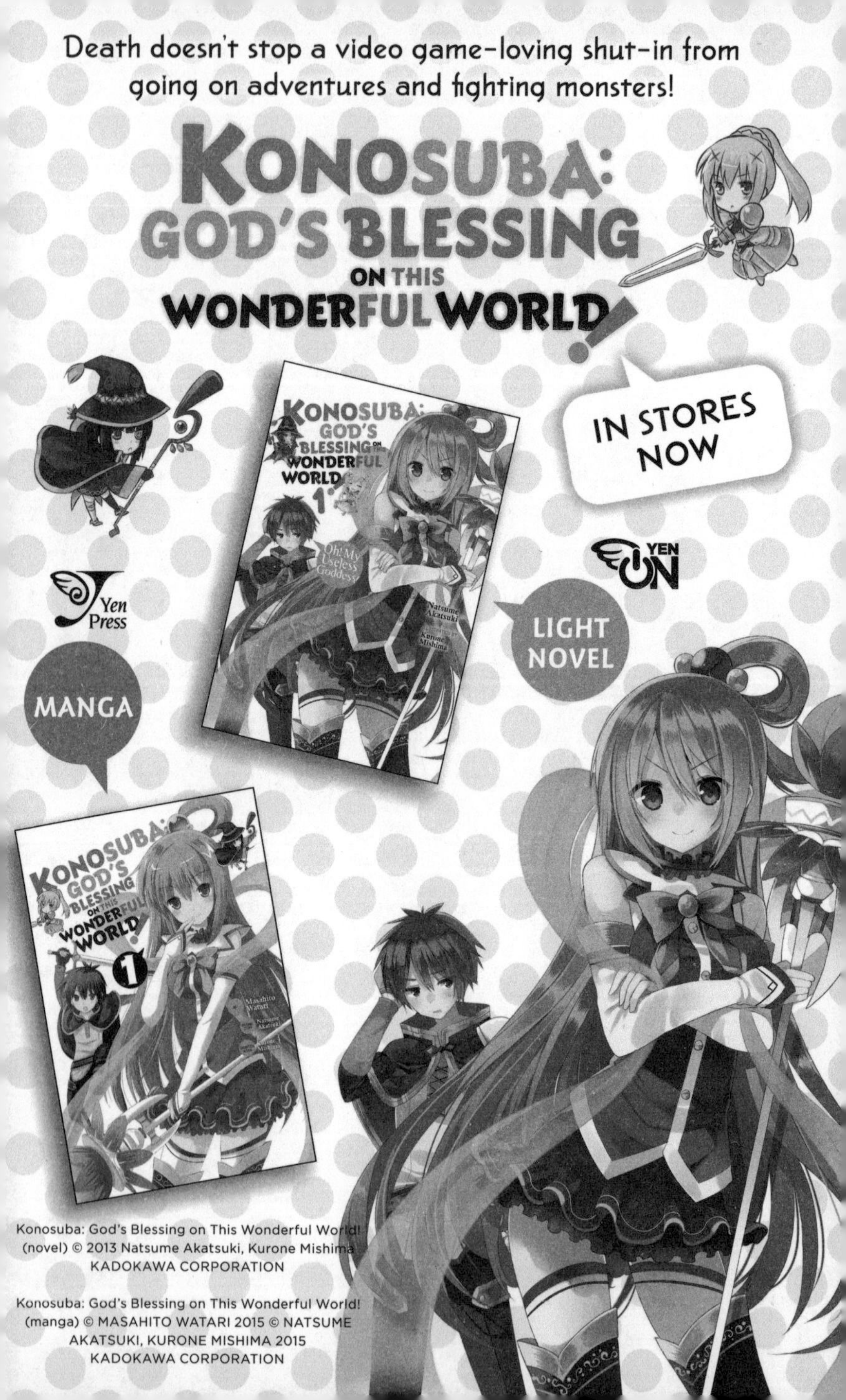

Death doesn't stop a video game-loving shut-in from going on adventures and fighting monsters!
KONOSUBA: GOD'S BLESSING ON THIS WONDERFUL WORLD!
IN STORES NOW
YEN ON
Yen Press
LIGHT NOVEL
MANGA
Konosuba: God's Blessing on This Wonderful World! (novel) © 2013 Natsume Akatsuki, Kurone Mishima KADOKAWA CORPORATION
Konosuba: God's Blessing on This Wonderful World! (manga) © MASAHITO WATARI 2015 © NATSUME AKATSUKI, KURONE MISHIMA 2015 KADOKAWA CORPORATION

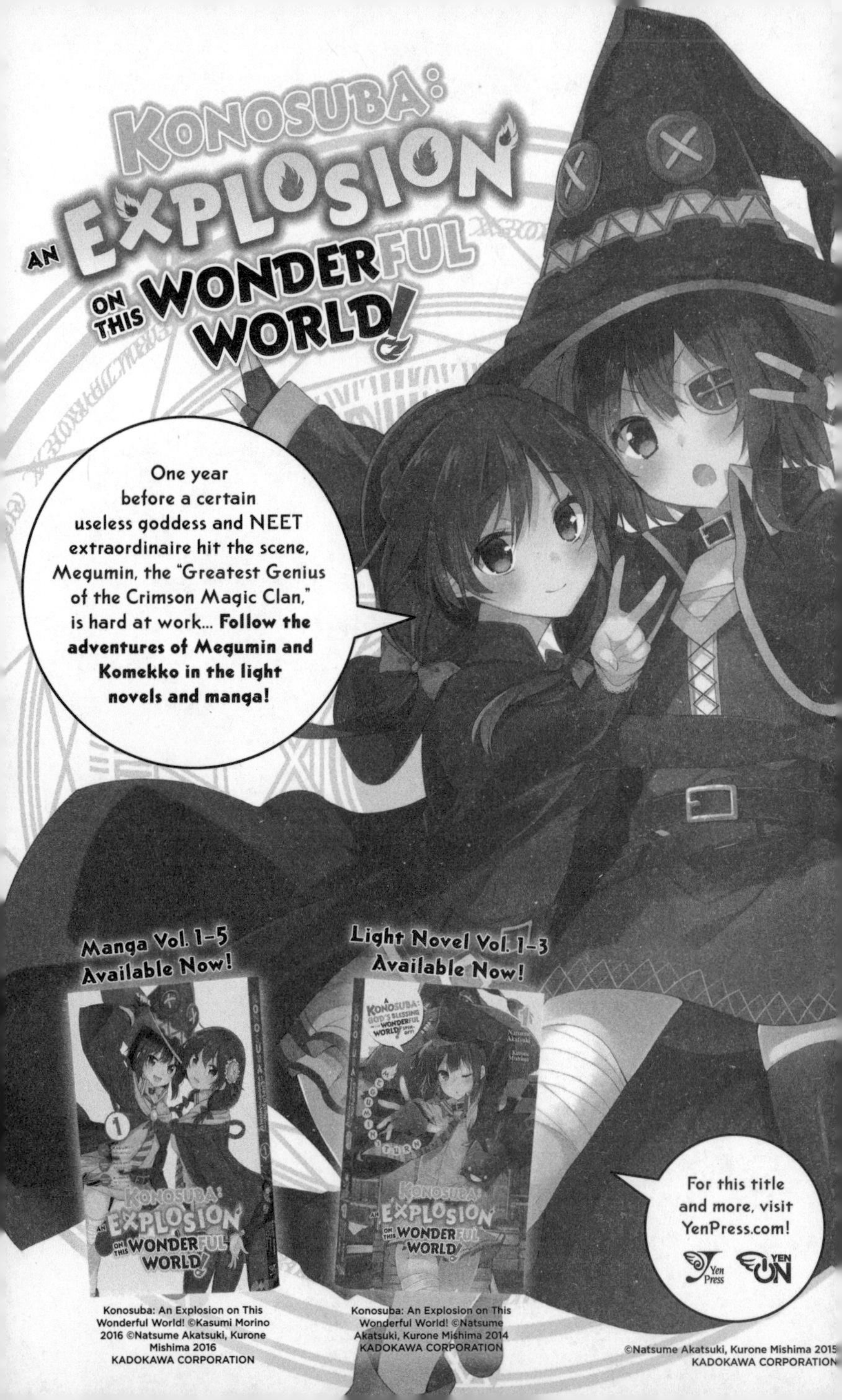
KONOSUBA: AN EXPLOSION ON THIS WONDERFUL WORLD!
One year before a certain useless goddess and NEET extraordinaire hit the scene, Megumin, the "Greatest Genius of the Crimson Magic Clan," is hard at work... Follow the adventures of Megumin and Komekko in the light novels and manga!
Manga Vol. 1–5 Available Now!
Light Novel Vol. 1–3 Available Now!
For this title and more, visit YenPress.com!
Yen Press
YEN ON
Konosuba: An Explosion on This Wonderful World! ©Kasumi Morino 2016 ©Natsume Akatsuki, Kurone Mishima 2016 KADOKAWA CORPORATION
Konosuba: An Explosion on This Wonderful World! ©Natsume Akatsuki, Kurone Mishima 2014 KADOKAWA CORPORATION
©Natsume Akatsuki, Kurone Mishima 2015 KADOKAWA CORPORATION

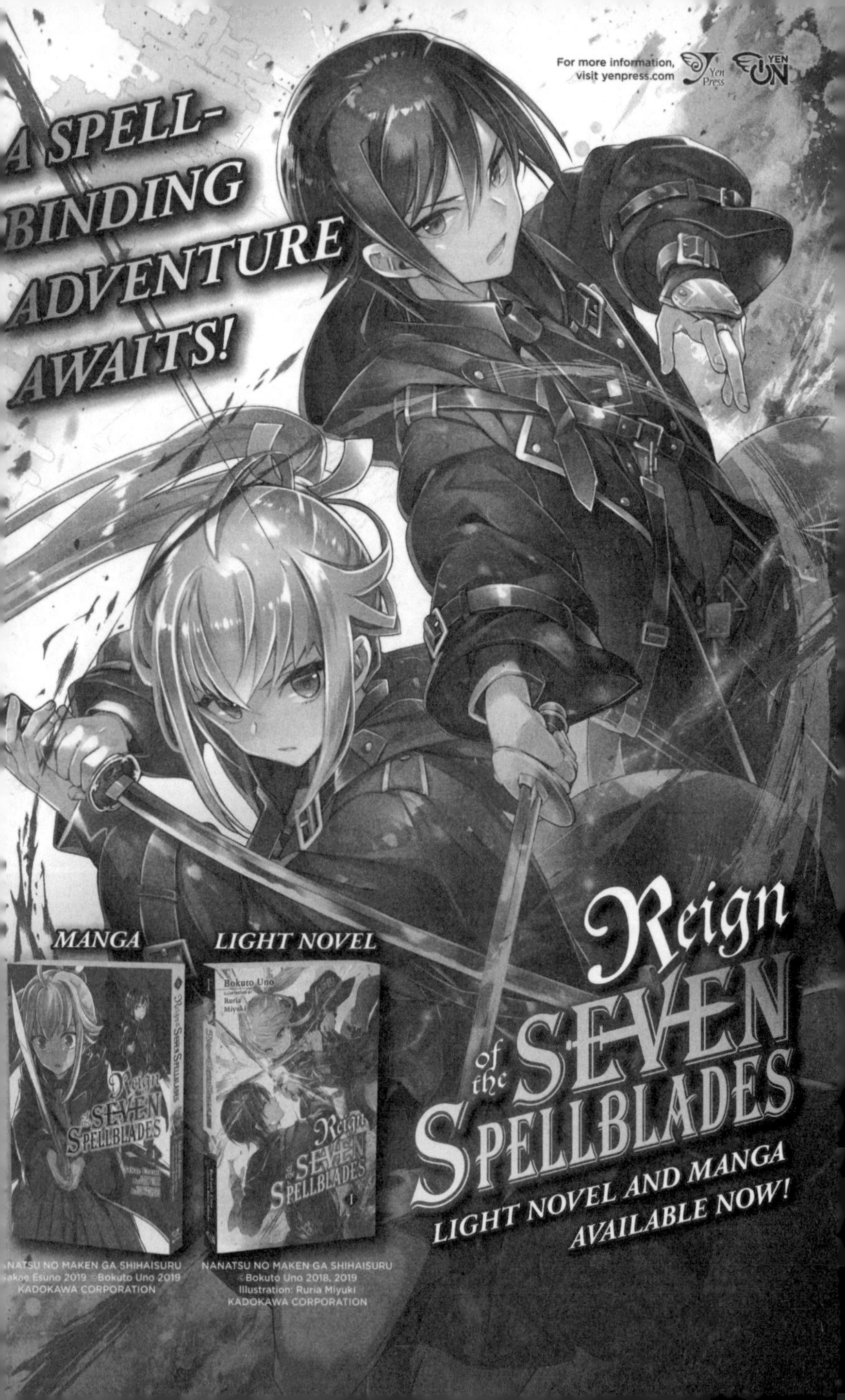
For more information, visit yenpress.com
Yen Press
YEN ON
A SPELL-BINDING ADVENTURE AWAITS!
MANGA
LIGHT NOVEL
Bokuto Uno
Ruria Miyuki
Reign of the SEVEN SPELLBLADES
LIGHT NOVEL AND MANGA AVAILABLE NOW!
NATSU NO MAKEN GA SHIHAISURU
akae Esuno 2019 ©Bokuto Uno 2019
KADOKAWA CORPORATION
NANATSU NO MAKEN GA SHIHAISURU
©Bokuto Uno 2018, 2019
Illustration: Ruria Miyuki
KADOKAWA CORPORATION

So I'm a Spider, So What?

I'M GONNA SURVIVE—JUST WATCH ME!

I was your average, everyday high school girl, but now I've been reborn in a magical world...as a spider?! How am I supposed to survive in this big, scary dungeon as one of the weakest monsters? I gotta figure out the rules to this QUICK, or I'll be kissing my short second life good-bye...

MANGA VOL. 1-12

LIGHT NOVEL VOL. 1-16

AVAILABLE NOW!

YOU CAN ALSO KEEP UP WITH THE MANGA SIMUL-PUB EVERY MONTH ONLINE!

YenPress.com

Reborn as a Vending Machine, I Now Wander the DUNGEON

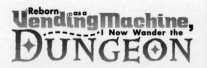

"Okay, I will! But only for as long as I can."

"Yes, yes. We'll work as quickly as possible. Hmm… Ah, there you all are. Menagerie of Fools, I'd like your help rescuing Boxxo."

The Fools all stood at once, and as they did, confidence filled their expressions.

"Leave this to us. With the Menagerie of Fools on the case, failure is not an option."

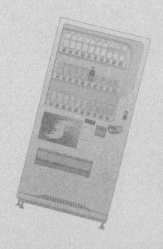

When she did, she heard things thudding to the ground. Startled, Lammis looked down—slowly. The Menagerie of Fools all stared back up at her, rubbing their hips.

"Anything you'd like to say, Lammis?" asked the captain.

"I... I'm sorry!" said Lammis, bowing deeply in apology.

"I get that you want to rush in, but haste makes waste. In situations like these, we've gotta keep cool heads." The captain flicked the brim of his hat and grinned.

"Wow, he actually said something sane!" exclaimed Shui.

"Next thing you know, it'll start pouring."

"More like *snowing*, Red."

"Nothing he says will be 'cool' as long as he's sitting there on his rear."

As the captain struck a pose, the other members continued to poke fun at him.

"Just what do you all think I am, anyway?" he demanded.

"Are you *sure* you want an answer to that?" said the vice-captain.

"Urk." The question put him at a loss for words.

Ignoring their conversation, Chairman Bear walked up and knelt to meet Lammis's gaze. "There are hunters and staff members searching for their whereabouts as we speak, and we're assembling a rescue team with all haste. Would you do me the favor of trusting us and waiting for them?" he said to her, gently putting a hand on her shoulder and kindly narrowing his eyes.

The group of three reluctantly changed course and headed off to the Hunters Association to follow Lammis.

When the Menagerie of Fools arrived at their destination and tried to open the doors, they burst wide open from the inside, and out flew Lammis.

She glanced around, spotted the Menagerie of Fools, pointed in a random direction, and opened her mouth wide. "There you are! We're all going to get Boxxo back from the kidnappers!" she cried, getting so close to the captain he could feel her breath.

She didn't let them have a moment to speak before she hoisted the captain and vice-captain onto her right shoulder and Red, White, and Shui on her left.

"Get away from me, Captain," complained Filmina.

"Can't exactly do much about it!"

""What the heck?!"" cried both twins.

"What's going on?!" added Shui.

Ignoring whatever the Menagerie of Fools was saying, Lammis braced herself to set off right then and there.

"Wait! Calm yourself, Lammis!" came the voice of Chairman Bear from behind her, causing her to stop in her tracks.

"But…! But we have to go! Or else Boxxo will—"

"Boxxo is skilled in defensive techniques, yes? And they need him because he's a magic item. They won't simply break him."

"Aww…" Lammis calmed down a little, then started taking deep breaths. "You're right. If we're going to save Boxxo, we have to do it the right way," she said, smacking herself in the cheeks to cool off.

Lammis settle down a bit. She turned back and called to the captain, "You can do the explaining, right?"

"Good work, Shui. Lammis, I have a message from Chairman Bear about Boxxo. If you have any questions, wait until I'm finished to ask them. Understand?"

Lammis nodded without a word.

The captain took a rolled-up letter from Chairman Bear from his pocket. "Let's see," he said. "'It seems Boxxo has been taken away by a gang of thieves. I've tasked hunters with tracking them down. Once you hear this, come to the Hunters Association. I'll explain the details there.'"

"Got it! The Hunters Association!"

"Hey, wait just— Great. She's gone."

Lammis had broken into a run without waiting for the captain to respond. In moments, she was just a speck on the scenery, and then she was out of sight.

"How does she move that fast?" wondered one of the twins aloud.

"It's *really* important to her," said Shui.

"A magic item?"

The captain seemed to get it. He saw the direction in which Lammis had disappeared, and he rubbed his scraggly facial hair. "That's the chairman's request all wrapped up. What say we grab a few drinks?"

"We'll come with you!" said the twins in unison.

As the three men of the group tried to leave, Filmina slipped in front of them and cast an icy glare their way. "Captain, Red, White. I assume you've forgotten, but the chairman told *us* to come as well once we'd relayed the message."

"He did!" chimed in Shui from behind them.

somewhere safe and delegate, not go down and *do* stuff. The dangerous work is supposed to be handled by the grunts."

"You're awful!"

"This is dereliction of duty!"

"Literally the worst boss ever!"

Crushed under the sheer weight of their protests, the captain shrank with a reluctant look on his face.

The vice-captain continued to watch, seemingly entertained, but finally, she had to say something.

"While I'd love to watch this play out further," she said, "we have a more important problem. Someone needs to get Lammis to calm down—and fast."

Vice-Captain Filmina was the quiet sort, but when she spoke, it was with strength and authority. The four quarreling members immediately stopped.

"Right… Yeah, you're right. I'll head over!" said Shui, resolving herself before trotting over to Lammis.

Though Shui yelled her name several times, the girl seemed too absorbed with finding Boxxo to hear her. Finally, Shui went around in front of her, grabbed Lammis's face in her hands, and forced Lammis to look at her.

"Lammis!"

"Huh? Oh, Shui... Have you see Boxxo anywhere?!"

Up close, she looked like she was about to burst into tears. Shui offered a kind smile. "Settle down. That's what I want to talk about, so listen."

"Oh... Okay." Lammis nodded several times, for some reason unable to object to being spoken to like a little kid by Shui.

"There, there. Good girl," Shui said, noticing

Red and White were usually agreeable and eager to help people. If it had been any other girl, they would have gladly talked to her. But Lammis was far too dangerous to approach when she was worked up like this.

"Well, then," said the man in the hat. "Filmina, you're vice-captain. I order you to—"

"Nope," came the flat, immediate refusal from the spellcaster with striking blue wavy hair.

"You leave me no choice, then. Shui, you're up. You're friendliest with her, right?"

"No can do. I'm so hungry, I can't move."

The girl with short hair and a bow on her back made a show of rubbing her supposedly empty belly.

The scraggly man stared at what she was holding in her left hand—a hunk of bread clearly missing a few bites—and heaved a sigh. "How is an organization supposed to function if no one follows the captain's orders?" he muttered bitterly, shoulders drooping.

Everyone else pretended not to hear him, which made him heave an even bigger sigh.

"This is an easy job. Anyone could do it. Just explain where Boxxo went. Even a five-year-old could manage that, so get to work already!"

"If it's so easy, why don't *you* do it, Cap?!"

"Yeah, that's right! Negotiating is part of your job!"

"And you always say you're great with women!"

The three youngest members offered their complaints one at a time, with Shui joining in at the end. The vice-captain took no sides; she only stepped back and watched.

"No, you listen to me. The captain's *job* is to stay

Boxxo Goes Missing

By Hirukuma

"Boxxo! Boxxo, where are you?!"

Lammis's cry could be heard all throughout the village. It caught the attention of all who heard her, but she didn't notice. She just kept running around and calling Boxxo's name.

"If you're hidin' somewhere, just come out! I won't be mad!" she shouted, slipping into her accent as she lifted a big boulder to check underneath it. But he wasn't there, so she tossed it aside and looked somewhere else.

Each time she moved to a new spot, she'd leave tremors and dust clouds in her wake, causing nearby folk to run away from her in haste.

A certain group watched her from a short distance away—the Menagerie of Fools. They wore troubled expressions, unsure of what to do.

"So…who's gonna be the one to break it down for Lammis?" asked a man with scraggly facial hair, sighing as he toyed with the brim of his hat. "Red, White, you two take this one."

""No!"" exclaimed the two young men at the same time. Aside from one of them having red hair and the other having white hair, they were identical twins. They waved their hands wildly, desperate to convey that they were *not* up to the task.

But soon, each was trying to foist the task on the other.

"She won't listen to me in that state! White, I'll let you handle this one."

"That isn't fair! You should go, Red! Chances to talk to cute girls don't come around often!"

Reborn as a Vending Machine, I Now Wander the DUNGEON

ORIGINAL SHORT STORY

Boxxo Goes Missing
By Hirukuma